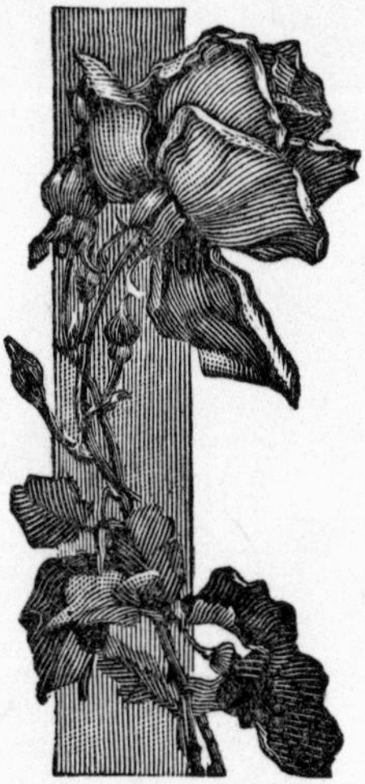

*Ex Libris*

[redacted]

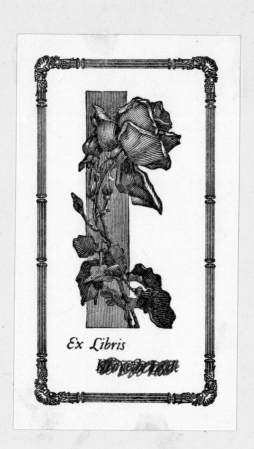

George Washington Carver

*Painting by Betsy Graves*

DR. GEORGE WASHINGTON CARVER

PRINTED IN THE UNITED STATES OF AMERICA

CL

# GEORGE WASHINGTON CARVER

## *AN AMERICAN BIOGRAPHY*

BY RACKHAM HOLT



1946
Doubleday and Company, Inc.
GARDEN CITY, NEW YORK

*To my daughter*

MARGARET V. HOLT

*who will help to make the new world a better one.*

# *Acknowledgments*

MANY FRIENDS of Dr. Carver in his childhood, youth, and manhood, whom I have never seen, have been generous of their time and effort in supplying recollections and data for this biography, and have been especially helpful in enabling me to augment his own scattered memories of his early days. Those to whom I am indebted for aid in gathering material compose such a large number that they cannot be listed, but I am deeply grateful to them all.

I should like also to acknowledge the assistance of Sara Coffin in preparing the manuscript and of P. H. Polk, photographer of Tuskegee Institute, who made the illustrations possible.

Finally, I wish to thank the publishers of the *Christian Science Monitor* and the *Saturday Evening Post* for their kind permission to reprint certain passages which have previously appeared in their pages.

# *Contents*

# *Illustrations*

# George Washington Carver

# CHAPTER I

## *"Oh, Mary, Don't You Weep!"*

DECORATE THE CITY with Stars and Stripes. Let every man know that on this eleventh day of January, year of our Lord, one thousand eight hundred and sixty-five, "by the irrevocable action of the Convention slavery is abolished in the State of Missouri, now and forever." None hereafter shall "know any master but God."

Illuminate the city with bonfires. Warmth has been sent into the stone-and-iron crypt of Lynch's slave pen where human feet were chained; light has been sent down dark and narrow streets to the ominous river they will not have to travel any more.

The inalienable gift of song swells. A new spiritual is born which holds all joy, all sorrow, all yearning, all endeavor—the humility of man before his God, the majesty of man who owns a living soul. And the beginning and the end is but one word. Free!

St. Louis rejoiced, but who beyond the levee could know or was prepared to obey that edict?

"Hush." Mary swayed in lullaby rhythm. "Hush," she whispered to the wail that rose from her arms. The January night was cold and the fire before which she warmed her sick baby was small. It flickered over James, half buried in his trundle bed, a callously healthy child who slept where he was laid. Their father used to come over from the Grant place times like this to be with her. But he was dead now. He had been hauling wood up to his master's house. "There's been an accident." they had told her. ". . . a heavy log."

Hush, little George. Doesn't your mother have sorrow enough?

Little George coughed and choked and strangled, and Mary poured honey she had doctored with tansy into his mouth. Other children had whooping cough and were none the worse for it, but he was so tiny and puny. He had been born in January of 1860 and had spent the first year of his life during the brutal days of border war between Missouri and neighboring Kansas, when farms lay desolate, men hid their families and their animals in the deep woods, and nobody had enough to eat.

A scream stopped in her throat as the door burst open and a chill blast crashed it back against the outer walls of the cabin.

"Run, Mary!" cried Moses Carver as he scooped up the sleeping James, and was gone again into the woods.

Mary knew what she must do, but icy, naked terror held her in a monstrous grasp, freezing her muscles fast. Heavy panting was around the cabin now, and men were in the doorway. Hands dragged her onto a horse. The baby's choked crying was lost in the pound of galloping hoofs. They were all gone, leaving the bitter wind to whirl through the room and beat against the futile little fire.

This was the year 1861, and jungle law prevailed in Missouri—a bloody melee of plundering and pillaging, burning and murdering. At one time or another during this savage period, the hot breath of fire blew over every settlement in Newton County. The Missouri Compromise, so hopefully passed by Congress in 1820 to settle the question of slavery, had not settled it at all, and the proslavery adherents and the Free Staters continued their bitter struggle.

From Kansas, wellspring of hatred, scourged by drought and famine, outlaw bands of jayhawkers and redlegs raged back and forth like rabid animals. In reprisal, Missouri bushwhackers and guerrillas rode under the banner of the black flag. The belts of Cherokee and Choctaw Indians were hung with dripping scalps. All set torches to hay and homes alike, destroying buildings and railroads, seizing stores of shoes, coats, blankets, and Negroes. All used "the knife, the cord, the bowl," as freely as the gun, shooting or hanging unarmed men before or after surrender.

There was lead in that corner of the state—lead for making bullets. Some had come in search of it, but now the countryside was filled with hungry men who killed their own officers for horses and arms. They were sick with smallpox and desperate for specie or greenbacks.

Hatred was especially violent against the Black Republican abolitionist Germans—the "lop-eared Dutch"—who had immigrated into the state in 1830. The same or other raiders that had stolen Mary and little George returned to Diamond Grove, and this time they caught Moses Carver, who had been among the immigrants and had prospered.

"Where's your money?" they demanded. But he refused to answer.

They strung him up by his thumbs to a branch of the walnut tree that stood against the house where he and his wife had lived in busy peace until the war. His muscles screamed in pain, but he would not answer. They took live coals from the fire and put them to his feet. Sweat ran down into his beard, but he still would not answer.

Finally they left him.

Susan wept as she put plantain leaves on her husband's burns, not from fear, because she, too, was a pioneer. She wept for Mary. Moses Carver did not approve of slavery, but hewing a home out of the wilderness required labor. There was only himself and Susan, and both had reached middle age. Susan, in particular, needed an extra pair of hands around the house and he knew their owner would be better off with Sue and himself than with many another. Twenty-five years after he had moved from Illinois to the prairie and timberland of southwestern Missouri he had become one of "those who caused money to be passed over a person's body," as they said in Africa. He had paid his neighbor, Colonel Grant, seven hundred dollars for a girl about thirteen years old, called Mary. She had had a home with the Carvers for six years, and her loss was the loss of a member of the family.

The raiders had not broken the spirit of Moses Carver; he was still fierce. A rumor reached him that a bushwhacker named Bentley knew Mary's whereabouts and would steal her back, though it would be expensive. He sent for the man. "Go after them, Bentley. I haven't as much money as they think, and I wouldn't give any of it to them. It's hidden under a beehive. But bring Mary and the baby back and I'll give you forty acres of my best timberland and Pacer—he's a good horse. Sue'll show you where he's hid."

With eight hundred dollars' worth of timberland and three hundred dollars' worth of race horse to spur him on, Bentley started in pursuit, riding fifty miles across Newton County and across McDonald County and over into Arkansas.

When, after a few days, Bentley came back, he had a bundle wrapped in his coat and tied to the back of his saddle.

"No sign o' Mary. Lot o' people think the Secesh ain't licked yet, nor slavery neither. First I heard she was dead, then somebody said they saw her goin' north with some soldiers, and somebody else said she was sent down river to Louisiana. Guess they didn't want to be bothered with the baby. Coupla wimin had it. I wouldn't want to take the timberland since I couldn't get your girl. I'll just take the horse for my trouble."

He untied the bundle and handed it over to Susan, saying doubtfully, "Guess it's alive yet."

# CHAPTER II

## *"I Was Young When I Begun"*

THE FIRST BRIGHT DAY of spring a few years later a little boy was in the woods gently scraping at the earth. He came to a piece of bark and when he had raised it he peered into the hollowed space beneath. One by one, handling each with anxious care, he lifted from the snug hole the cans and gourds from which sprouted young shoots. He lined them up on the ground and then sat back on his thin haunches and raptly watched the twinkle of yellow sun on the brave green leaves and fronds of his ferns and his particular treasure, a begonia. The temperature in the foothills of the Ozarks sometimes fell to fifteen below zero and the ground was frozen for a foot. George had protected his plants from this winter cold, bringing them out for sun and then covering them over again. Now it was spring, and they were ready to live once more.

The neighbors knew the child had a magic way with growing things. They called him the Plant Doctor, and he made house-to-house calls in Diamond Grove to prescribe for ailing plants; sometimes cuttings wouldn't root, some were wilting, some drying, and he would recommend more or less water, more or less sun. If they were seriously ill he carried them away to his secret garden. It was far enough off and hidden by bushes and nobody knew about it but himself. There he would prune or knock out the soil and shift until he had nursed them back to health and bloom. He never lost a plant in his sanatorium.

George did not know how it happened that he had a green thumb. There were a good many things he did not know.

The first thing he inquired about was rain. What was rain? What made it? Then what were hail and snow? Why, for instance, was a flower? Out of one box of rose moss came different colored flowers—yellow, white, rose, pink, striped, spotted—all from the same piece of earth. "Why?" he whispered to himself. "I wish I knew."

It was in the nature of this boy to cherish his plants in solitude and, besides, Aunt Sue Carver would not allow him to bring his trash into the house. Sometimes he smuggled in a fistful of flowers or grass or even a few heads of oats, going to bed with them gripped in his hands and waking in the morning still clutching the withered remains. Usually she would exclaim as he appeared in the doorway, "George, what have you got there?" and out would come toads or frogs, grasshoppers that leaped among the hot wheat stalks, or dragonflies that zoomed above the little stream rippling down below the cabin. Or it might be some pretty feathers or interesting-looking rocks—very much the same sort of litter he was to pick up on his rambles and bring into his laboratory all the days of his life.

As he walked back from his garden through the tall trees of walnut, oak, and hickory—people preserved their timber then—taking short steps because he was undersized, or as he hopped across the rutted fields sniffing the wet smell of damp earth freshly turned up to the sun, he piped in a high, childish falsetto. He had an impediment in his speech, the result of the whooping cough in infancy and violent attacks of "croup," which he had over and over again. He stammered, and half the time no one could understand what he was trying to say, but he was forever singing. He sang, too, about his duties, which were never-ending.

The Carvers had two houses a few feet apart, one room each, the roofs of hand-split boards, and the cracks between the logs chinked with mud. But the "big" house was just for company, and when it was occupied George trotted across to it carrying the meals. In the little house lived George and his brother Jim, Aunt Sue, and Uncle Mose Carver. Most of the country people called each other after this fashion; the older folk were "Uncle" or "Aunt," and the younger ones were "Cousin" this or that, though lacking any blood relationship.

No plants bloomed in the Carver home; it had no decoration of any sort. The furnishings were merely two wide wooden beds, a small spinning wheel with a treadle for fine linen and a big one for heavy wool, some stools, and a cross-legged table on which were ranged the pewter, blue- and pink-flowered dishes, and stubby, bone-handled knives and two-pronged forks—very elegant for their time. When the rains came or the autumn chill, the door and the window shutter, usually swinging wide on wooden hinges, had to be closed, and the family ate and worked by the light of tallow dips. At all seasons they went to bed with the chickens and rose at four in the morning.

Work was the order of each day. George liked some of it. He would walk down the rows in the cornfield very fast with Martha Jane Williams, Uncle Mose's niece, carrying a little bucket of corn, dropping kernels in perfect rhythm—two steps, three grains, two steps, three grains.

He could not keep up with Jim, who was not merely two years older but big and strong and very active—a handsome fellow. Being so much more healthy, Jim did the heavier work and was not around the house very much as George was. The frail and rather pathetic little boy was sick a good deal. Nevertheless, he had to do his work whether he felt well or not; there could be no lagging on a farm. The garden had to be planted and weeded and the fruit picked, the cows had to be milked, the sheep sheared, the horses fed and groomed. George often carried water to Pacer's grandson—a pretty animal.

Uncle Mose was more than a trader in fine horses. He bred and trained his racers and trotters so carefully that they brought high prices; three hundred dollars in Missouri in Reconstruction days was the equivalent of three thousand a few years later. Men came from far distances to buy them.

His bloodhounds, too, which he kept for fox hunting, were well bred, and there were seldom less than twenty. Twenty hounds can make considerable commotion, with a mess of little puppies yelping in soprano and the big fellows baying in bass. When this sort of din arose, more often than not it was because George had stirred them up by chasing or being chased by them; they would run a man as quickly as they would a fox, once they got the habit, and Uncle Mose would soon appear and put a stop to it.

He was a strict disciplinarian in some ways. The stick-and-mud chimney of the house had cracks and niches in it, and in a certain convenient hollow a certain hen was determined to nest. One of the hounds made this joyful discovery and neglected to destroy the evidence of broken shells lying about. A sucking-egg dog was unpardonable to Uncle Mose. He switched it until it was broken of the evil habit.

Though he was a stern man, he would not tolerate cruelty. He did not swear as a rule, but anyone who wanted to hear what he could do in this respect had only to abuse stock. He learned that one of his neighbors, who had recently moved into the countryside, did not feed his horse properly. One day the fellow came driving up behind the poor rickety animal, its ears poked through a big straw bonnet on its head. George thought the hat was intended more as a decoration than as a protection against the sun and looked apprehensively at the scowl already spreading over Uncle Mose's face; even his beard appeared to bristle.

The man didn't know him very well and greeted him affably, "Mornin', Uncle Mose."

Silence was the only answer.

The man tried again, "Mornin', Uncle Mose."

Silence.

He tried to lighten the atmosphere with conversation, "What d'ya think o' my horse's bonnet?"

"Well, now, Ben, since you asked me I'll tell you. I think if the horse had less millinery and more oats it'd appreciate it more." Then he stomped away to the barn, growling in his deep voice, "A man that'd be mean to his horse'd be mean to his wife."

The Carver farm of one hundred and forty acres was almost self-contained. When someone was sick they didn't send for a doctor; they gathered roots, herbs, and barks, and prepared their own medicines. It was George's job to peel the bark from the north side of the tree; the bark was then boiled and sweetened with honey to make a drench for horses with botts. He also had to collect sassafras bark and spice bushes to put in the lard and make it smell good. Ashes were saved in a hopper, and at fall hog-killing time stacks and stacks of soap, both hard and soft, were made.

Fields of flax stretched away and hemp grew in the fence corners. Now that George's mother was gone, Aunt Sue did all the spinning on what had been Mary's wheels. She wove the cloth of flax, hemp, and wool, making heavy working garments for Uncle Mose and Jim, George's little short dresses, and her own long, billowing skirts for wearing about the house and hoopskirts for visiting—no lady ever went out without her hoops. To dye the clothing, oak bark was used for black, hickory for yellow, and chestnut for browns. They tanned their own leather and made shoes to wear in the winter from the hides of deer, which were as plentiful as rabbits.

George learned little of what sort of person his mother had been. He could not ask Aunt Sue because she always cried when Mary's name was mentioned. He did know that she had been honest in speech and upright in all her ways. Once Aunt Sue commented on George's remarkable co-ordination between hand and eye, saying he was like Mary that way. Mary had not been able to read; she could not tell one letter from another, but if she had ever seen a certain almanac before, she could find any page in it more quickly than Aunt Sue.

George's hands seemingly were intended for making things. He had often seen Aunt Sue knitting with her four shining needles. Then of a sudden he thought, "I can do that!" So he stood for a while watching just how her fingers moved, and went outside and picked up turkey feathers. He stripped the barbs until just a little tuft was left at the end. Then he took the top of a mitten and the top of a stocking, raveled them out, and started knitting long strips of the different colors with his improvised needles. Occasionally thereafter he knitted something practical, but chiefly he knitted just because he wanted to know how.

The boys were allowed to do pretty much as they pleased during the intervals between tasks. The split puncheon floor had to be scrubbed every Saturday morning. George followed the prescribed routine faithfully and then settled down out of doors to the churning. That had to be finished before they could go fishing. He and Jim took turns beating and beating the old dasher, but one time it simply would not get warm enough to make the butter come.

In order to hasten the processes of nature George scooped up a dipperful of hot water from the big iron pot in which the clothes were washed and dyed and stealthily poured it in. He had tried this before and in his impatience had poured in so much the butter was spongy. Consequently, he knew that if he and Jim were caught Uncle Mose would lint their jackets and they would be made to stay at home. But the fish were waiting down in the spring branch.

This time he was more careful, and finally the butter came. He presented it to Aunt Sue. She looked at it suspiciously. "Why is it so white?"

Did George reply, "It has been scalded"? He did not. He remembered the answer of the little girl whose father asked her if she knew what a lie was: "An abomination unto the Lord and an ever-present help in time of trouble." A boy who wants to go fishing is not always responsible. He had recourse to this form of help and stuttered innocently, "I d-d-don't know."

Since there was the butter to prove he had worked, and it was not too white, no further reprimand was forthcoming.

He grabbed his miscellaneous assortment of worms, crickets, crawfish scales, and pieces of fat meat, and dodged down to the branch.

When George fished, often the flapping object on the end of his string was only a sucker, and nobody cared to eat it, because it was so full of bones. But he never went fishing without catching something, and his perch or catfish or sunfish or occasional eel Aunt Sue cooked in the ashes of the fireplace.

It was years before a "parlor cook" stove was brought in—a great wonder, and neighbors came from miles around to admire it. Before that, all of the cooking was done in the fireplace. Aunt Sue beat the batter and shaped it in a skillet. Then she fitted the skillet with a tight lid, set it on the coals, and piled more coals in the hollowed place on top. Out would come a savory loaf of fatty corn bread four inches deep.

As a little boy George used to make sandwiches, though he had never heard of such things. Often for dinner the family had dodgers—corn meal wet with water, patted with the hands into an ellipse, and baked brown. George would take one of these dodgers which had been left on the plate, split it, lay strips of home-cured fat meat between, and start for the woods. On the way he would pull a wild onion and add it to his sandwich. Thus fortified, and with no inclination to work, he could stay out all day until suppertime, and then meander home.

Once, way back in infancy's dim, distorted memory, there was a time when no food was to be had except corn, and not much of that. It must have been some time after the raiders had returned to the farm, tipped over the beehives one by one until they had found the money. But the hard days and hungry nights had passed, Uncle Mose's industry had made him prosperous again, and now corn, corn was everywhere. It hung yellow and drying from the smoke-blackened rafters; they ground it for gruel; they boiled it like rice; they parched it to eat as children do popcorn. They had hazelnuts, butternuts, pecans, and walnuts from the woods. Uncle Mose had plowed the fence rows, dropped in walnuts, and stepped on them. Now he had great walnut hedges around the farm.

He would have no timber cut and no holes dug on the place. A company drilled once and found a heavy vein of lead, but he would not allow them to go further. They offered a good sum to open it up, but he said no. And he made them cover the shaft and go away.

Nothing was bought save coffee and sugar. And these were bartered for farm products. The Carvers were good livers, though no waste was permitted. On Sundays they had the usual chicken dinner, and if it was not all eaten it appeared on the table for Monday breakfast; then it came on again for dinner and for supper. Uncle Mose would say as he reached for the neck, "Got to eat it sometime. Might as well do it now."

Nothing was thrown out; nothing was burned up that an animal could eat. Extra supplies were put away for use during the winter. The huge smokehouse was full of meat, butter, and lard. Apples, peaches, pears, blackberries were laid out in the sun to dry before storing. Vegetables were banked. Cabbage plants by the hundred were turned down in trenches in the fields where they had grown, covered with six inches of dirt, and only their roots left sticking up. George would dig these as needed, slough off the outer leaves, and there would be a nice white cabbage head.

Home canning was in its infancy and none too easy. But Aunt Sue had three cans she kept year after year and opened only for most unusual company. The lid of the can had a groove which she filled with a half-spun roll of cotton and covered with sealing wax.

But first you had to make the sealing wax out of beeswax. Uncle Mose, an expert bee hunter, had fifty or sixty hives. He would go out with a pan of bait of honey and bee bread and burn it on live coals. The bees smelled it four or five miles away and came to sip. Then he watched which way they went, followed, and located their tree. After nightfall he and Jim smoked them out with a fire of rags and tobacco and cut the tree down. Sometimes they got a washtub full of honey. Then they cut off a section of the log, and put a top on it, and that would be the hive.

George did not participate in this operation; he watched from a distance because the bees would run for him. As it was, he was swelled up most of the time with stings. Uncle Mose did not even wear a net. Often the bees took a notion to pick out another tree for themselves, and he scraped around with his hand until he found the queen. Then he clipped her wings to keep her from wandering off in search of a new home and taking the whole swarm with her.

Wild turkeys and wild geese abounded, and once Uncle Mose killed a bear, which the family ate for a long time.

Colonel Grant and his slaves had not survived the war, and his farm was now owned by the Baynhams. There was a big cave on the Baynham place from which a spring continually gushed forth, and it was full of bears. George would not venture too near it on this account, but he did commit a daring act of another sort one day. The Baynham place was one of the finest farms in that section, and the brick-and-frame house one of the most imposing. George was tolerated by some of the neighbors as a comical little chap; he could make them die laughing just looking at him. Others thought his prankishness pathetic and gave him special liberties. Nevertheless, he knew he had no business going beyond the kitchen. In some way, however, he got into the parlor where the family portraits were hanging on the wall—the first paintings he had ever seen.

The lines and colors appeared very beautiful to him, and through an involved system of questioning he discovered that they had been made by someone called an "artist." He thought to himself, "He made them with his hands, he made them with his hands. I want to do that."

All the way home he said it over and over and finally, as though the thought took complete possession of him, he stammered the words aloud: "He made them with his hands, he made them with his hands. I want to do that." And the refrain sang through his head for days.

After that he was always drawing. He had nothing to draw with, but wherever he found a blank space on a stone or board or even on the ground he scratched something or other. He made colors out of pokeberries, roots, and bark, and painted on cans, wooden pails, pieces of glass, anything. This occupation was as secret as his little greenhouse in the woods; he would not dare bring any such foolishness into the house.

Uncle Mose was no more severe with Jim and George than he would have been with his own sons; boys were brought up that way. He did not teach them by the negative method—don't do this and don't do that. Once a year each would be given the privilege of going to the town of Neosho, the county seat, eight miles away. But they could not go together, lest the older influence the younger. Furthermore, it was rightly judged that two children together could concoct mischief one would not think of alone.

About a week before it was time for Jim or George to embark upon this great adventure Uncle Mose would call them to him and pronounce a parable: "Once upon a time there were two boys in the same family. One was a spendthrift. He threw away all his money on gewgaws, jewelry, and prize boxes. The other saved his money and bought a setting of eggs. He raised chickens and sold them until he had enough to buy a pig. He raised piglets and sold them until he had enough to buy a heifer. He raised a couple of calves and sold them and bought a colt. It grew into a horse, and by that time he had enough money for a saddle and bridle. Finally, he was able to buy a suit of clothes."

At that point Moses Carver would stop. There was no need of his going further because that was the highest peak to which anyone could climb.

When the time came for Jim or George, whichever was having his turn, to start for town he emptied the blacking box he used as a bank, free to spend its contents as his fancy led him. But when he returned Uncle Mose would say, "Let's see what you bought." If the old gentleman was pleased with George's straw hat or five cents' worth of fishhooks he exclaimed with much gusto, "That's good!" He did not quite understand when the boy brought home a steel-and-bone crochet hook, so he said nothing. But he would look at Jim's big glass heart or jew's-harp and merely remark, "A fool and his money's soon parted." And that was the end of that. No scolding was necessary to drive the lesson home.

George never explained the reason for his early return from one of these trips. At first it had been exciting. He had encountered the big ornamental wagon of a medicine man and slipped through the crowd collected to hear the banjo pickers and listen to a spiel about wizard oil, which would cure anything. To hear the medicine man talk you could cut off a pup's tail, sprinkle a few drops of oil on it, and the tail would grow again in five minutes.

When this palled, George had gone walking along, his eyes delighted with such items of interest as the brick courthouse in the public square, which had two stories, one on top of the other. With so many new scenes pulling his attention this way and that he could not be expected to watch where he was going. Suddenly, as he turned a corner, he bumped into the legs of a Negro, big and powerful. George had never seen a black face before, except his brother's. He was completely terrified and turned and ran for home without any purchase at all.

Any inclination toward gambling George may have had was nipped at his first venture. Uncle Mose's nephew Dick was full of pranks and jokes. He came over one Saturday afternoon and exclaimed, "Jim and George, come here! I'll betcha each fifteen cents ya kin put on your shoes an' tie 'em any way ya want—hard's ya kin—an' run aroun' the house three times an' they'll be ontied."

Both Jim and George promptly put on their shoes and tied the rawhide laces in hard knots. Gaily they ran around the house—this was easy money—three times. They came back panting but triumphant.

"Jest like I said," shrieked Dick. "Yur shoes is on an' tied!"

Jim declared it was a swindle and wouldn't pay. But George offered no argument. He went to his box and fished out ten cents in paper money and five big copper coins, which he silently handed over. Gone was his little hoard, but he was cured of betting.

George did not have much time for play, but he did sometimes join the other boys at shinny. He always bore a nick in his shin where a tin can swiped him. There was no such thing as a ball. Balls made of rags were used for throwing purposes, but one of these would not have lasted long under the furious assaults of shinny. Instead, a tin can was knocked back and forth between the two teams with sticks of hickory or anything else that had a knob on it. You had to keep it going, and if you managed to knock it through the other boys' line, you won.

When George did play, he had so much fun that, like any other boy, he was likely to keep shoving off the fact that it was growing later and later and he still had to get the stock in. One particular time Uncle Mose was making one of his rare trips to Neosho and probably wouldn't be back for quite a while yet.

Finally it was unmistakably twilight, and George had to stop. But by this time the barn was so dim he couldn't see to fork the hay down. He slipped into the house, abstracted the tin lantern, and lit the candle. It was strictly forbidden to have a light in the barn with all that hay about. He was working as fast as he could by the feeble light that flickered through the holes punched through the tin when he became aware that Uncle Mose had arrived and was standing there watching him. He hurried even faster; one word of back talk and he would have been in for it. But Uncle Mose let him finish and put the lantern back, apparently counting on fear to take the place of a switching.

Ordinarily George was deathly afraid to set foot outside

the door at night, because Raw-Head-and-Bloody-Bones was lurking out there. But one evening he got so mad nothing could frighten him. The other boys, knowing he was a victim of shyness, used to tease him about the girls, and when they did that he threw rocks at them or jumped on them and gave them a good killing.

Then one night there was going to be a party at Mrs. Selby's. George knew what it would be like; they would have 'Pon Honor games in which someone would lose a forfeit and to redeem it would be ordered to turn and bust so and so. They asked him to come, and at first he said no. "You want to get me there and make me do something I don't want to do." But they crossed their hearts and promised they wouldn't. So he went.

When the games started, they called off sides and found they lacked one person. They begged him to come in, but he was suspicious. "You want to make me kiss a girl."

"Oh no. We won't do that."

"Then I'll come in."

Almost the first thing, George lost a forfeit. "Heavy, heavy hangs over your head. What will the owner do to redeem it?"

"Bust Clarissa three times."

Clarissa Swan was rough and ugly to the minute. George said he wasn't going to kiss her or any other swan and started to walk off. They pulled him back and tried to make him, so George went to fighting. Clarissa grabbed him, and he slapped her.

At this point Mrs. Selby stepped in. "You told a story," she said severely to the other boys. "And I don't blame George."

George didn't wait for the argument to be settled. He picked up his things and started for home, tramping over a mile across the fields, so mad he forgot to be frightened of the dark.

Parties then were for young and old together. More often than not they consisted of husking bees, apple parings, log rollings, wool pickings, or quilting parties. Uncle Mose was the best fiddler thereabouts. A really first-class party could not be held without Uncle Mose playing his fiddle. He tried taking George to one of these gatherings, but the youngster was alarmed by the crowd and the noise; he slipped out and walked home.

Little boys made cornstalk fiddles the same way little girls made rag dolls. "Cornstalk fiddle and rausum bow makes best old music you ever did know." Young stalks had a better resonance than old, dried ones, and with a bow strung from a wisp of a horse's tail George could produce a sort of rhythm to jig to. He did not know anything to speak of about music, but he knew more than anybody else except Uncle Mose, and willingly showed some of the women in the neighborhood how he made music come out of an organ or guitar.

He had a wonderful memory, and at what they called their "literaries" was good at singing or debating on some such subject as, "Was the mother of a chicken the hen that laid the egg or the one that hatched it?"

Shooting matches were the big thing for grownups. The men would chip in and buy a sheep or an ox and then shoot for the parts—hindquarter, foreside, and so on. If anyone hit a bull's-eye, he had another shot. Uncle Mose was so good that if he got the first try, he was sure to drive the animal home. Jim practiced until he reached the same point; he, too, was ruled out, to give the others a chance.

George, on the other hand, was completely helpless with a gun. His long suit was to bring down game with rocks. He was a center shot with a rock, and no rabbit could get out of his way. Whatever he threw at he hit. He used to throw at snowbirds, little birds that came to pick up bits of grain and seed scattered in the course of feeding the stock. He took pleasure in doing that. Then one morning he threw a sharp pellet and knocked off the top of a bird's head—scalped it. He ran and picked it up and the blood trickled over his hand. He stood and looked at it for a while until the tears started. He cried and cried and couldn't seem to stop. That was the last of the murder of the innocents.

George himself was very much like a young bird, all head

and mouth. And he looked like one as he sat way out on a limb, where the huskier youths did not dare to follow, and laughed at them. His body was so slight it could go anywhere his head could go. When he was the one to be chased, he was always far ahead; muscular farm lads could climb a fence pretty fast, but George could go through any crack in it. Then he would dodge out of sight in some small hiding place and rest until he had strength to light out again. He could have kept this up all day and they could never have caught him, because they would be all worn out with steady running.

Once he came back from a chase crying. The old folks asked why he wept, but he wouldn't answer. He wouldn't tell them he had poked his head through a crack and stuck there; he couldn't wriggle through. His frame had begun to grow a little, as it ought, but this was a distinct calamity to George.

With one of Uncle Mose's hunting knives George contrived to fashion some crutches for a crippled boy, so that he might play with the others, but you couldn't just manufacture a knife. For George, a knife of his own was an impossible wish. Then one night he had a dream. He dreamed he saw a watermelon lying in a cornfield. It had been cut and partially eaten and the rind was lying at the foot of three cornstalks. Also lying at the foot of the three cornstalks was a tiny lady's knife, not much larger than a pencil, with a black handle and two blades.

George could hardly swallow his breakfast, he was in such a hurry, and it was just growing light when he made a direct line over fences and across furrows to the place of his dream. There were the three cornstalks, there were the remnants of the watermelon, and there was the knife—his to polish in the earth, his to use for whatever purpose he wished, his to keep by him always until he was a man.

This vision did not seem strange to him then, nor did he thereafter consider his special gift of sight at all odd. He merely said, "It is easy for me to foresee things." He did not speak of it as a child because it tied up somehow with faith and religion and the Proverb, "Those that seek me early shall find me." But Uncle Mose did not believe in the Bible.

The Locust Grove schoolhouse, started during Reconstruction, was less than a mile from the Carver home. Here church was held each Sunday morning, a Methodist or Baptist or Campbellite or Presbyterian coming out from Neosho on horseback to conduct the services.

Though practically all the community life in those days centered around the church, and the Carvers were considered infidels because they did not attend, Uncle Mose was of sufficient quality and substance to be respected in spite of his unbelief.

If a neighbor had malaria just when the grain had ripened, Uncle Mose joined the other neighbors who came to help with the harvest. When death carried some away, he gave a piece of his land not far from the house to be used as a graveyard. Though he himself did not attend the buryings, George did. The little group of mourners stood on fence rails laid about the fresh grave to keep their feet dry, but he had been born to stand apart. A little way off from the others and alone, his feet in the mud, he watched with solemn eyes the earth reclaim its own.

The new Constitution of Missouri provided for free school instruction for all between the ages of five and twenty. But that, somehow, did not seem to include George. Though he could not go to school with white children, he was permitted to attend the Sabbath-school class which was held before the church services, and afterward he could sit on the steps and listen to the singing. Even as a very little boy he had a studious nature. He was quiet and a good listener and accepted the Word in a serious manner, wandering about afterward and holding a solitary communion with Nature.

Sundays as well as weekdays he made a faithful pilgrimage to his three-by-six garden plot, occasionally digging up his plants to see if they were growing. He brooded over questions he could not answer: how roses became double, why the leaves on the same tree were different, why clover and oxalis folded at night and on dark days, what insects were doing in the flowers. He longed to be able to "mix" flowers, as he called it, and planted them close together, hoping they would mix.

From the time he was virtually a baby in the woods he wanted to know the name of every stone, insect, flower he saw. He had a book given him by Aunt Sue—Webster's old blue-back Speller—that had a picture of a man climbing a high cliff on the top of which stood a temple of learning. Few people thereabouts could even write, but George had studied the Speller until he knew every word. However, it did not reveal the names of the birds, so he made up names to suit himself. Having once tasted of the fruit of knowledge and caught a glimpse of the mysteries hidden in words, he could not rest content.

He had not made knowledge a part of himself until he had done something with it; abstractions had to be made concrete. When stray copies of *Little Women* and *Little Men* found their way out to those parts, he said, "I can do that. I can write a book." And straightway he wrote a long, long story after what he considered was the general manner of Miss Alcott.

George looked with longing at the doors of the schoolhouse closed to him and announced grandly that someday he was going to have a school of his own where boys would learn to do cooking and housework the same as girls. He was going to teach the things he himself could do with his hands. This was childish prattle and laughed at as such. He was told he didn't know what he was talking about, which was quite true, but he stubbornly continued to cherish the notion in secret, and never entirely relinquished it.

George had had no contact with the rest of the four million lately emancipated who were stirring with a vast racial longing for education, which would free their minds as well as their bodies. It is probable that the yearning within him was an individual thing and would have driven him on regardless of his color.

When he finally stammered out his consuming desire, the Carvers did not seek to hold him back. Accordingly, this frail boy, smaller than his theoretical ten years, placed his bare black feet on the road to knowledge. Abandoning the security of home and the safety that lies in familiar things, George set out so willingly to school.

# CHAPTER III

## "The Young Lambs Must Find the Way"

THE IMMEDIATE MECCA of this little pilgrim was Neosho. Eight miles was not much of a walk for a country boy, though it was uphill and down and up again. By late afternoon George was trudging along the city streets, dressed to kill in his Sabbath suit, the rest of his possessions tied in a big bandanna handkerchief. He had come this far successfully, but had no notion what to do next. He just kept on walking, around and around, until the ache of weariness crept up his legs. Still he couldn't think what he was to do with himself for the night.

Finally he stood still. Before him gaped the broad open door of a barn. Barns he knew and horses he knew. He dodged into the shadows and found, almost by instinct, the boards nailed to uprights that led to the hayloft. He burrowed into the dusty pile and lay there while the rats gradually and cautiously resumed the patter and scurry which had been interrupted by his invasion. Breathing the familiar and comforting smell of horses and leather, he finally fell asleep and slept away his loneliness and tiredness.

When George awoke he listened for the occasional thud of a horse's hoof and the soft switch of a tail and a heavy body rubbing against the stall. He peered over the edge of the loft into the open carriage space of the barn, which was coming to life in a faint gray way. It would soon be daylight, and someone would approach his sanctuary to fork the hay into the mangers. Like a small black shadow he slipped down and out to the sweet, fresh air of dawn.

George wandered about for a bit, and then sat down on a

convenient woodpile to think what he should do about the hunger that was contracting his stomach. In the big grassy yard sunflowers and tiger lilies were beginning to glow in the light of their brother, the sun. The small house was unpainted, but neatness shone about it. Presently there appeared in the doorway a small wiry woman with dancing eyes in a light brown skin. Starting with quick steps for the woodpile to build the breakfast fire, she spied the thin and timid little figure perched upon her kindling. She recognized his look as one which a full belly would help and drew him into her home and her warm heart.

Mariah Watkins was a woman with a fine expression, swift and bold of speech. There was no nonsense about her though. Her deep kindliness and great goodness declared themselves in direct and immediate action. When she had satisfied the first needs of the stray she scrubbed him shining—being a conscientious midwife, she knew the virtues of hot water and was lavish in its use. Then she wrapped a big apron around him as though he were a girl and proceeded with the third step toward salvation—work.

No children had resulted from Aunt Mariah's marriage to Andrew Watkins. Uncle Andy, short, stubby, brown-skinned also, and above the average in intelligence, did general job work in the community. He, too, was a person of character and had a clear tenor voice which George admired and tried to emulate.

Aunt Mariah had delivered the orphan from fear and want and she particularly cherished this foster son, whom she always spoke of as "my George." In the broad net of her love, however, she also held hundreds of children, both white and colored, whom she considered her own, whom she had delivered over the years as a midwife. The esteem in which Aunt Mariah was held spread far out to where the streets of the town changed to country roads. These she would travel, sometimes a hundred miles, for a lying-in. Her clientele was chiefly among the well to do, who respected her forcefulness and relied upon her efficiency. Once, when she was very old and gave a party for her white children, some thirty cars were parked outside the little house, and the "best families" of Neosho and Joplin, twenty miles away, were there.

Aunt Mariah always said she would rather have "my George" about the house than a girl. Under her aegis he learned how to wash clothes until they gleamed on the line and how to press the iron smoothly into intricate corners. Most important, when he whitewashed the walls or scrubbed the floors, he was learning how to make a home. He did not need to be taught thrift, industry, and self-reliance. Life had done that for him. But the molds could be solidly set, and this, if they needed doing, Aunt Mariah and Uncle Andy did.

Sometimes she took George to the African Methodist Church which she attended. The preacher, whose name was Givens, could not read a word and had to have someone else read the text for him, but he was such a good man. He actually lived what he preached, and made a profound impression on George. Aunt Mariah was one of those who "Do believe, without a doubt, that Christians got a right to shout." She shouted with the rest in church. Nevertheless, she liked quiet—children must not laugh on Sundays, and George crept about his duties like a mouse. He was, on the whole, a quiet child and became a quiet man.

It is doubtful whether Aunt Mariah could read—perhaps a little—but she prayed a great deal and instilled in her foster son her devotion to the Word of God. When he was nearly eighty he was still reading the Bible she gave him, keeping the place with the bookmark he embroidered under her vigilant eye.

Reconstruction days were hard for white and colored alike in Missouri. It was still staggering from the impact of the war and what might almost be called its own private civil war within its own boundaries. Nevertheless, the Freedmen's Bureau was operating, and schools of a sort were being started.

Just over the fence from the Watkins house was the crude

frame building of the colored school of Neosho. Its first teacher, a white woman, had been replaced by a Negro, Stephen S. Frost. In the one room of the Lincoln School, a tumbledown cabin fourteen feet by sixteen, he did the best he could with his own limited education for the seventy-five children massed on the high, hard benches before him.

Into this throng George was promptly inserted. Being now admittedly a "person," despite the Dred Scott Decision, he was entitled to a surname and, according to ex-slave custom, Carver's George was transformed into George Carver. He was an absorptive sponge whose thirst for more knowledge was increased with the salt of fervor. This was what he had left home for. When the bell rang for recess, he hopped over the fence which separated the Watkins house from the school ground with his book in his hand. He propped it above the tub and read as he scrubbed. The bell rang; recess was done. George dried his hands, picked up his book, and hopped back over the fence to sit at the feet of learning and transcribe such learning onto his little six-by-nine slate. When the day's classes were finished and the other children trooped homeward, over the fence he went once more to help Aunt Mariah and Uncle Andy with the milking or bringing in the wood. And, immediately after the chores, the book was open again before him.

Some time after George had come to Neosho, Jim had followed and he, too, attended classes for a while. But he was not a scholar. Before long he abandoned school and started to learn the plasterer's trade, at which he was much more apt. The town had a large colored population. It was pleasant for Jim to be in a community of his own sort. He felt the difference and was at home. He was physically older than his years; he seemed a young man, and a very well-liked young man. He himself liked the Jefferson girl who lived next door, but Stephen Frost got there first and married her.

This incensed George, who didn't think much of the teacher anyhow. He wasn't old enough to know many things

Moses Carver, owner of Mary, mother of
George W. Carver

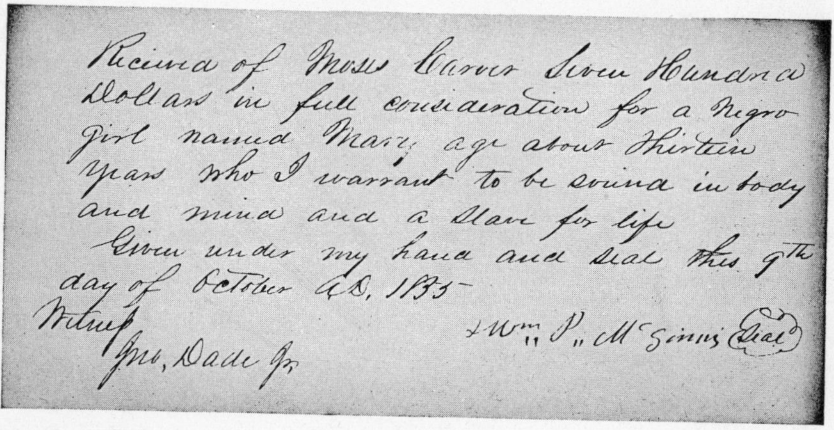

Received of Moses Carver Seven Hundred
Dollars in full consideration for a Negro
girl named Mary age about Thirteen
years who I warrant to be sound in body
and mind and a Slave for life
Given under my hand and seal this 9th
day of October AD, 1855
Witness
Jno. Dade Jr.
Wm. P. McGinnis (Seal)

Bill of Sale for Mary

Dr. Milholland, who befriended George Carver as a young man

*Courtesy of Cal Jefferson, Neosho, Mo.*

Mariah Watkins, foster mother of George when a little boy

Lucy Seymour, in whose home George later lived

about people, but there were certain ones he disliked instinctively—Mr. Frost was ashamed of being a Negro.

George was devoted to his big brother and, though no two boys could have been more different, they were always good companions. One thing they had in common was the gift of mimicry. They clowned with each other, and when they walked back together on Saturday afternoons to visit the Carvers and happened on a party they were called on for comic recitations.

Fred Baynham had given Jim a book of choice selections, and George had bought one also—*The Dime Ludicrous Speaker*. Each had his favorites and willingly rendered them, George's performances, as was natural, given their different temperaments, possessing finer shadings. Jim would oblige with the "Hard-Shell Sermon" and George with the "Lecture on Woman's Rights"; then Jim with "Where the Hen Scratches, There She Expects to Find the Bug," and George with Mark Twain's "Good Little Boy." As the book advised, George delivered Josh Billings' "Uncle Toby" with "serio-mock solemnity," and, as the book promised, his small audience found it "very laughable."

With the town boys of his own age George did not spend a great deal of time. They were not like those at home, and he was shy of strangers. Boisterousness alarmed him. He was still delicate, half sick most of the time, and he shrank from shouts and noise. They would tease him to join their rough and tumble, and sometimes he would play for a little while before bedtime, but it would usually be with little girls, or in quieter games in which he felt more sure of himself.

They soon learned to stop competing when he fished out his pocket knife that he had found in the cornfield and started to practice mumblety-peg, flipping it nimbly over his left shoulder while he held on to the lobe of his right ear. No one could beat him at that game and, moreover, he was said to be pretty good at marbles. They played for keeps, and his bag of mibs swelled and swelled as his one real agate rolled unerringly for its mark.

But these diversions were infrequent as compared with other children's playtime. George had a living to earn. Work was his natural lot. Aunt Mariah was an unusually fine cook. She prepared the meals herself when she was at home, and George, by standing around and watching her, absorbed some of her technique. At least he could take over and keep house for Uncle Andy while she was away on her frequently long trips.

Whenever he could find jobs he went out to work for other people about the town. One of these was Mrs. Slater. Though there was little Mrs. Slater could teach George in the way of cooking, like Aunt Mariah she had a hand in educating him in fundamentals. She trusted and depended on him and, in spite of his lack of years and size, gave him a good bit of responsibility. Once she and her husband went on a trip to St. Louis and she left him in charge of the house. They were away longer than they had intended, and George occupied the time fixing this and cleaning that and polishing the other. When they returned, eagerly and enthusiastically he started an account of all the things he had accomplished. But she soon stopped him with, "Now, George, don't tell me the number of things you have done, but how well you have done them." This was a little lesson he took very much to heart and always remembered.

There was one period in which George thoroughly enjoyed himself. He had the mumps. He was not sick enough to feel bad, and for once was free from labor of any kind. He didn't have to cut wood and he didn't have to scrub the floor. He had no chin at all and was the funniest-looking thing. If he swallowed anything sour he yelled and carried on, but that was all that stopped him. He romped and cavorted and stood on his head and talked back and was babied until he nearly burst with self-importance.

Soon thereafter he was allowed his first experience in poultry raising, entirely on his own. He set a goose on thirteen eggs. He stayed awake on hatching night, and kept running out to see it every few minutes—such an exciting experience.

In the morning his score was 100 per cent perfect—all thirteen were hatched.

They were, however, to cause him grief later. The kitchen garden had been started in January; the lettuce bed was coming along nicely and the leaves were almost ready to eat. The young goslings could squeeze through the picket fence which guarded the growing vegetables, and George was expressly charged to keep them out. But once again he fell into the trap of childhood: one afternoon he went to shoot marbles. He was in good form and was cleaning all comers out of their mibs. He stayed too long. When he came back, the plot was as bare of greens as the palm of his hand.

He screamed at the goslings, which made for the pond as hard as they could go, he after them crying and throwing stones. But he was so furious over their audacity that he couldn't hit anything, and threw one rock so hard he lost his balance and tumbled into the pond himself. He clambered out, a sorry figure dripping with tears and muddy water. Aunt Mariah was cross, as she had every right to be, but she was not one to do more than scold. That was punishment enough. In fact, instead of her incisive, condemnatory voice, George would have much preferred a strapping and have it over with.

Aunt Mariah fostered the handicraft talents of her foster son, but she did not really need to teach him how to mend clothes with fine stitches, to knit, or to plait rag rugs. His fingers adapted themselves almost insensibly to the things they had to do. Having been born with knowledgeable hands and a quick brain to guide them, he could walk uptown and see a set of collars and cuffs on a woman's dress, come home, and crochet the same without having any notion of the process by which the originals had been manufactured. He could effect a like result without being shown. Just as simply he hemstitched the first handkerchief he had ever owned, and made patterns with knotted pieces of string, with cross-stitch, and with rickrack.

He did not know how other people made patterns, either

for crochet or living. He had learned by now that he was a Negro, and as such had nothing to look forward to in the way of a better life. Little Negro boys could not dream dreams of being rich and famous someday, or even of achieving some fine purpose. But having no optimism nor hope to obscure the design, he plodded on, weaving it in his own fashion. The particular kind of world into which he had chanced to be born was grayly lit with trouble, but the beauty inherent in order and design was a satisfaction and a compensation. A huge, insatiable question mark had been in his mind ever since he could think at all: "I want to know." He fed it fuel constantly, and it was never satisfied. But it did repay him with energy; his "I want to know," followed by its corollary, "I can do that," was the dynamo which powered his life.

In short order George had mastered all Stephen Frost could teach him and more. But he continued some time longer hopping the fence to school and back again. Though he was growing older, he was not growing much larger, and he was weak and tired all the time. He kept thinking, if he could only go away somewhere, a change of climate or something might make him get better.

When he was thirteen or so he learned of a family that was moving to Fort Scott in Kansas, and they agreed to take him with them. Uncle Andy made a will leaving everything he had to George, and George solemnly returned the compliment, leaving to Uncle Andy the pennies he might amass someday. He and Jim tramped back to Diamond Grove to pay a last visit to the Carvers, and they had their pictures taken, George in his first store shirt, with ruffles. Then he bade farewell to his brother, climbed aboard one of the mule wagons, settled himself gingerly on the shaky pile of furniture, and set forth upon his travels.

Both wagons were stacked high with beds and chairs and tables, and pots and pans jingled all the way to Fort Scott. They were so loaded that the family took turns walking or riding when one would give out. Many days passed before they had covered the seventy-five miles, and when they did arrive, George knew nobody. Having a healthy stomach and taking a lively interest in keeping it occupied, he had to hustle around for a job. Mrs. Payne, it seemed, needed a hired girl, so he went to her house, a fine large one, the sort he had known only from the outside. He approached with apparent confidence.

"I heard you wanted someone to do housework."

Looking at him rather dubiously, Mrs. Payne agreed, and then added, "But do you know how to cook?"

George's cooking had been chiefly of the corn-and-pork variety, but this was no time for hesitation, and he was utterly certain of his ability to do things with his hands—anything. So he stoutly answered, "Yes ma'am."

"Very well," said Mrs. Payne, "I'll give you a chance, but my husband is very particular. He likes his meat and his greens just so, and the pudding must be right or he won't touch it. I hope you make good coffee. You can start dinner now."

George was taken aback at the unwonted length and variety of the menu ordered, but gave no hint of his unfamiliarity with the dishes. Instead, he said cannily, "Mrs. Payne, I'm so anxious to do this just like you're used to. If you show me how you do it, I'll be sure to have things just the way you like them."

So Mrs. Payne, innocent of his stratagem, showed him how much of this she put into her biscuits and how much of that, quite unaware that she was showing him actually how to make biscuits. Then the performance was repeated with the bread pudding, which he had never even seen before. He stumbled through that meal successfully and went right on in like fashion. Mrs. Payne never knew how inexperienced he had been, because the second batch of biscuits—and these he made entirely by himself—was much better than her own. "I can beat you all to pieces," he thought to himself, and did so.

In no time George was expert in dealing with ovens. And

when a bread-making contest was held, he took prizes with his yeast bread, salt-rising bread, and yeast and buttermilk batter biscuits.

Whenever George had saved a small sum he went to school. He learned with extraordinary rapidity, and managed to crowd a lot into a few weeks here and there. As his money ran out, he sought other jobs, usually finding little difficulty, being hired in different houses just as a girl would be.

George was working for a colored blacksmith whose wife was an invalid when he encountered stark horror. He had been sent on an errand to the drugstore one afternoon about four o'clock. Around the jail, which was not far off, a crowd was gathering ominously. Darkness was falling as he returned, and more and more men were joining the mob. Its roar mounted in a bestial crescendo until the citizens of Fort Scott finally tore the Negro prisoner from the jail.

On the sidewalk directly before the blacksmith's house they beat out his brains. Women and children snatched at bits of him for souvenirs. They dragged the bloody mess to the public square, poured oil over it, and set it alight. The stench of burning human flesh rose in a noisome pall. It filled the boy's nostrils and seeped like a black cloud of terror into his brain. He shuddered through the night, and before daylight could reveal the scene of man's ferocity he was away out of that place forever.

## CHAPTER IV

## *"Sometimes I Feel Like a Motherless Child"*

FROM THEN ON George was truly a wanderer. He went from town to town and countless little places, sweeping yards, sawing wood, sandwiching in a bit of schooling when and where he could. Someone would say, "Come with me and you can get a job," so he would go with that person, perhaps to another part of the state entirely. He was so skillful at homecrafts that he could usually get work which paid at least enough to keep him alive.

Sometimes he stayed a week in one place during harvest-time. He loved to bind wheat and oats; he could walk behind the machine, pick up the bundle as it fell, make a double tie in a steady whirl, and never pause in his walking. He could keep up this strange performance all day. At other times he got jobs in greenhouses; it might be for no pay if he had a few pennies saved. The opportunity to handle flowers and plants was enough.

George's progress at school was just more of the same thing—extending his knowledge of the three *R*'s. Some were colored schools and some were mixed, but there was not much to choose between them. Often he could not get what he needed to finish a grade in one place, so he would try to fit it in somewhere else. Or his little means would run out before certain lessons were completed, and he would have to make them up at some later date. Much of his time was spent studying where he was going to sleep the following night, how to get his next meal, how to get a book he needed. There were no free books for colored children. Often he had to study with somebody, or even share the same slate.

Always he wanted to learn, to know. He thirsted for something, and whenever he saw a chance to satisfy that thirst, he moved automatically toward it. At Diamond Grove he had not questioned why he could not go to school with the other children—he just knew that he could not. But as he went about now from place to place, the reason was borne in upon him. Though he was aware of the reason, it still seemed the embodiment of nothingness—he could see no point to it. He didn't want to be somebody else, he didn't want to change in any way. He simply wanted to be what he was. He wanted the opportunity to develop along the lines ordained by his nature and not be told, "You may go thus far and no farther." Therefore, he proceeded, to the best of his ability, as though he were not going to be stopped.

George was an insignificant little chap, and most people thought he was rather cute. Many had a kindly feeling toward him and would give advice, though he had no real shelter. If he landed among those who were not kindly, he had to put up with it. He learned what it meant to be stormed at like an animal. Sometimes he thought that a mule was more fortunate than he, because it could feel only blows of the body and not of the spirit. Not only was he an orphan, but he had no more birthday than a hog would have. Imagine a wagon or other chattel creaking out the glad tidings of its birth! No one had ever told George the day he was born, he was not even sure of the year. He never thought to consult the census records, so he never knew that it was 1860.

His orphaned state had some advantages. Since he had nobody to look after him, he learned to depend on himself alone. He learned that self-pity is a destructive force, and that if he were able to stand the blows they would help develop him and he would make progress; if he couldn't, he would just flatten out.

In the process his independence flourished. He would not allow anyone to give him anything. Even in his early teens he became enveloped in a stiff and almost violent pride. If a man asked him to draw a bucket of water and then held out a quarter instead of a nickel, he would pull back from the outstretched hand, even though he might have a clamoring belly and not a penny to his name. All he asked was work to do and fair payment. This was not caused by a shame of accepting charity, but by a logical mind that balanced things —so much work, so much pay—and he did not want his mind to be warped out of shape. Sometimes he was laughed at, but he remained stubborn. He agreed it was kind of people but not reasonable to offer something for nothing.

Whatever came, George accepted his lot without whining; it was simply the way things were. People of his own race were poor, too, and they had problems of their own and children of their own to occupy them. In self-protection he put the pain aside, and just kept scurrying around, scratching for something to eat.

George was almost always on the move, consequently almost always among strangers. He left a trail of gifts behind him to those who had been kind. It might be his reading lamp, it might be a pen, but his gratitude would usually find some means of expression. Sometimes he completed a filet collar to give away, but chiefly he made his lace just as pieces of design, for his own pleasure. It was his form of expression.

He had a compulsion to create with his own hands the things he saw about him; he would always find a way to do them, and not from books. Once a man came through the country making horsehair watch chains with big open links. George followed his movements intently, then went away and snipped off a wisp of hair from a horse's mane where it would not be noticed and made a horsehair watch chain with big open links.

Somewhere in his travels he had picked up an accordion, for which he paid the vast sum of seven dollars, and this inanimate but noisy object gave him a lot of satisfaction. It was a huge thing and difficult to manipulate, having two bells on the upper right-hand corner operated by a lever he pressed with his right forefinger. These bells he interpolated into the score wherever he thought they would be most effective. At least he thought he could play, though he was more than likely to strike a flat where a sharp should be and alarm the whole neighborhood.

In the town of Paola he had an upstairs room and would sit at the window, the accordion resting heavily on his lap. As soon as he saw someone coming he started to play furiously until the passerby looked up, admiringly, as George believed. One day he saw a man approaching—the music teacher who lived directly beneath him. This was a real chance to show his ability. He seized his instrument and dashed into a spirited rendition of "Home, Sweet Home." The teacher paused and stood staring upward. George, very pleased with himself, pumped away more energetically than ever. But the teacher was not expressing approval; he was shaking his head sorrowfully. George slowly eased the thing down to the floor; he had lost his taste for it. He decided then that he would play it right or not at all, and meanwhile he would wait until he learned how.

The boy was alone, but not lonely in the sense that he particularly desired human companionship or aid or comfort. Since all outdoors was his home, he never lacked for one. He had country roads that were free to walk on and fields and woods full of fascinating and mysterious life. Would he ever know what rocks were made of? Why this soil should be red and that black or yellow or mottled? Such thoughts occupied him incessantly; his hands and his brain were too busy to leave room for brooding.

In the course of time he arrived in Olathe, still following the steep trail of learning, cut by plenty of sharp gulleys along its course. In search of work and education, he lived for a while with a barber and his wife. With some forty colored children he went to school in an old building which had once been a grocery store. The family shortly moved away, but George was taken in by Mr. and Mrs. Christopher Seymour. At first this was chiefly that he might continue his school without any more interruptions, but the Seymours were childless, as the Watkinses had been, and soon George occupied the place of the son they lacked. He was a son to be proud of, being gentle and considerate and able to keep house as well as a girl.

Aunt Lucy Seymour was precise in her habits. She had been accustomed to bake one biscuit each for herself and her husband. Now there were three in the family. Accordingly, she baked three biscuits and placed them on the table. But before she could sit down George's was gone and he was asking for bread and announcing that he hadn't even begun to eat yet. But all the food he consumed didn't seem to make him grow much. She thought, rather helplessly, that if she could hobble him he might put on weight, but he was never still—he was going all the time.

In his wanderings George had never fallen into bad company. He inclined far less toward rowdyism than toward religion. Uncle Seymour was a devoutly religious man and George went with him to morning and afternoon services on Sundays, wrapped in his big shawl to keep out the cold of the unheated Presbyterian church. He became a member at this time, and supposedly that remained his denomination, since he never heard of being turned out. Though, actually, all denominations were alike to him and he always attended whatever church happened to be available.

Aunt Lucy was a lovely character, but firm. She had belonged to a Virginia family and considered her background socially superior to that of colored people who had had less exalted associations. George, however, was permitted to join her nieces and nephews in their recreation, and spent many evenings at the old games of checkers, tiddlywinks, and dominoes. Daytimes he devoted to school, going through the fifth grade and the sixth, playing his accordion for the Friday exercises—a studious, neat, reserved lad.

Eventually the Seymours moved to Minneapolis, Kansas, taking George with them. At that time he was still so undersized that he could ride on half fare, but suddenly his length began to stretch out to the six feet he was finally to attain. He accomplished the entire feat practically in one year.

He was quiet, but not solemn. On the contrary, he had a merry heart. He belonged to the local melody bands—quartets or quintets made up of elocutionists and fiddlers and virtuosos on the jew's-harp or mouth organ, though he never could perform on these last because the metal against his teeth set his nerves rasping. His description of Rubinstein playing the piano was generally considered a masterpiece of humor and pathos.

There were still a few words he could not say without stammering; nevertheless, he was the prize performer in local dramatics, and such foolishness. Though he had reached a man's stature, his voice was as high as a girl's, and once in a small play the young people were to put on he was to have the female lead. When they gave the show in a near-by town, it was decided he should have his picture taken in wig and bustle and leg-o'-mutton sleeves. He fell into his part so completely that not even his enormous hands and feet gave him away, and the lady photographer thought he was of her own sex and chattered away as one girl to another.

He kept up the ruse until he realized her confidences were such as a boy should not hear, and then he became frightfully embarrassed at the thought of how embarrassed she would be if she discovered how he had fooled her. His hat was not at the correct angle, according to female canons, and as she patted his chignon and adjusted his bangs, sweat poured off him. And indeed he was thankful when he made his escape without her discovering the fraud.

In the school of life George was attending he learned much about human beings. A man in Minneapolis had been living in a two-room shack of straight up-and-down boards, the cracks not stripped and lacking whitewash. He had made money and had built a fine house up on the hillside above the street. The Seymours moved in as the white family moved out, their furniture piled on a wagon. At that very juncture somebody in search of a laundress came asking for Mrs. Seymour, and the wife pointed contemptuously to the tiny place and said, "Down in that shack," neglecting to mention that it had just been her own home.

That summer George left long enough to take a job on a farm about four miles from town. It was his first experience in driving oxen. He learned to say "gee" and "haw," and the beasts would go obediently as directed. There came a beautiful day and hot, ideal for an excursion to Rock City—and he could always say he was going to haul water. Rock City was a strange and fantastic freak of nature, a tremendous pile of boulders which seemed to have been dropped out of the sky. There sat the stone mountains in the midst of a flat, level expanse of prairie. You could drive or plow all around or dig underneath and not find anything to account for their appearance there.

As he came up to this extraordinary sight, he ordered the oxen to "haw" that he might consider the phenomenon. Instead, they made a burst for the water, the wagon rocking dangerously, and plunged into the pool, which must have been six or seven feet deep. The wagon was nearly under water and so was George, up on the fodder, hollering and waking the echoes. But his shouting did not budge the oxen. They just stood there and drank until they had all they wanted. Then they dragged the wagon about, almost upsetting it, George still yelling at them, and started the slow, ponderous plod for home. That wound up George's ox driving; they were obviously unpredictable animals. Theoretically he said good-by, never to drive again.

Once back in Minneapolis, George resumed going to school and helping Aunt Lucy with her laundry work. She was the best shirt ironer and polisher in the county, but pretty soon he was allowed to iron dresses for her. It might take half a day to finish one properly. She charged four or five dollars for it, but nobody fussed at her prices. He loved to do them when they were really beautiful fluted ones of white organdy. Such pretty things. Sometimes the bodice had little fine tucks and he had to iron down and in between them so that when they were opened they would puff. He remembered that his first store shirt had been puffed like that. Then there were the fancy underskirts, and he thought, what a pity that all that exquisite work would not show. He tested these when they were finished. He would take one by the top and set it on the floor. It had to remain erect, just as though there were someone inside it. If it could not stand that test the owner, when she came to claim it, might wad it up and throw it back in the basket.

George was now ready to branch out for himself, and embarked on his first business transaction. Small as the town was it had room for two laundries. He, too, was going to have one. He had his eye on a little house a few blocks away on Main Street, down in the bottom below the street, one room with a kitchen lean-to. He opened negotiations with the owner, who made out a bond. To secure title George had to pay five dollars a month. "But," said George, well knowing that life was an uncertain business, "suppose I don't always earn enough to pay that?"

"That's all right. Just pay what you can and then make it up later."

George took his word for it, moved in, and opened for business. Sometimes he had enough money to make the five-dollar payments on the date they were due, and sometimes not. But the balance was always evened up before long.

No one had expected Minneapolis to grow as it did. But within a year a big hotel was built in the block above George on Main Street, which was graded. The grading left George even deeper in the hollow, but he did not mind; it was clear that the town was going to spread out in that direction, and George's property had risen in value from a hundred and fifty dollars to several thousand.

The owner stopped by one morning to call on George. "How do you do. I came to see whether you wanted to sell your property."

"No, I don't think I want to."

"I'd like to buy it. Think it over. I'll be back tomorrow."

The next morning virtually the same conversation was repeated. The owner came again the third day. "Well, what have you decided?"

"I don't want to sell."

"Tell you what I'll do. I'll give you another lot I have about a quarter mile down the street, and I'll move this house to it."

George thought he would rather keep the one he had.

"Do as you please," said the owner. "I can take this property back and don't have to give you anything."

When George looked his astonishment, the man explained further. "You've voided your contract, and it's not worth a cent. It says specifically you were to pay me five dollars a month, and there were several you skipped."

"But," George protested, "I always made it up the next month."

"It says specifically, five dollars the first of each month. I want this lot and I mean to have it; so will you or will you not take the other one?"

There was no recourse. George moved way back to the other lot, some distance farther from town, and as he walked the extra blocks, carrying his laundry back and forth, he cogitated over the sad but valuable lesson he had learned: that in business you can't take people's word for things.

George had several colored friends and a host of white ones, who thought him an unusually clever and thrifty young man. Sometimes people he had encountered on his way were interested enough to follow him with letters. These meant much to him. He, like the rest of the world, had days of waiting for letters that did not come. Some he had been so certain of. Then he discovered at least one reason. The town had another George Carver, a white man, who was receiving mail he was not entitled to. George could fix that little matter in a hurry, and did. At random he picked himself a middle initial—*W*.

Often he was asked, "What does *W* stand for? 'Washington'?" George was not at all sure the name as a symbol of truthfulness was applicable to him, but since the *W* did not stand for anything, it might as well be "Washington."

Not always had George reciprocated in kind with his correspondents because, for months on end, he had not been able to spare a penny for a stamp. This was one of the reasons why he and Jim were out of touch with each other for long periods—besides the fact that Jim was no letter writer, and he also had no fixed home.

George had not heard from Jim for a very long time indeed, when Mrs. Seymour told him she had sad news; she had just learned that his big brother was dead. Jim had died of smallpox nearly a year before and been buried in Fayetteville, Arkansas.

The last link with childhood was gone. George would soon be a man. He had come a long way, and at last he approached in triumph a momentous milestone. He had studied assiduously and believed he was ready for college.

Highland University, which had been founded under the sponsorship of the Presbyterian Church, had a coeducational enrollment of less than one hundred students. It was small, but George was not particular about that; he only wanted to go to college. He sold his property, which left him at least enough to get there, and gave no thought to "working his way through"; he had always worked his way through everything. He wrote the usual letter of application and received the usual form, which he filled out, stating that he had finished such-and-such studies, had such-and-such recommendations. These were pronounced satisfactory, and the university would "be happy to have him with them."

Before the great day of his matriculation George still had the summer ahead of him, and he was not one to waste time. Chester Rarick had been at school with him in Minneapolis and had later gone to Kansas City and opened a business school. George followed, to take courses in shorthand and typing. He also bought a typewriter, a towering contraption lacking refinement; its entire mechanism was exposed, and it sounded like a threshing machine. In return George tried to teach Chester to play the organ, but Chester was music blind and could not tell "Columbia, the Gem of the Ocean," from "Yankee Doodle."

George did not follow his shorthand and typing any further, but was able to use them as implements to make possible what he wanted to do along other lines. Old men see visions and young men dream dreams. He was young and dreaming of the future.

By way of bidding farewell to his childhood, George made a nostalgic tour, first of all visiting Jim's grave in Fayetteville, and then on his way north to Highland stopping at Diamond to see the Carvers. He went to the Locust Grove Sunday school and church dressed in a light gray checked suit, quite slender and as usual so very polite and courteous.

That evening he spent with some of his old playmates. They had no musical instrument save a harmonica, but George had brought along his accordion. They all sang most of the evening, mingling "Tenting on the Old Camp-Ground" and "Just before the Battle, Mother," with gospel hymns and "Swing Low, Sweet Chariot." George joined in the family worship, and the father prayed for his health and his happiness in the Christian faith. He concluded by reminding George that he could make money and lose it, but when he got an education no one could take it from him. George bowed profoundly and thanked them for a delightful evening.

He stopped in Olathe, too, where his friends looked with a sort of awe at little George, now grown to a tall young man with a great future in store, going off to prepare for it.

This modest youth, gentle in speech and manner, was very proud and burning with eagerness when opening day came and he presented himself. The principal was busy and looked up sharply from his desk. "Well, what do you want?"

"I am George W. Carver, sir. I've come to matriculate."

"We take only Indians here, no Negroes."

# CHAPTER V

## *"A Long Ways from Home"*

GEORGE TURNED and went out the door which had opened only to close again behind him. All expectation was destroyed. He longed to leave that place forever, as he had left behind the place of the lynching. But he had used up all his money to get there; he had none left, and still he had to go on living. He therefore followed his accustomed rule—proceed from the Known to the nearest related Unknown. Temporarily, at least, he had to stay in Highland.

The story of his rejection at the college spread. A few good women who attended church and believed its teachings were indignant; they gave him what jobs they could find to do about their homes. Their sympathy was, perforce, silent, because he himself never spoke of the wound he had suffered to his pride and to his dignity as a human being. He was one whose natural reticence automatically commanded privacy. He lived alone, more quiet and reserved than ever.

Mrs. John Beeler became a real champion. Her husband had a big fruit farm about a mile south of town, shipping apples by the carload and keeping a number of pickers busy. George was taken into the house in his familiar role of general helper.

Mrs. Beeler was a first-class cook. Nobody else could satisfy her husband; he had no teeth and was hard to please about his food. Almost immediately she had to go away for a day, leaving George and Della Beeler, their daughter, faced with the problem.

Della was better at playing the piano than she was at dealing with a stove. She said, "George, we'll have to get Father's dinner. He probably won't eat anything we cook, but I'll make the pudding if you'll make the corn bread."

So George got a little round pan and baked the bread. It came out golden crisp, and he cut it in pieces like a pie. Then he and Della stood off and waited to see what Mr. Beeler would say. He didn't say anything. He just ate and ate. His mouth was so full he couldn't speak, but he kept motioning for more until he had finished the panful. The two young people were so enthralled they forgot about the pudding. It cooked too fast and boiled up until it resembled nothing except a bread-and-milk poultice. But Mr. Beeler's appetite had been satisfied, so it didn't really matter, and they threw away the mess.

His friends urged George to attend the church socials and small entertainments in their homes. Wherever he went he was a general favorite. He had a pleasant, likable, if somewhat shy, manner, and he cheerfully played his accordion when asked; a person who makes music is welcome in whatever society he finds himself. Though he hid his despondency it absorbed all other feeling in him. He had forsaken hope as it had forsaken him.

As soon as he could, George tried to escape the immediate pain that pressed upon him night and day. The Government had opened the Western plains of Kansas for settlement in 1878 and the rush there had begun, to be followed by another flood of immigration in 1886. Young Frank Beeler, who was about the same age as George, had gone out to Ness County, had established a town consisting almost exclusively of his store, and called it by his name. To the Great American Desert George also fled in 1886 and filed on a homestead of a hundred and sixty acres two miles south of Beeler, built a sod house, and put in crops.

He had to have work while he was waiting for his acres to produce so he approached the adjoining Gregg-Steeley Livestock Ranch. Mrs. Steeley eyed him with keen suspicion and kept him standing outside while she talked to him. She admitted someone would be needed, because she had merely been visiting her son, the owner, and would soon be leaving. She would not be back for some time and the house and her son must be looked after. "Have you any recommendations?" George pulled out four or five, but her distrust evaporated as soon as she had read the first one. "This is recommendation enough."

Very early the next morning Mrs. Steeley put George on a horse and told him he was to go to the post office five miles away. There were no roads, but he started in the right general direction and prayed that he would arrive somehow. The desert prairie was utterly new and strange to George. As to trees, they were practically non-existent. The nearest were a half-dozen or so poplars thirty miles distant. In that great expanse there was not a switch to be seen—nothing higher than a sunflower stalk.

Suddenly, just a little in front of him, George saw a great lake with a ship on it and people on the ship. He could stand still and watch them moving about. As he advanced upon this fantastic scene, it kept easing away from him. Always it was there, just ahead. Later he learned that this was a mirage and might last for hours without changing its appearance.

When George came upon the post office, he had no difficulty in identifying it, because it was the only building in the county that was not made of sod. It was of white magnesia limestone, sawed into blocks, and he never did find out its origin.

A man came out of this structure and when George, by way of making conversation, politely asked whether this were the post office, he, also by way of making conversation, started to swear. George had learned that when people cursed him for being black, they were laying the curse of ignorance upon themselves. And this man's aimless blasphemy so tickled him that he nearly fell off his horse laughing. The man could do no less than laugh with him.

Mrs. Steeley's attitude, though it had some of the same surface characteristics, differed in fundamentals. She was proud of her knowledge of how to treat colored people. They were born to be servants, and she knew how to keep them in their place. Day after day George had to suffer petty indignities in silence.

*The toad beneath the harrow knows*
*Exactly where each tooth-point goes,*
*The butterfly upon the road*
*Preaches contentment to that toad.*

His food was the same as hers and her son's, but he could not partake of it at the same time. He was unable to see why a difference in skin pigmentation should make this necessary. Sometimes he could swallow his bitter bread, and sometimes not.

The leader of the religion George followed preached the twice-turned cheek. He had to argue with himself a good deal, reminding himself that life forces some people into a lonesome valley. He warned himself that when he had hateful thoughts about Mrs. Steeley, he was ruining his disposition and becoming just as hateful as she. He urged that at heart she was a good person, but was afflicted with a feeling of being inferior, which forced her to dominate somebody or other to try to prove she was superior. At great length he repeated to himself that he must not carry a chip on a thin-skinned shoulder. Weeping was not invited. "Why do you care?" he remonstrated. "Don't waste your time that way. If you carry your feelings on your sleeve, some blunt fellow is sure to run against them. Keep them on the inside and you won't get hurt."

The hurt was already there, but he sought ways of covering it. Animals returned affection to anyone who was kind to them. Every stray horse looked for George to gather grass or hand out sugar to it. The team with which he worked during the week became his Sunday playmates. They knew each other well. Immediately after breakfast he would escape from the house. With sugar in his pocket he would start out, calling "Hi-yi-yi" as he went. Jessup, the gray, and

Yacob, the white, were sometimes way off, it might be a quarter of a mile. When they heard his voice, they raised their heads and stared. They stood thus a moment and then came tearing, full tilt, as though they were going to trample him.

"You'd better not run over me!" warned George.

Then, as suddenly, they planted their forefeet and stopped.

"Well, you'd better!"

If they had come in from the red clover they were likely to be slobbery. George would scold, "You ought to have a handkerchief." He would pull out the one he had brought, already dampened, and wipe off their big, flat lips. Then he would put his arms around Yacob and hug him, laying his cheek against the animal's hard velvet one. He would put his hand in Jessup's mouth, look the creature in the eye, and say, "Hold up now. Don't bite or I'll smack you." And Jessup would let his teeth come softly together. Both would poke their heads into his pocket and nose around and scuffle and carry on until they had found the present he had brought them.

For want of other companionship, George talked to the horses by the hour. When Mrs. Steeley sold his playmates, he could say nothing, but he was full of grief. It was like selling children. In the dark nights, he wondered how they were being treated and if their new owners were kind to them.

Pretty soon, Mrs. Steeley went away and George took charge, doing the housework and cooking during the day-time and going to his own little house to sleep at night, in order to fulfill the legal requirements of his claim. Now at last Mr. Steeley and George could be pals. They sat down to meals together and had a good time talking about pleas-ant and interesting things.

Mr. Steeley, being county commissioner, had a house a degree better than the new pre-emptors, though only a slight degree; his table was of boards, his dishes of tin, and the baking was done in a Dutch oven. However, the house did have glass windows brought from Larned, the nearest town where supplies could be purchased, seventy-five miles southeast of Beeler, on the Missouri Pacific Railroad.

Together, Mr. Steeley and George erected barns, poultry houses, tool sheds—every sort of building needed on a farm—all out of sod. Making houses of dirt was a novel experience for George, and he enjoyed experimenting. With a plow they cut the buffalo sod four inches thick and twelve inches wide, then cut the strips in twenty-four-inch lengths. These were laid, alternating with each other as bricks would be, until the walls were nine or ten feet high. On the ridgepole and the rafters was laid more sod, then dirt, until it was a foot thick, and raked smoothly.

George became so expert he could show newcomers how to trim the walls down with a sharp spade and whitewash with lime to stop the dirt sifting in. He had the reputation of being the best builder in the county, and his own hut was so neat and clean and so decorated with flowers that no other soddy could compare with it. He built a lean-to on the south side of the Steeley house, a sort of conservatory, and here he kept his flowers and plants blooming luxuriantly through the most bitter cold.

The desert floor was green and beautiful in the spring, and its charm held until May. That was what fooled the tenderfeet. They would plant their acres in corn and it would spring up straight and flourishing, would tassel and silk perfectly. They would point to it with pride and exclaim, "Who says corn won't grow here? I guess you folks just don't know how."

Then would come the period of the hot winds. Beginning about ten o'clock, scorching, burning blasts, almost as bad as the fine dust of later days, would sweep across the prairie. Non-saccharine sorghum could stand the winds after its fashion—it could curl up and stay for weeks without water—but by nightfall the corn would look as though a barrel of boiling water had been poured over each stalk. For weeks and weeks such weather continued, with nothing to relieve it —no shade, no rain. All work had to be done in the early morning and late afternoon; if a farmer stayed out during midday, he also would be cooked.

About halfway between Beeler and George's house lived a settler called Cyclone Munn. He lacked the neighborliness which made life bearable on the desert. A little creek running through his land enabled him to grow a small garden, so rare and so highly prized in the midst of the heat of the plains where almost all food came out of cans. But he kept it strictly for his own enjoyment, violating unwritten homesteading law by refusing to share his delicacies.

Frank Beeler and George fastened covetous eyes on Cyclone Munn's three rows of green corn—eating corn. The ears began to swell, and the boys kept careful watch. They had to judge just right between the time it ripened and the time Munn would start to pluck it. A cloudy night came along—perfect for the deed they were to do, and they crept into the garden with a gunnysack. They pulled the tender ears quickly and quietly until they had enough for a fine feast. They were starting back toward Frank's store when a gun banged behind their flying heels—the theft had been discovered. However, they dodged about and managed to reach the store safely with their loot.

Out back of the building George lighted a fire in a shallow hole and heated water in an old tin can. The can was not very large, so he could boil only a few ears at a time. He would bring them in to Frank and then go back to prepare more. Finally he discovered the stock was not inexhaustible. As fast as he had carried them in Frank had devoured them, and on his last trip, to his great disgust, only three were left for him. This was a tribute to his cooking, but one he could have done without.

The weather was more than a topic of conversation in Ness County. It spelled the difference between financial ruin and success. If a rare day in June brought nineteen hundredths of an inch of rainfall, everyone exclaimed. "What wonderful weather!" Often also it was a matter of life and death.

Early in George's first winter, Mr. Steeley had to go to Larned for supplies; he would not be back for about a week. Though cold, about thirty below zero, it was a beautiful, bright day, and George was astonished when Mr. Steeley cautioned him to get the stock up every night because a blizzard might be coming. "And," he added, "when you get the stock in the barn, stay in the house. Don't go out for anything." George felt slightly insulted at what to him was a warning for children, and said, "I've seen blizzards before."

"No, you haven't. Where you come from, they have storms but not blizzards. Don't dare to go out!"

With this final admonition, Mr. Steeley started off in the clear, sunshiny morning.

For fuel the homesteaders used sunflower stalks or cow-chips dried by the sun, which almost melted the stove, they burned so fiercely. One of George's tasks was to gather these and pile them in a corner of the house to be used as stove-wood.

The second day, after he had tidied the place, George took his team and went out for chips. Until two o'clock he dug fuel, then he noticed a peculiar strip of bluish cloud lying way off on the horizon. It was just a little strip, but so queer that it caught his attention. He had never seen anything just like it.

He continued gathering chips, glancing occasionally at the sky. By three, the strip looked a yard wide, and he decided it must be the blizzard.

Quickly, then, he rounded up the stock, got them into the barn, and closed it tightly. This took about an hour. The cloud had widened enormously by this time and had begun to spit snow a little bit.

George stood and just looked for about half an hour in a kind of awe at this strange sort of weather. Because, in that brief time, the barn, which was less than a hundred yards away, had been completely blotted out. He tied a rope to the bedstead, got the door open, and stood outside, clutching the rope. The wind was blowing terrifically. He could hold his hand up six inches from his face and not be able to see it. He took a few steps from the house, not more than three or four, but could see no trace of the building. At last he could understand some of the tales he had heard in that country, that after a blizzard, when daylight had come and the snow had ceased, men were found frozen to death within a few feet of shelter.

Clinging to his life line, George eased himself back into the house. It snowed all night, and he had little sleep. The window glass had a crack so fine you could not put a pin through it. Nevertheless, the snow was finer still and sifted in, keeping him busy scooping up the pile and shoveling it out. Next morning it was clear and sunshiny again, with only a howling wind and a solid sheet of snow to prove that the storm had come and gone.

When Mr. Steeley finally returned, he remarked, "So you thought you'd seen a blizzard! What did I tell you?"

George was thoroughly humbled. "You're right, I only thought I had seen a blizzard."

The houses were about a mile apart, but most of the pioneers contrived to be neighborly. Evenings were often devoted to music. Mr. Steeley played the violin, Mr. Gregg the guitar, Frank B-flat cornet, and George created harmony among all from his seat at the organ. They made the soddy quiver with every song they could think of, from "Buffalo Gals" to "Nearer, My God, to Thee." Frank has written, "I look back with a great deal of satisfaction to the concerts we pulled off in the sod houses and also in my store after business hours. Those were the days of real joy."

During the hours of farm inactivity George wandered over the countryside, picking up Indian relics and botanical and geological freaks. Once he met a friend of Mr. Steeley's and remarked, "Sometime they're going to find something under here. I don't know what it'll be, but I've been all over these hills. There's a big dome under here, and they'll find something, you mark my words." Fifty years later the Beeler oil pool was tapped, just where he said it would be, and it was believed to run under his own quarter of land.

When the weather kept him indoors, he made lace, copying the intricate designs of spider webs, or turned to his books. He continued to study and continued to paint because he could not help himself. He was always putting paint on something—tin or anything he could get hold of.

He would go any number of miles to see and paint a particular scene of which he had heard. If he learned that Castle Rock, forty miles from Dighton, where he happened to be at the moment, was a view worth looking at, he somehow managed to get there and come back with a picture of it. He had always been smearing and daubing, but quite without direction.

Now he was given some help in this constant industry. Clara C. Duncan, one of the first teachers of Talladega College, which had been one of the first institutions opened for the higher education of Negroes, came out to Ness County to homestead. For her he made his first drawing under instruction—a pencil sketch of a rabbit. She showed him how to correct certain lines and then, still under her direction, he made a little painting two inches by three of a fuchsia, and followed this with a gaillardia.

In an unusually solemn moment, even for him, George had composed a poem and typed it with a green ribbon on his ponderous machine. This he titled "Golden Moments":

*Whilst I was sitting one day musing*
*On Life's book, each page perusing,*
*I heard a whisper softly sighing,*
*"Lo! Time's sickle is near thee lying.*

*The rich and poor, the great and small,*
*By this same sickle all must fall.*
*Each moment is golden and none to waste.*
*Arouse thee then, to duty haste!*

*O! sit not down nor idly stand;*
*There's plenty to do on every hand.*
*If you cannot prosper in work like some,*
*You've at least one talent, improve that one."*

It went on like that for forty-two stanzas. These, also, he took to Miss Duncan. When she handed the poem back to him, it looked as though a cricket or grasshopper had dragged it around. She had cut it down to twelve stanzas. He looked so crestfallen that she tried to reassure him, "That part's good, what I've left."

"But," George protested, "you didn't leave anything."

"But that part is very good."

George got as far as the gate with his mangled manuscript when she called after his dejected figure, "Come back, George." Again she tried to reassure him. "What you have here is very good." But George was not to be consoled. He started away again, and once more she called him back.

"Now listen, George, and remember what I say. It's always better to be a good prose writer than a poor poet."

George believed her so implicitly that he decided then and there that he was cured of his poetry-writing affliction and was grateful that she had corrected what might have developed into a terrible disease.

One by one the things he could not do well were being pruned away, to leave the things he could do supremely well.

The desert had its compensation in the way of beauty. At night the aurora borealis lit up the sky in fountains of brilliance. George had never seen any color so rich. To him it was a marvel of marvels. And at certain times in the early morning and late afternoon a mirage might appear. Never was anything more wonderful than to stand and look at great rivers and open seas, or a woodland stream in which people were fishing or canoeing.

George could bear most things, but not being deprived of the cool richness of foliage and verdure. He took to dreaming of flowers he had never even seen. One was of orchids growing on an old fence post that had become a mossy stump. Another night he dreamed of some exquisite *iris prismatica.* An old log had fallen down in a little pool which had collected after a rain. It had made a grassy, damp place, and the iris were coming up alongside the log.

It was undeniable that agriculture which would give any sort of return was almost impossible in this arid country—the land was really fit only for grazing. George labored long but unprofitably. He proved upon his claim June 25, 1888, but did not live on it the required five years to get it free. Instead, he took out a mortgage for three hundred dollars.

As the greatest contrast he could think of to the burned expanse of western Kansas, he had a vague idea in the back of his mind that he would open a greenhouse in some likely spot. He had been wandering around Kansas for nearly a dozen years; now he started northeast for Iowa, taking with him various specimens of cactus. He would rather throw away his clothes than those.

But even a bird with a long neck cannot see the future.

# CHAPTER VI

## *"The Trumpet Sounds Within My Soul"*

IN VILLAGES along the way, when George had accumulated a few dollars, he would set up a laundry business. It didn't take much capital. He could buy a washboard for fifteen cents and a big tin tub for twenty-five cents, or, if he lacked the twenty-five cents, he could take a barrel and saw it off and make a tub.

One of the towns in which he stopped to look about was Winterset, Iowa, not far from Des Moines. It was a pleasant place but not quite large enough to support a greenhouse. However, he could always turn his hand to cooking, so he applied for a job at the Schultz Hotel.

The proprietor's son had been the cook, but thought he would rather play the violin, and had gone off with a traveling troupe. Mr. Schultz said George could take his place, though he warned, "If my boy comes back, he gets his job again."

On that condition George took complete charge of the kitchen; he was the chef and did the buying also. Mr. Schultz said that he cut the expenses in half, and the guests were pleased with the food.

Early in life George had to learn that when one door closes two will open. Occasionally he forgot this, but he soon picked up courage. And so many people in the world were pleasant and kind and helpful that he did not have to pay any attention to those who were not. He had trained himself not to hope but to be prepared for disappointment, then if a bumptious person returned a pleasant answer, he was agreeably surprised. This faith had given him much comfort.

It never mattered to George what church he attended.

Everywhere he went he sought the Y.M.C.A. or the nearest Sunday school or prayer meeting. On a certain Sunday evening it happened to be the Methodist Church. He sat in the back near the door and listened appreciatively to the clear soprano of the choir leader, Mrs. Milholland, his own tenor high above the untrained voices of the congregation.

The next afternoon he was summoned from the kitchen of the hotel; Dr. Milholland wished to speak to him.

"You like to sing, don't you?"

George admitted that he did.

"Well, my wife heard you at church last night. She sent me to fetch you around to the house."

George went, and Mrs. Milholland's interest in the young man was enormously increased. He had a quick gaiety whenever it was allowed free expression and a warm outgoing nature that responded instantly to anyone who gave him a welcome. She was an enthusiastic gardener and had her own little greenhouse; she was also an amateur painter who delighted to splash color on canvas, though she had had no training. George was horrified at the state of her palette, stiff with dried paint, and could not help exclaiming, "Oh, your brushes, your brushes!" Immediately he set about reducing her worktable to cleanliness and order. Mrs. Milholland was properly grateful for this assistance.

Obedient to her request, George had gone to the piano and sung for her. Now she had a suggestion to make. When his day's work was over he was to come to her house and give her instruction in painting, and she would exchange with singing lessons. This was, in reality, her own gracious way of helping someone in need, by putting it on a reciprocal basis. And the really important thing was the exchange of friendships.

From that time the Milholland home became one for George too—a place where he could be sure of helpful understanding. At holiday time he was a part of the family festivities, and at Christmas his was the function of dressing up and creating merriment as he distributed the gifts.

Mr. Schultz's son was not so good a violinist as he had thought, and presently he was back again to claim his job, leaving George without one.

George could polish collars and cuffs until they shone like glass. A laundry where the townspeople could be sure their best clothes would not be faded or shrunk or scorched would be a boon to Winterset. He found a tiny cottage on the edge of town with a kitchen shed and a parlor cook where he opened a small hand laundry, paying a little cash for his equipment and securing the rest on credit, vouched for by Dr. Milholland. He had never bought on credit before, because he could not be sure he would be able to pay for it. And having a debt of fifty dollars nearly threw him into spasms. He hurried at the double quick in an effort to wipe it out, and took on all sorts of outside jobs.

Every evening he had to report to Mrs. Milholland on what he had accomplished during the day—tell everything in detail. She would call her two children in to listen, using him as an object lesson. Then she would laugh and say, "Who ever heard of anyone doing half that!"

George had learned to be punctilious about appointments and to fulfill promises, however slight. Any old time wasn't worth shucks, and "sometime" meant no time. Nobody particularly cared for the reason if he were there at nine o'clock and you were not. An excuse was only one of the ways of saying you didn't do it. "Just get George to promise and you can rest easy"—this was the reputation he had built up.

Once he was out in Mrs. Milholland's yard beating carpets. A neighbor came and asked if he would do the same for her.

"What did George say?" Mrs. Milholland inquired of her.

"He said he'd come if he could find time."

"That won't do. He's in great demand. Didn't he promise?"

"No, not promise."

"You'd better go back and get a promise out of him. Then you can rest easy—he'll be there."

George kept his cottage-laundry immaculate, with his usual fastidious care. Passersby who chanced to glance in through the open door could see him seated at his supper table, set as precisely as though he were entertaining.

The little black-handled knife he had found in the cornfield was not sturdy enough for his constant toy whittling; for this he used a ten-cent "Buckhorn handy Barlow blade, best old knife that ever was made." Often he carved corner pieces of picture frames to give away as souvenirs.

Mrs. J. M. Robbins had chanced to be at the Milhollands' when George had made his first appearance there, and she was another who helped hold his hand up. One day she found him working on some crochet patterns he was copying from a magazine and, seeing her interest in the lace, he had brought out a large box of samples of designs he had found in various places. She looked at him in amazement and asked, "But what are you going to do with all these patterns? Why all this work?"

"I'm going South to my people later on," he replied, "and I expect to use them in teaching in the schools there." With his own particular brand of tenacity, George had never quite forgotten his childhood announcement that someday he was going to have a school where he would teach the things he himself could do with his hands.

The cottage was on the southeast rim of the city with the open country almost at hand. To be back in the woods again was his chief joy. Long hours he spent in utter content rambling with his basket on his arm, picking up flowers and leaves to take home—the same sort of litter he used to bring in as a child. Only now he could study them, identify and classify and arrange them on shelves. For years he had sat in libraries finding a little bit of information here and a little bit there; then he had gone to a lecture perhaps and pieced it in and found something to connect it up with.

Mrs. Robbins' son Fred, in his late teens, was at home then. He found George one day strolling in the woods on the hill above their house, bearing the inevitable basket, looking for botanical specimens. He was not carrying the basket with his usual ease. He was becoming stooped, and someone had told him that it would help him to straighten up if he walked two miles a day with a stick across his back, held by his elbows. This he was faithfully doing, though he was suffering from a bad case of tonsillitis.

Fred took George home. Mrs. Robbins had a remedy that she used with good results, so she asked him to stay. In the Robbins home he remained until he was well. Being a busy housewife, she left his entertainment to Fred, who was completely fascinated by George's conversation.

George had developed a special method of polishing stones. Gladly he showed his rocks, or perhaps a piece of asbestos he had dug up, to callers who might be interested and explained as much as he himself knew. He had gathered quite an amazing store of knowledge which he freely shared with any who cared about it, and these were many, because he had a happy gift for making the things which were exciting to him seem important also to others. Garden lovers were his natural friends, and to all such he was guide and philosopher. If anyone expressed the slightest desire for a certain fern or bulb it was sure to be forthcoming—George spared no effort in securing it.

For a while he left his books alone; he was too much absorbed in acquainting himself with natural objects. But, according to Mrs. Milholland, "he very soon started what might be called a private school for himself, and the hours for each branch were as rigidly enforced as in a school where there were many students."

Mrs. Milholland was worried for fear George's talents would not reach their full realization without more formal guidance. She agitated the subject constantly. "Now, George, you've got to go back to school. You ought to be in school."

And George would answer, "Yes, but how can I? I've just got a start with my laundry here. I still owe forty dollars on the equipment I bought. How can I go back to school?"

But her words kept sounding in his ears, and the idea kept

bothering him until it came to be an almost continual voice ding-donging in his mind: "You ought to go back to school. You know you ought to be in school." Though it was out of the question, from George's point of view, all the summer of 1890 Mrs. Milholland kept insisting. He was so troubled that he didn't want to go see her, and she sent the children to find out what was the matter.

One bright, clear day during the latter part of July he was polishing a shirt bosom before the open window and at the same time comforting himself by saying, "I know I can't." He brushed this aside and then had a vision of that forty dollars. Its place was taken by a new vision. "You'd better go back to school." "No, I can't go to school." He went into a sort of daze and forgot what he was doing. He abandoned the cross-barred polishing iron—there it sat on the shirt bosom.

He left the board, walked over to the window, and stood looking out for many silent, thoughtful minutes. At last he heard his own voice speaking aloud with sudden determination: "Well, then, I will go back to school!"

A great burden seemed to roll away. From then on George never had so much work. He could do any amount of it, and by fall had paid off the forty dollars. He gave his paintings on tin to Mrs. Milholland and sold his little belongings for enough to pay his tuition.

As George walked the twenty-five miles toward Simpson College, he fed his hopes on the information contained in the catalogue that the Science Hall had "an elegant art room immediately under the skylight."

## CHAPTER VII

# *"That Promised Land Where All Is Peace"*

SEPTEMBER 9, 1890, George arrived in Indianola, Iowa, "unusually quiet and pleasant, presenting to the students as few unworthy attractions and allurements to vice as any town in the state." Simpson College, which had been organized under the auspices of the Des Moines Conference of the Methodist Episcopal Church, consisted of three buildings, and its faculty numbered seventeen. Its president, the Reverend Edmund M. Holmes, was also Professor of Moral and Intellectual Philosophy.

No one is more alone than a young person entering a new school, where everybody seems to be calling greetings to everybody else. He is certain he is the only stranger and that the magic circle of already-existing fellowship can never be penetrated. Even academies of higher learning generally omit courses in friendliness from their curricula.

George came to school carrying little with him to make him welcome. He had only a satchel full of poverty and a social timidity resulting from a constant struggle with poor health, his falsetto voice, which went so strangely with his height, the never-ending need to brace himself against that first antagonistic gaze of strangers, and the uncertainty as to whether he would be allowed even to work toward his heart's desire.

Rebuffs were more familiar to George than meals; he knew he was going to meet them, and was seldom wrong. But Simpson was an exception. He was not precisely welcomed; the other three hundred students stared at him briefly, and then ignored him. But at least he was not turned away with an unalterable, "No."

For all his varied learning he lacked certain fundamentals—mathematics, for one, a subject which offered no appeal to him. He therefore enrolled as a special student in the preparatory school and registered in arithmetic, grammar, essays, and etymology.

However, he bumped squarely against a heavy obstacle when he applied for permission to register in the art course. This was an unheard-of thing—that a colored person should want to study art—and he was looked at in astonishment. It seemed a great pity that he should even consider spending his time in that way; didn't he realize he should be studying something at which he could make a living? No. Definitely, tuition would not be accepted for the art course.

George could appreciate their attitude; if he had no talent, studying art would be a waste of time. But how could he find out without trying? He remained stubborn, even in spite of the teacher who said she thought the whole thing disgraceful. At first he only paused wistfully in the doorway of that "elegant art room immediately under the skylight," but finally he ventured within and presented his plea directly to Miss Etta M. Budd, the art director. She was not very encouraging, but said he might attend classes for two weeks, and at the end of that time she would let him know whether he had any talent. With that George had to be content.

The women at Simpson lived in the Ladies' Hall, but the men boarded in private homes, and President Holmes gave George permission to occupy an old abandoned shack not too far from the campus. When George mentioned the fact that he must have work, Dr. Holmes said further that he would urge the other students to give George their laundry. With this assurance he entered a little store and bought two tubs, a washboard, soap, and starch. These purchases had to be arranged on credit because after he had paid his modest tuition of twelve dollars he had precisely ten cents left.

In a meat market on the north side of the square he bought five cents' worth of beef suet. That cut his capital in half. He walked on to the grocery on the northwest corner of the square and spent the remaining five cents for corn meal. He carried his tubs and board to the shack and waited for customers. They didn't come and they didn't come; Dr. Holmes had forgotten to make the announcement of the new laundry in assembly. As day after day went by and the suet and meal diminished George grew hungrier and hungrier.

Mrs. Milholland has since mourned, "Had his Winterset friends known of the very slender purse he carried, his first days there might have been very different. But because of his constant resourcefulness, his friends did not dream but that the college laundry work which had been promised him would amply provide for all his needs."

George, however, was more tormented in his mind than by his physical state. For the first two weeks he was in a sweatbox of worry as he struggled to shade a sphere properly; would Miss Budd decide he had talent and let him stay on?

At the end of the second week he awaited the fateful decision in a perfect agony. But Miss Budd made no comment, and he was afraid to ask her, for fear she would say no. Finally, his nerves were in such a state that he could bear the uncertainty no longer. Timidly he ventured, "Miss Budd, you said that if I showed any special talent I could stay in the class. May I?"

"I don't see why not. You may start doing landscapes."

A day or so later Miss Budd could be seen walking purposefully along North Howard Street and turning in at number 805. She was paying a call on a former pupil, Mrs. Arthur W. Liston. Miss Budd stated her object, "I have a talented boy who wants to study painting. He has asked to saw my stovewood for the tuition and will you find him a room? He is a very promising young man and we must help him."

Mrs. Liston started out almost at once for George's tumbledown home. But when she rapped on the door and he opened it and stood before her, she scarcely knew how to approach him. Something in his quiet manner made it difficult for her to state her real errand. Then a sudden thought came to her and she found herself asking aid instead of offering it. Could he do some sketching for her? She wanted to paint her flower garden, but her drawing was not good enough. Would he help her with it?

Of course he agreed immediately, and while they were arranging for the best time her eye took in a battered black pan half filled with corn meal and water and a discarded old stove on which was a boiler empty and gaping for something to be washed in it. She suggested that a room nearer the campus might be better for his purpose and that she knew of one belonging to some friends of hers. It was on the corner of Buxton and Detroit Avenue, just opposite the canning factory; she was sure he couldn't miss it, and it would be much more suitable for his laundry.

Mrs. Liston's next act was to busy herself making his needs known to the students, and after those grueling early days George had all the work he could manage. As one of them expressed it, "He took on the job of keeping clean a bunch of dirty roughnecks." And he was eminently successful at it.

From that time also he was seldom at a loss for friends. Merchants cheerfully gave him goods boxes, and from these he constructed his furniture. Then one afternoon, when he returned from school and opened the door, an astonishing sight greeted him. He wrote Mrs. Milholland, "The people are very kind to me here and the students are wonderfully good. They took it into their heads I was working too hard and had not enough home comforts so they clubbed together and bought me a whole set of furniture—chairs, table, bed, and such things as I needed. I never found out who did it. Of course I had my suspicions and accused a number of boys, but they stoutly denied it."

That was their biggest tangible contribution, but they also paid him the honor of realizing he would not knowingly accept material aid, and consequently performed their charities in secret, slipping a nameless ticket for a lecture or an anonymous fifty-cent piece under his door when they were sure he would not catch them at it.

On one occasion George fell out with Miss Budd over this matter. A musicale was to be given and after the morning class she asked him if he were going.

"I'm afraid not," said George. "I can't afford it."

In the afternoon she sent for him. "Here, George," she said, holding out a ticket. "I don't think I shall be able to go tonight. It would be a pity to waste this, so you take it and go."

George thanked her with his customary courtesy, dressed in his best, and went to the performance. And there, almost the first person he saw, was Miss Budd. After that he was more on the alert, so she could never play that trick again.

Nevertheless, it was through such manifestations of a new spirit that George began, as he expressed it, for the first time to look upon himself as a human being. Individuals had been kind before and had liked him once they knew him. But George did not want kindness any more than he wanted brutality. He wanted to function simply as a human being with the privileges and obligations of other human beings. Here at last he was in the environment he had so long been seeking, and in the entire community he was accepted in full fellowship.

The offer of friendship extended by the other boys was not mere kindness on their part but a response to a superior quality they recognized instinctively. One who visited him in his room found him first stirring the boiling clothes, then taking a bite of his dinner, then reading a sentence from a textbook. Then again he would stir, bite, and read. Afterward the student said, "That man will accomplish something in this world, if it's nothing more than to rub off some of the black."

His room, as usual, was decorated with stones and flowers and cacti he had brought back from the West. Many of the boys spent long hours with him while his iron moved ceaselessly and rhythmically over the board, asking questions on a multitude of subjects and receiving answers from his more mature mind that whetted further their youthful curiosity.

Though George was kept so busy with his laundry and his studies that the beam of his oil lamp shone late through the night, on Saturday and Sunday afternoons he followed his favorite pursuit of walking in the woods and, to those who joined him, such afternoons never seemed long enough.

They were comrades in sports also—an ultimate test. He would not have made a big-league team, but he loved to play baseball and was a welcome addition to the college team. He was invited to join the literary societies and help furnish the music for school concerts in neighboring towns. His general popularity was enhanced by his excellent voice, particularly in the student Y.M.C.A. He was one of the four leaders at a convention of the organizations of the vicinity, a noteworthy group racially, consisting as it did of himself, a Chinese, a Japanese, and a white American.

If George was rated highly by his fellow students, the faculty, more conservative but equally laudatory, considered him "an excellent student with perseverance, clear insight, and amazing patience." To quote again from Mrs. Milholland: "George was with us over the Sabbath once when Dr. Holmes preached at the Methodist church, and through the happy greeting exchanged by president and student one could readily recognize the warm friendship existing between them."

Since George could not often spare time or money to pay visits to Winterset, long letters were exchanged between himself and Dr. and Mrs. Milholland, the sort of unstudied, naïve letters a boy writes to his family, who will understand his little vanities and rejoice in his success.

Gardening remained a close bond: "If you are thinking of investing much in orchids I think you will regret it as they are very hard to raise. However, I will send you the names of two of the cheapest; they belong to the butterfly family, come very highly recommended, and are said to be of easy culture. One is spotted and the other is a beautiful purple—very fine."

When he made a vacation trip to Des Moines, which "was

muddy, but I had a nice time," he reported on the health of the Milholland relatives there. He kept the flowers as well as his friends in mind and inquired after their health also: "I hope your orchids are doing well. I saw some of that variety in bloom while in Des Moines. They are very pretty indeed. I wish you would send me a bulb of that oxalis we got from Miss Siders last fall. You can put it in a tiny box and send it by mail; I lost mine. I have two double-fringed purple petunias (slips) and I think they are both growing. If you haven't any I will send you some. I thank you very much for the seeds; part of them are up. I lost all my foliages during the holiday vacation by putting them in a cellar that was too damp for them. My roses are just beginning to grow again. I want to try to root one of each for you if I can."

In the spring George wrote:

> You will doubtless be surprised to learn that I am taking both vocal and instrumental music [piano] this term. I don't have to pay any direct money for my music, but pay for it in paintings. They are very kind and take especial pains with me. I can sing up to high D and three octaves below.
>
> My health is very good with the exception of a bad cold I contracted yesterday by working in the studio when there was a draft blowing through. However, I will take some quinine tonight and hope to feel better in the morning. I have trebled the work I had last term and it keeps me very busy.
>
> I beseech you, Doctor, to wait until I come up, and I will tell you the joke I have on you; it is very good indeed, so much better than the key.

The origin of this joke was lost in obscurity. Presumably it referred to George's use of the key in the back of his arithmetic book. His marks in his other subjects seldom fell below ninety, but arithmetic went down and down until finally he received no mark at all.

Raillery on the subject remained a bright thread running back and forth through the correspondence: "Well, Doctor, you may expatiate as much as you please on the key question; I hope you enjoy it and will keep right after your turkey. You will not when I come up again, for my joke on you is so good it will monopolize all the time." It finally died on a note to Mrs. Milholland: "You can't imagine how much good the reading of your letter has done me, and tell Doctor I enjoy his preaching very much and that I will finish arithmetic this time, key or no key."

George was buoyant with enthusiasm when he reported progress in painting, but he was so fearful that his retailing of compliments would smack of braggadocio that he attempted a not-too-artful deception of substituting dashes for the first person singular. "I am getting along very well with my painting, will begin flowers soon, and then I will send the model for yours. My teacher says she is very sorry she did not know —— when I came here or she would have let my talents run as they liked. She further paid me two very pleasing compliments today. She said that in all her contacts with people she never met anyone like —— and that I was going to excel in flowers. She further told me she had never seen me get them stiff and ungainly, and she is not going to let me copy a thing, but make my own designs and paint from nature. And she is painting a large panel from one of my original drawings."

Finally he smothered his pride with: "Well, the subject of myself is getting very monotonous and was before I began it, but I thought you would like and be interested in knowing what they thought of me. Please don't let anyone see this letter but the home folks. My teacher sends her best respects to you and also repeated invitations for you to come down."

He felt closer to Miss Budd than any of his other instructors, because painting was nearest his heart. But even Miss Budd was limited in her understanding of him.

He had been set to doing landscapes, because that was the routine, but he didn't really care about them. And as for the marine, which was his assignment in April, he hated it. One young woman, the only one from the Art Department, was going to graduate in May, and her finishing work was to be of dark red roses. Day after day she struggled with these, while George looked on enviously; it would be a very long time before he would be allowed to paint red roses.

One day Miss Budd shook her head over them, and said, "Alice, I'm afraid you have no talent." Then she went out to dinner, leaving George and Alice alone in the studio, he with his detested marine and she with her hopeless botch of roses.

Poor Alice suddenly exclaimed, "I can't do it!" and threw down her brush.

"Here, let me help," offered George.

Alice handed him the brush and he started to work with swift and certain strokes. He had never looked on the sea, but he had studied roses from babyhood. Both were so intent on the picture that they forgot about Miss Budd's return, until Alice heard her step in the corridor and cried, "Look out!"

George was startled. He jumped up and backed away hastily, knocking over a statue of Ajax, which he loathed. It smashed to bits, and in the general confusion Miss Budd said severely, "What *is* the matter with you, George!"

Without answering, George bent to gather up the pieces, and Miss Budd's glance caught Alice's picture. She was nearly as startled as George had been at her arrival. "Why, Alice, that's the best work I've seen you do. I really believe you've caught the spirit of it at last!"

George looked up from the shattered plaster he was gathering together, and he and Alice grinned at each other, then burst out laughing.

Alice explained. "It isn't mine. George did it."

Miss Budd turned to George indignantly. "Why didn't you tell me you could do flowers like this? I've a good notion to give you a Scotch blessing! Go get another canvas and start a still life!"

George was happier than he had ever been before.

After this experience Miss Budd continued to assign different subjects to different students according to their several abilities but, recognizing George's special gifts, she allowed him to go his own way. He could not copy; he was very poor at that, but he made his compositions from memory. He could bring to life again any flower he had once seen, from bud to full bloom, and started at once on the yucca of the plains which he remembered from his desert days.

Art and Nature being thus inextricably allied in George's make-up posed a pretty question. How could his predilections be best put to use in the matter of earning a living when college was over? This problem bothered Miss Budd more than it did George. He did not wish to look behind the curtain of this happy present.

Miss Budd was a wise woman brought up in the academic tradition, her father being J. L. Budd, Professor of Horticulture at the Iowa Agricultural College at Ames. According to popular report, artists died poor, and she did not see much future for George in painting. A man named Sargent in the United States Department of Agriculture made wax models of fruit as outstanding as the Harvard glass flowers, and George thought he might do something like that. But Miss Budd did not consider it enough. She wanted his education to rest on solid foundations of practicality. And yet to be successful he must do something in which he would be content; he must follow a natural bent.

George had felt the cruel shocks of being a Negro in a world ruled largely by white prejudice. The scars were hidden under a natural optimism, but he had also been endowed with a strong social conscience.

This significant note occurred in one of his letters to the Milhollands: "I am taking better care of myself than I have. I realize that God has work for me to do and, consequently, I must be careful of my health." And always he signed himself, "Your humble servant in God," an attitude he did not take lightly. If the time should come when he could help other members of his race toward unfettered minds, he would need more than the ability to make pictures.

Together Miss Budd and George talked things out, and at last George decided he would go to Ames to study agricultural science. It was a hard decision, and when he told Dr. Holmes he was going to put away his brushes and paints he could do nothing else that day. For once in his life he sat idle.

# CHAPTER VIII

## *"And the Walls Came Tumblin' Down"*

IN 1891 the Iowa State College of Agriculture and Mechanic Arts was already an eminent institution and, under the presidency of W. M. Beardshear, prided itself on being excelled in agriculture by no other college. It was the seed bed from which sprouted three men who were to rule the agricultural destinies of the United States for twenty-eight years.

James G. Wilson, director of the Agricultural Station, was soon to become Secretary of Agriculture in the cabinets of McKinley, Theodore Roosevelt, and Taft; Henry Cantwell Wallace was Assistant Professor of Agriculture, later to become Secretary of Agriculture in the cabinets of Harding and Coolidge until he died in 1924. His son, Henry Agard Wallace, was to fill the same post during the first two administrations of Franklin D. Roosevelt, though the present Vice-President was at that time only a small twig being bent in the right direction.

The school term had already started when George arrived in May; it extended from Washington's Birthday to Thanksgiving, and the long vacation occurred in the winter when farmers ceased from farming. Professor Budd, who had been prepared for the coming of his daughter's protégé, directed him to the dining hall to arrange for his mealtime. There he was bluntly told he could not sit at table with white boys; he would have to eat with the field hands in the basement.

George shrank from yet another blow. "This, too, I can bear," he thought, but he did not want to be turned away from school again. In all simplicity he wrote his good friend

Mrs. Liston back in Indianola asking what he should do. The response was equally simple. Mrs. Liston put on her hat and boarded a train which speedily covered the fifty miles to Ames. She spent the day with him strolling about the grounds, admiring the buildings and their appointments and equipment as though she were walking through catalogue and prospectus. Between statistics she dined in the basement with George and the servants.

That day marked the end of his isolation, and from then on things went very much easier. Miss Budd had asked Dr. Louis Hermann Pammell, Professor of Botany, to find some work for George, and so North Hall was given a new janitor. Dr. Pammell it was who also solved the problem of sleeping quarters; or it may have been Professor Wilson. Such arrangements were often made behind George's back. The necessities which occasioned them were unpleasant things which it was not necessary he should know. Sometimes he learned of them years later, sometimes never.

The college was state supported, and consequently tuition free, but there were other expenses. Under "How to enter" the catalogue stated, "Write to steward enclosing three dollars to retain room, and ask for dimensions that you may bring proper furniture, carpet, etc." George had been unable to keep up the payments on his Ness County homestead and had deeded it to the man who had financed his loan. Consequently, he was propertyless and moneyless once more. He had arrived in Ames without even bedding, nothing, in fact, except faith. Whoever was responsible for finding him sanctuary, George was installed in Dr. Pammell's office downstairs on the first floor of North Hall, and Dr. Pammell moved up to the second floor.

George could not later recall that anyone at Ames was ever unkind to him. When he was waiting on table in the dining hall one of the women students rose and left the room as she saw his black hand serving her. But her name is not engraved in history, and that of George W. Carver is. Eventually other students followed the accustomed pattern of respect, admiration, and affection. He has said, "If one pessimistic note ever reached my ears there were a dozen optimistic ones urging, 'Yes, you can do it. Go ahead.' As a result the thing was accomplished."

So George was allowed to continue his geology, botany, chemistry, bacteriology, zoology, entomology, and kindred subjects.

The college was a part of the National Guard and subject to call by the governor. "To fit young men for positions in the state troops as line officers and company instructors," male students in the lower classes were required to become members of a college battalion and wear the prescribed uniforms of navy blue with brass buttons during military exercises. This was slightly ironic from George's point of view, since he would never, under any circumstances, be permitted to be a line officer; nevertheless, with the other students he attended lectures on military tactics and, on Wednesday and Friday afternoons, maneuvered to bugles in drill and parade, which would give him a "dignified carriage of the person, gentlemanly deportment, and self-respecting discipline with habits of neatness and punctuality."

He was scared to death of General James Rush Lincoln; you'd better not make a mistake or the general would bless you out! But then everybody else was terrified also. At first George thought the general took a special delight in making things disagreeable for George alone; he was wrong in this and wrong in that and wrong in the other. The general was the meanest man anybody'd ever seen! But as time went on and George had a chance to bring his knowledge of human nature to bear on this vexing problem, he found that General Lincoln was no more strict with him than with anyone else. Then the general's military brusqueness began to amuse him.

Though George could by no means be called a martial man, he dearly loved uniforms and bands, and he applied himself to mastering military science. He rose steadily from private to second lieutenant to first lieutenant to captain—

the highest rank among the student officers. And in the process General Lincoln became his warm friend.

Students were encouraged to join one of the seven literary clubs, and George was made a member of the Welch Eclectic Society, the purpose of which was "development in science, literature, and the art of public speaking." "The art of public speaking" offered him a distinct challenge. He was already sensitive about his speaking voice, because he had so little control over it. It would stay subdued for a while and then break unexpectedly into an embarrassing falsetto. The first time this happened in his elocution class, the teacher exclaimed, "Of all the ridiculous voices I ever heard, none has ever been quite as bad as yours!"

George took exception to this, but she let him sulk. And when he had pulled himself together they went to work on it. They were so successful that after he had achieved a balance he was offered a scholarship in singing at the Boston Conservatory of Music. Since this was not his intended career he did not accept, but it did represent a triumph over a handicap which had long hindered him.

The literary societies did not merely announce meetings in bald letters on the bulletin board, but embellished it with fine printing and scrolls. When George got through with one of these it was a thing of beauty. They also vied with one another in adorning the rooms in which they met. The Eclectic Society naturally outdid all the others, because George became the Committee on Decorations, and his arrangement of ferns and flowers achieved a harmony no one else could equal.

Another thing which made the Eclectic Society outstanding was the nature of its monthly meetings, usually legal in tone. A court was held in which certain offenders were tried —criminals who had disobeyed the rules of the table in the dining hall. The hall was furnished with a multitude of big square tables, each seating eight, two to a side, and students chose their own table mates. George no longer had to weave his way around the pillars serving others, but sat at the most envied of the student tables. It was envied for the merriment which emanated from it and spread throughout the room.

This group made up special games. One was to divide the table in quarters, and no one was permitted to pull a dish over the line. If caught violating this provision he would notify his lawyer. The fun at table was carried on to the club meetings. He would be prosecuted and tried and, if he lost, his fine would be no dessert for the next day. If he protested and carried it to a higher court and lost, the punishment was serious—no pie for a week. Often the professors came in to hear and applaud the debates, carried on with great solemnity and courtroom punctilio.

Another table rule required everyone to ask for what he wanted by its scientific name. If you could not remember that black pepper was *Piper nigrum,* you could sit there forever, sans condiment, and nobody would pay any attention. Or if you forgot *Triticum vulgare,* you could call and call without result; others would comment on the particular richness and tastiness of the bread, but the forgetful one would have to eat potatoes. Or if you requested NaCl instead of ($C_{12}H_{22}O_{11}$), no matter how politely, you drank your coffee with salt instead of sugar.

This sort of jollity relieved the monotony of putting food into the stomach and at the same time helped to sharpen the students' wits. They must use the terms they were learning in chemistry, mineralogy, botany.

Chemistry George liked, because it permitted him to tear things to pieces and find out what they were made of.

And algebra he liked, because it dealt with unknown quantities. He was supposed to be studying in the same classroom where an algebra class was being held, but he found something so fascinating about the letters and signs, he listened to that instead of attending to his own work. Finally the teacher said, "You aren't accomplishing anything just sitting there like that. You might as well join the class." This George was delighted to do, though he was not supposed to have algebra until the next year. But the experiment was highly successful. The more unknown quantities there were the better pleased George was; he could run them down with ease and satisfaction.

Geometry, however, was another matter altogether. Here he bogged down completely, after getting off to a good start. The day of the first test he was given the easiest proposition in the book, and he jumped at it like a bull terrier at a rat. He had only that one, and whizzed through it so fast that he met some of his classmates coming in as he was going out.

"Are you through already, George?"

"Oh, yes, and I made a four," he announced airily. Papers were marked on a scale of four hundred; three hundred and seventy-five was passing. Exit George.

The next day he took his place in the front row. Professor Edgar W. Stanton was round and jolly looking, but George didn't know him very well, or he would have sat in a corner. Mr. Stanton started to read the marks. It did not take him long to reach the *C*'s. George straightened up. He wanted to hear that four read out loud so everyone could hear. Mr. Stanton had a little black book, and he kept turning pages and looking up in the air and turning more pages. Finally he said, "Mr. Carver, I give you zero."

George could not believe he had heard correctly. "Zero!"

"Yes, zero."

"But, Mr. Stanton! I had the answer right, I looked it up afterward."

"Having the correct answer makes no difference. You went wrong on your first statement. You can't arrive at a right result from a wrong hypothesis."

Though George was outraged at the moment, he soon realized the correctness of this attitude and its applicability to other aspects of life. A path might straighten out at the end though it had been crooked on the way; but if you retraced your steps it would still be crooked. You could not build truth except on a foundation of truth.

George waded through geometry somehow, but did not

accomplish very much. He was not what might generally be called enthusiastic over mathematics.

He also hated history, all history except the aboriginal history of the United States, in which he took a special interest. Ancient history he got only after his fashion, which was poor. He later claimed he had never been guilty of remembering a date. When asked to "describe briefly the significance of the reign of Queen Anne," the spreading flower of Queen Anne's lace (*Daucus carota*) drifted delicate and white across his mental vision.

And he was just stupid about United States history—he wanted to go to the woods instead of study. Once he decided not to be the fool of the class any more; he would get at least one lesson right. He read a certain aspect of the Washington administration and learned it as though he were learning poetry. Fortunately he was called on, and rattled it off, word for word. The instructor stared. George sat down abruptly. It was just as well she did not question him further the next day, for he would not have known anything at all about the Washington administration.

George was by no means meek in classes which interested him, but argued persistently, usually on the side opposite that of his instructor. "I don't see why I should have to learn why a leaf is orbicular lobed or ovate serrate. I want to know what the plant is."

"But you have to learn that first."

"I don't believe it. Having to learn all that is the reason for most students hating botany. Why can't you put plants into groups and say that all in that group will have certain characteristics? In the begonia family the leaf will always be shield shaped."

The speculations which began to stir in him then and were clarified by having to answer argument in controversy became the basis for his later group theory in education.

As George climbed the long flight of steps that led to the big red brick building which housed the agricultural classes, he was entering a new world, one in which science was being applied to farming. The empiric truths of Vergil's time had long been forgotten, and the renascence of agriculture had started only about fifty years before when Justus von Liebig, being a chemist, had begun to apply chemistry to his studies of vegetable physiology.

He taught that plants were nourished by carbonated nitrogen which they received from the carbon dioxide and ammonia present in the atmosphere, and that their potash, soda, lime, sulphur, phosphorus, etc., came from the soil. The function of manures, therefore, was to restore to the soil those minerals which plants withdrew from it for their growth, and he astonished his associates by preparing artificial manures. The result in England had been the use of nitrate of soda, Peruvian guano, and superphosphate of lime in the form of bones dissolved by sulphuric acid. The Agricultural Society, having as its motto, "Practice with Science," had been founded in 1838, and the first experiment station in England had been established in 1843, only half a century earlier.

In the United States, Americans began to exert their mental powers on agriculture with the same energy they had applied to industry. Science and agriculture joined hands, found themselves compatible, and were now bustling along together at a rapid rate. During the decades in which George was growing up many aids to agriculture were being perfected: ensilage, as a result of the disastrous rains of 1879; inoculation against Texas fever in cattle and cholera in hogs; tuberculin tests; an array of farm machinery; and new methods for testing soils to determine which constituents were best suited to the new plants that were being introduced from all over the world.

Science in agriculture was at the spring of its year, and George was beginning to understand something of that "trinity of relationship existing between the plant, the soil upon which it grows, and the human being or animal consuming it." In 1936 he wrote:

Mr. Wallace [H. C.] was one of my beloved teachers, and while his special subject in the A. & M. College was dairying in all its phases, he was a master of soils. Many are the invaluable lessons I learned from him. He set me thinking along lines practically unknown at that time, but which are now found to be almost, if not quite, as astounding and important as the exploding of the theory of spontaneous generation by Justus von Liebig more than a half century ago.

Henry C. Wallace, son of the Reverend Henry Wallace, founder of *Wallace's Farmer,* who was loved throughout Iowa as "Uncle Henry," inherited from his father the conviction that agriculture is the great mother science and industry of the ages; in commerce it is the basis of civilization. He was expressing an intellectual concept of agriculture when he said, "Nations last only as long as their topsoil lasts," but he applied himself also to the immediate problem of farming, and when he became Secretary of Agriculture in Harding's cabinet, launched the phrase, "Farm Relief."

A certain destiny was shaping George. Though he had endured hardships and loneliness, simple and fine people such as the Watkinses and the Seymours had arisen in the path of the orphan to act as mother and father to him; he had found such guiding friends as the Milhollands and Listons; and equally simple and fine teachers were now continuing the process of molding him mentally and morally.

One of the most potent of these was James G. Wilson. The cheerful, Scottish-born Dean of Agriculture and director of the experiment station had already taken a turn at politics in the State Legislature, and was the first farmer congressman in Washington, where he was known as "Tama Jim." Now he was exercising his gifts as a truly great teacher. He was a father to all the students, both boys and girls; all felt free to go to him for advice at any time and without any hesitation.

Wilson had been informed of George's unusual gifts as a painter, and wanted to make sure the young man was not sacrificing something rare. He asked, "Why not push your studies along this line to some extent?"

But George replied, "Because I can be of more service to my race in agriculture." This, as Wilson later said, he considered a magnificent statement. The friendship which followed was founded on mutual respect.

James Wilson and George Carver had a peculiar affinity, despite their differences in age, condition, and race. One was as deeply religious as the other and believed in carrying his Bible in his heart and not merely under his arm. Professor Wilson was a noteworthy Biblical scholar and George was in the process of becoming one.

Being a state school, Ames had no compulsory religious training, but students were strongly urged to attend the Bible classes and prayer meetings held under the auspices of the Y.M.C.A., or the Sunday-school classes conducted by certain members of the faculty. Everyone wanted to be in Professor Wilson's group, which grew so large he was embarrassed for the other teachers, who had only a small attendance. Privately he asked certain ones, including George, to change to some other class but, after two or three weeks, one by one they drifted back until they were all together again, and Professor Wilson was helpless to break up the company.

The Y.M.C.A. held a summer school at Lake Geneva, Wisconsin, and during George's junior and senior years he went as a delegate to represent his college. The daily lessons emphasized order, precision, promptness; over and over, they reiterated the need for accuracy and system.

One of the purposes of the Y.M.C.A. was devotional—George devoutly believed that the knowledge of God is the beginning of wisdom. A second aim was evangelistic—to gather other college men into the fold. It was said, half in fun, that George brought religion to Ames, but there was much truth in it. In August of his first year the first meeting of the Volunteer Band for Missionary Work had been held, with George and two others in attendance. Before he graduated it had expanded to thirty, with three volunteers for foreign service. A third purpose was educational—the Volunteer Band had its own library and issued bulletins—and the fourth was practical—its records contained such items as "1 bbl. clothing consigned to Pleasant Hill, Tennessee."

The first time George went to Lake Geneva he had for tent-mate an Englishman named Ashby, an excellent athlete. He was a magnificent swimmer, and George abetted him when he slipped down to the lake for his nightly swim after lights out. The rising bugle at the camp sounded at 6:00 A.M., retiring at 9:30 P.M. These hours fitted in admirably with George's long-established custom. His habits had always been in accordance with Nature's own, and he kept very much the same hours as the sun.

George modestly thought he could play croquet a little, but Ashby was a star performer and had never been beaten. One morning Ashby was not up in time for the first seating in the dining hall and George waited for him to join the second. They still had some time, and Ashby challenged him to a game. George had no inclination to match his feeble play against the skill of Ashby, but had to accept the challenge when the latter taunted him with, "You're afraid!"

"All right then, come on. I'll play, but I'll probably beat you."

"That's the spirit. I'll give you first shot."

So George placed his ball and shot through the first two wickets. His double play sent him through the side wicket and back to the middle. And so on. He just couldn't miss this morning. Every extra shot sent him through another wicket and earned him another bonus. He hit the far peg and started back. Inwardly he was jumping with glee, but outwardly nonchalant, as though this were the most usual thing in the world. He came back the same way, and hit the home peg, where Ashby was still standing with his mallet in his hand without having made a single shot. George threw down his own mallet and said in a superior sort of way, "I told you I didn't want to beat you."

After that he rested on his laurels; he never trusted his luck in another game with Ashby.

Not long afterward honors were evened. George, himself unused to water sports, admired his friend's smooth handling of boats. Rowing with Ashby looked so easy, and one evening he thought he, too, would take out a rowboat. But a sudden breeze sprang up, as it does in those waters. The waves rose higher and higher until they were jumping like fun. George had a mental picture of the hundred-pound muskellunge which had been caught there the day before, and also remembered that someone had let down a flatiron hundreds of feet without being able to touch bottom.

His heart was sinking, if the waves weren't, when he saw Ashby coming after him; nobody had ever looked so good. The expert swung his boat around and hopped into George's, giving him the rope to hold. They started for the shore, rising over the waves and down as smooth as oil, and meanwhile Ashby started to tell George how to do it. But George recognized his limitations and stated emphatically, "You needn't give me any instruction, because I'm never going to try it again!"

At Iowa Agricultural College the manual of labor was divided into two kinds: uninstructive was paid for in money; instructive was compensated by instruction given and skill acquired. Both of these were made available only to the most faithful and meritorious students. However, they were expressly warned that they were expected to pay in cash for the main part of their expenses while at college; the opportunity for earning money was merely to help out a slender purse.

But George's purse was flat, and an exception had to be made for him. The ledgers contain such items as:

G. W. C. in account with the student department.

Scrubbing one day 8 hrs.
" " " 3 "
" " " 5 "

One of his extracurricular activities was to act as professional rubber for the athletic teams. He had to see that runners and football players ate the right kind of food and not too much of it, that they slept the prescribed number of hours and at the right times, that they performed the right exercises in sufficient quantity. When the exercising was over, he really went to work, massaging, thumping, stretching, feeling out muscles, and incidentally learning much about the anatomy of the human body. With his incredibly long fingers, almost twice as long as those of any ordinary man, he gently wiped away soreness and fatigue. He could bring healing to pulled ligaments, but only as long as there was no serious injury. He could not bear to see anyone in pain, and went completely chickenhearted at the sight of blood.

George became known as the man who would not use anything he had not paid for. If he sent away for a book he unwrapped it to verify the fact that it was the one he had ordered, and then put it aside until he knew his money order had been received. Not until that time did he consider it his, nor would he open it and read.

Professor Wilson was the only person who could break down the barrier erected against unearned aid. One day he happened to glance at George's feet. The shabby, broken shoes caught his attention. Without a word he reached in his pocket and held out two dollars. "Go get a pair of shoes!" he ordered sternly. "Not a word out of you! Go! Get out!"

In the face of that sternness, George was for once unable to talk back. Meekly he took the two dollars and bought himself a pair of shoes.

He had been so occupied and absorbed during his first year that he had neglected the Milhollands, but when he did write in August the response was immediate: "Your letter from Ames did not come any too soon as we were thinking of sending a tracer after you." The orchid was growing, geraniums were profuse, the expensive begonia had not lived. Mrs. Milholland had not done any more painting since he left. Dr. Milholland added a postscript: "We are glad to hear that you are well, and, of course, busy. Satan will never get you. You have the *key* to the situation and can lock him out. Will you return to Indianola or remain at Ames this fall? We are glad to remember you in our prayers and desire that there may be a mutual remembrance."

The pull of George's paints and brushes remained stronger in him than he had realized. He was like a mother who leaves her baby at a foundling home one night and then goes back to fetch it in the morning. His first winter vacation of 1891–92 he hurried back to Indianola and enrolled as a special student in the art course at Simpson.

With a delicate and discerning eye he translated into another medium the beauty he saw about him or remembered from some past time. It might be crab-apple blossoms, pond lilies in a deep blue shade, or a character sketch of the *Mentzelia ornata* of the desert. Miss Budd said she could correct his faulty coloring but could teach him nothing about form. Sometimes he felt he could not make a mistake; the picture grew before his eyes. At other times he wept with the pain of creation.

When his second winter vacation came around, he registered again at Simpson, but a doctor stepped in and forbade it. He had anemia, and his nerves were in a shocking condition. He was ordered not to touch his brushes and paints for at least a year. He walked the floor in agony, but the decree was inexorable.

Presently George picked up his courage again and resumed work, which he had always with him. Thanksgiving Day came and passed, and so did Christmas, while he went about his accustomed duties. The day after Christmas he was supposed to go to Professor Budd's house in Ames, a mile away from the campus, to clean up after the disorder of merrymaking. A light snow had fallen during the night and a sleigh had been sent for him. He put on his old scrubbing clothes and climbed in. Some of the other students jumped aboard and said they, too, were going to town, which George

George and his older brother, James

George Carver as a young boy

Captain George W. Carver of the National Guard at Iowa State College

George Carver with painting which won honorable mention at the Chicago World's Fair, 1893

*Courtesy of P. H. Polk, Tuskegee Inst., Ala.*

Dr. G. W. Carver painting at Tuskegee Institute

George Carver in art class at Simpson College

thought a little odd. As they jingled along he saw still others walking, and thought it stranger still that so many people should be going to town all at once.

The snow had stopped and the sun had come out clear and bright. The sleigh drew up in front of the biggest store in Ames, and one of the boys suggested, "Let's go in."

George had on his oldest rags and objected vigorously, but they were too many for him and half pulled him into the store and into the men's clothing department. "Here, what's this!" protested George. "I don't want to buy anything." His overcoat was worn and covered even worse tatters.

"Just try this suit on."

"There's no need to fool this way. I'm not buying a suit."

"We just want to see how it looks."

Still struggling, they got him into a gray suit and added the rest of a complete outfit—shoes, hat, gloves, everything. George was bewildered and upset, but he was given no time to think. Professor Wilson thrust a railroad ticket into his hands which read, "Ames to Cedar Rapids," and at seven that evening he was on the train, carrying four of his paintings.

From December 27 to 30, 1892, an exhibition of Iowa artists was being held in Cedar Rapids in connection with a meeting of the Iowa Teachers' Association. Professor Wilson and George's other friends were determined that his work should appear, and had chosen this method of circumventing his inevitable protestations and insuring that he got there. G. W. Carver was duly listed in the catalogue as the author of No. 99, Yucca; No. 25, Roses; No. 43, Peonies; No. 186, Vase of Flowers.

When George presented himself and his canvases, characteristically and with his usual adaptability, he offered to help install the exhibits—an offer which was gratefully accepted and which contributed to the general excellent showing.

His paintings at once brought him into state fame, which was confirmed when the judges selected all four to be shown at the World's Columbian Exposition in Chicago the following summer, but he could manage only one, and chose the Yucca gloriosa. He carried it himself to the White City, where it received an honorable mention.

Incidentally, he saw the World's Fair. The first time he went, he thought he knew all about it beforehand, and made a tour, rushing through one building after the other. But the second time he had learned how to get the most out of a fair. He devoted himself to only three buildings: Art, Horticulture, and Science—in that order.

Though George was not allowed to paint very much, he turned this insatiable desire of his into a field in which he could exercise his art, and produced mycological drawings that were exquisite in their perfection of detail and color.

And as a plant breeder, an explorer into the infinite, he could create fresh color and form in the living plants he loved so well. As a child he had planted his flowers close together, hoping they would mix. Then when he grew older he found out that this was the function of bees, but it was a haphazard method—so many specimens had to be discarded. Now he had learned how to crossbreed by hand to produce the desired result. He had performed most of his experimentation on bulbous plants, because during his migratory life they were so much easier to carry from place to place than root plants. The subject of his thesis for a bachelor's degree was "Plants as Modified by Man," and he selected the amaryllis as his special object of study.

The graduating class of '94 was called The Gourds, and its motto, "Ever climbing," was mysteriously printed on the top of the powerhouse smokestack one dark night. George, who was affectionately nicknamed "Doctor," because he "knew everything," was elected poet laureate. He had, perforce, to essay writing verse again and composed an "Ode to the Gourds."

He had been offered a job after graduation by a florist. This he gently declined. "I did not earn my education in order to arrange flowers for the dead."

After four years at Ames he was ready for his B.S., and Mrs. Liston was on hand for his triumph as she had been for his difficult initiation. He met her at the train, very happy and proud in his gray suit with the inevitable flower in his buttonhole, which he never was without, then or thereafter. She, for her part, was loaded with red carnations, the class flower, tributes to George from members of the art class at Simpson. He read the "Ode to the Gourds" and took Mrs. Liston to dinner in the student dining hall, where they sat at the professors' table—a place he had legitimately earned. He was the first colored graduate of the college and the only member of his race ever to be on the faculty staff.

School honors seem important at the time to most young men and women, and to George they might have appeared doubly so. But they had come easily, even unsought, and he knew very well that their value depreciated when schooldays were over; that such applause was heard no further than the college doors. However, he was not leaving those friendly doors just yet.

His correspondence with the Milhollands had continued faithfully, and in October 1894, a month before graduation, he wrote:

> The many good things the Lord has entrusted to my care are too numerous to mention here. The last, but not the least, of these is my appointment as Assistant Station Botanist. I intend to take a post-graduate course here, which will require two years—one year of residence work and one of non-residence. I hope to do my non-residence work next year and in the meantime take a course at the Chicago Academy of Arts.

The conflict between George's longing to devote himself entirely to painting and his equally strong desire to be of service seemed as though it would never end.

# CHAPTER IX

## *"On My Way to the Kingdom Land"*

SEVERAL APPLICANTS had offered themselves for the opening on the faculty as assistant botanist in the experiment station, but George Carver's qualifications were far superior to those of anyone else. Dr. Pammell called him one of his most brilliant students, the best collector, and the sharpest observer he had ever known, and in 1899, only five years later, Professor Budd in a published article in the *Iowa State Register* quoted G. W. Carver as his authority.

Carver was placed in charge of the greenhouse, where he performed various plant gymnastics in grafting, inarching, and crossbreeding. In accordance with the new agricultural developments in the country, Professor Budd's department was engaged in improving orchards; some fruit trees had been imported and were being added to the native stock. Carver's work with amaryllis had proved him a master at crossing, and he was employed by the Horticultural Society of Iowa during vacation in crossing and hybridizing fruits—apples, pears, plums.

During his two years on the faculty at Ames as assistant to Dr. Pammell, he devoted special attention to bacterial laboratory work in systematic botany. Dr. Pammell was an eminent botanist, and his monumental *Manual of Poisonous Plants* was an authority, not merely among botanists, but in veterinary science. Carver collaborated with him on two publications: *Treatment of Currants and Cherries to Prevent Spot Diseases,* Iowa Agricultural Experiment Station Bulletin 30, 1895; and *Fungus Diseases of Plants at Ames, Iowa, 1895,* Iowa Academy of Science.

He fully reciprocated the esteem in which he was held by

his professor. His *Progressive and Correlative Nature Study,* published in 1902, bears this inscription: "To Dr. L. H. Pammell, a distinguished botanist and great teacher; my constant adviser, not only as a student, but throughout the many years which followed. It is with grateful memory that I dedicate this book."

Under Dr. Pammell's instruction, Carver had started his mycological collection very early, a collection which grew to some twenty thousand specimens. And he had rapidly become an outstanding mycologist in his own right. When a new fungus disease is discovered, not even the mycologist can tell what it is going to do. He must get the range of occurrence and the extent of the damage. The lower plants (fungi) known as molds, mildews, toadstools, frogstools, mushrooms of simple structure and organization, reproduce by means of microscopic spores instead of seeds. They contain no chlorophyll and are therefore unable to live on inorganic matter like other plants, but must draw food from decaying matter or living organic tissue, and are likely to take charge of cultivated plants. Some do not spread, but others must be watched with a good deal of care.

When a very little boy George had been called the Plant Doctor, but now he was earning the title scientifically. As he tramped the wide distances of the nine-hundred-acre campus, up and down Squaw Creek and Skunk River, his eye, sharp as a bird's, detected plants which were sick, and he brought back the fungi which had attacked them. If he were intent on one kind he might see many others and collect them, but he put them aside until the time came to deal with them; he must keep his mind focused on one thing.

He was still possessed, as he had been when a child, by that unappeasable question, "I wonder why?" He liked to quote Tennyson's lines:

. . . . . .

*Hold you here, root and all, in my hand,*
*Little flower—but if I could understand*

*What you are, root and all, and all in all,*
*I should know what God and man is.*

Over and above Carver's scientific knowledge was his intuitive affinity with Nature. Animals, plants, insects, even minerals were his friends. Once he wrote, "Never a day passes but that I do myself the honor to commune with some of their varied forms."

Not only Carver's contemporaries, but also the very young found pleasure and stimulation in his society. The six-foot man and a six-year-old boy, Henry A. Wallace, walked in the woods together. The Vice-President has since said: "Because of his friendship with my father and perhaps his interest in children George Carver often took me with him on botany expeditions, and it was he who first introduced me to the mysteries of plant fertilization. He seemed to have a great sympathy with me. Though I was a small boy he gave me credit for being able to identify different species of grasses. He made so much of it I am certain now that, out of the goodness of his heart, he greatly exaggerated my botanical ability. But his faith aroused my natural interest and kindled an ambition to excel in this field; his praise did me good, as praise of a child often does. There is no doubt it is the gift of the true teacher to see possibilities before the pupils themselves are conscious that they exist. Later on I was to have an intimate acquaintance with plants myself, because I spent a good many years breeding corn. Perhaps that was partly because this scientist, who belonged to another race, had deepened my appreciation of plants in a way I could never forget. Certainly because of his faith I became interested in things that today give me a distinct pleasure. I feel I must pay him this debt of gratitude."

A lasting memorial to this companionship is the Wallace hybrid corn, which covers many acres of Midwestern farms, standing tall and unbent by storms.

Carver was spending more and more time with James Wilson. He was welcomed at the Wilson farm in Traer,

Iowa, and felt at home in the midst of this musical family. And more and more he traveled with the professor on short lecture trips; Wilson would talk on agriculture, and Carver on mycology, horticulture, or floriculture, describing the differences between window plants, hothouse plants, and store plants, emphasizing the fact that a plant could no more flourish in conditions unnatural to it than a polar bear could thrive in the tropics; you could no more put a tree or a plant in a place where it did not belong and expect it to develop naturally than you could put an Eskimo at the Equator or a Hottentot at the North Pole.

Though he was not a great orator he spoke clearly and directly and in a friendly manner about matters close to his heart, whether his subject was flowers or the Psalms. Sometimes he went alone, to little places in Iowa—Mediapolis, Nevada, Cambridge, West Liberty—and wherever he had been, he was affectionately remembered.

In West Liberty the Flori-Horticulture Society held an exhibition, and the West Liberty *Index* for August 20, 1896, stated: "Had that worthy Ames gentleman, Professor Carver, who would have doubtless known the names of all the plants and who must be credited with the organization of the society, been here, the display must certainly have delighted him."

Carver had been unable to attend because he was busy packing and finishing up his work at the college.

He had altered his plan to attend the Chicago Art Institute, skipped his non-residence year, and applied himself to his master's thesis. He was to receive his degree in November 1896. Though his desire to paint was not uprooted, it was taking second place; regardless of his gifts, the pull of obligation was becoming stronger and stronger.

On one occasion at a Y.M.C.A. meeting Carver had spoken of the needs of the colored people in his own land, but he had been a young chap then and knew little of what he was talking about; his was the brashness of ignorance. Never in his life did he discuss the race question publicly,

He was a thinker, not a fighter—a laboratory scientist, not a sociologist, and he realized that if once he should become involved in controversy he would have no time left for his work. Having accepted in silence the personal injustices that had come his way, he had succeeded so well in covering them over that the details were blurred and most were eventually lost to memory. He knew he could not even dwell upon them in his mind without losing energy which he believed might be put to a better use. And for him this better use signified a wordless service which would speak loud in accomplishment. The public plea for his race he would leave to others who were more fitted for the duty.

A man named Booker T. Washington had revolutionary ideas as to the sort of education which would best fit the necessities of Southern Negroes and for fourteen years had been vigorously applying them at a little town called Tuskegee in Alabama. Then on September 18, 1895, he had made a speech at the Atlanta Cotton States and International Exposition which had echoed across the country, "a platform upon which blacks and whites could stand with full justice to each other." This was the first time a Negro had been allowed to lift his voice in the South, and the audience was in an uproar, applauding and weeping, when he described his race as "the most patient, faithful, law-abiding, and unresentful people that the world has seen," and then held up his own hand and said, "In all things that are purely social we can be as separate as the fingers, yet one as the hand in all things essential to human progress."

Washington made a parable of the historical legend of the lost ship: "A ship lost at sea for many days suddenly sighted a friendly vessel. From the mast of the unfortunate vessel was seen a signal, 'Water, water; we die of thirst!' The answer from the friendly vessel at once came back, 'Cast down your bucket where you are.' A second time the signal, 'Water, water; send us water!' ran up from the distressed vessel, and was answered, 'Cast down your bucket where you are.' The captain of the distressed vessel, at last heeding the injunction, cast down his bucket, and it came up full of fresh, sparkling water from the mouth of the Amazon River. To those of my race . . . who underestimate the importance of cultivating friendly relations with the Southern white man, who is his next-door neighbor, I would say, 'Cast down your bucket where you are'—cast it down in making friends in every manly way of the people of all races by whom we are surrounded. Cast it down in agriculture, mechanics, in commerce, in domestic service, and in the professions."

George W. Carver was ready to cast down his bucket.

He was, of course, the best-trained Negro agriculturist in the country and, as a result of the bulletins issued by the station, was becoming widely known. In November 1895 a request came to President Beardshear from Westside, Mississippi, for Carver to join the faculty of the land-grant college of Mississippi—Alcorn Agricultural and Mechanical College. President Beardshear was cautious in his reply: "Mr. Carver has admirable tact and is universally liked by faculty and students. He is a thorough Christian gentleman and gives good promise of marked scientific usefulness in his chosen work. We would not care to have him change unless he can better himself." He inquired as to the salary offered and the nature of the work. "Please send me a copy of your latest catalogue and courses of study. In case your position proves desirable we can give him ironclad recommendations."

A second request was sent Carver direct, asking him to accept the Chair of Agriculture. He wanted to be sure that, if he agreed, he would be taking the right step, and he talked it over with his faculty advisers.

Some wrote unqualified recommendations. General Lincoln said that Mr. G. W. Carver, a "most gentlemanly and efficient cadet, rising to the rank of captain through merit alone," enjoyed the respect of all who knew him and there were none but wished him well. Dr. Pammell wrote: "I have great confidence in Mr. Carver's ability. This has been backed up by having him reappointed assistant with an increase in salary. I believe Mr. Carver has a great future before him." And Professor Budd: "Indeed we do not like to lose him. He will get next year as good a salary as you offer."

But the thought of parting came hardest to Professor Wilson, and he devoted many pages to his reply:

I do not want to lose Mr. Carver from our station staff here. . . . I have been more intimate with Mr. Carver than with any other student on the campus. I have to some extent befriended him when it was in my power to do so, and he has responded by doing a great deal of work among the students that has pleased me greatly. . .

In cross-fertilization . . . and the propagation of plants, he is by all means the ablest student we have here. Except for the respect owe the professors, I would say he is fully abreast of them and exceeds in special lines in which he has a taste.

Carver had attended Wilson's class in heredity

. . . and I assure you I would not hesitate to have him teach our classes here. . . . He understands the anatomy and physiology of animals thoroughly, and the effect of different feeds. . . . With regard to plants he has a passion for them, in the conservatory, the garden, the orchard, and the farm. In that direction we have nobody who is his equal. I had designed that he should experiment along the line of developing our native plants, cross-fertilizing, and introducing such new plants from over the world as would be beneficial to farmers and orchardists of Iowa. . . .

We have nobody to take his place and I would never part with a student with so much regret as George Carver. . . . I think he feels at home among us, but you call for him to go down there and teach agriculture and horticulture and the sciences relating to these things to the people of his own race, a people I have been taught to respect, and for whose religious education we consider it a privilege to contribute. I cannot object to his going. It will be difficult for me to find another student who will quietly do the religious work that Mr. Carver has been doing, who will bring the same gracious influence to bear on the boys coming here from the Iowa farms, in order that they may be started in the right direction. It will be difficult, in fact impossible, to fill his place.

These are warm words, such as I have never before spoken in favor of any young man leaving our institution, but they are all deserved. If you should conclude to take him from us I will recognize the finger of Providence and submit.

With respect,
JAMES G. WILSON.

The separation of these friends was to come, but not precisely as either had anticipated.

Carver's election to the chair at Alcorn was deferred until spring, and meanwhile another offer of service came to him, one which allowed of no hesitation in acceptance.

Booker T. Washington believed with Wilson that the farmer must be taught to think along the lines in which science had shed light upon his art. Agriculture being the root, trunk, branch, and twig of the Southern economic system, it was essential that just the right man be in charge of putting the Agricultural Department at the Tuskegee Normal and Industrial Institute on a scientific basis. On April 1, 1896, he asked Carver to join the faculty in that capacity, at a salary of fifteen hundred dollars.

In reply Carver wrote:

> Of course it has always been the one great ideal of my life to be of the greatest good to the greatest number of "my people" possible, and to this end I have been preparing myself for these many years; feeling as I do that this line of education is the key to unlock the golden door of freedom to our people.

In June, when Washington received an honorary M.A. from Harvard, he made another memorable speech: "During the next half century and more, my race must continue passing through the severe American crucible. We are to be tested in our patience, our forbearance, our perseverance, our power to endure wrong, to withstand temptations, to economize, to acquire and use skill; in our ability to compete, to succeed in commerce, to disregard the superficial for the real, the appearance for the substance, to be great and yet small, learned and yet simple, high and yet the servant of all."

These were sentiments in which Carver wholeheartedly concurred; it was clear that these two men would be able to work together harmoniously toward an identical consummation. Throughout the summer they exchanged letters and made plans. By arrangement, Professors Wilson and Wallace met Washington to add their verbal endorsement of their brilliant young friend.

Meanwhile he was packing everything except his mycological collection, which he was leaving to his alma mater—his library, his clothes, his scrapbooks, his amaryllis bulbs, his biological sketches, and his paintings. He had not utterly relinquished his dream; he still had a faint hope that at the end of two years circumstances would permit him to go to France to paint.

The school weekly, the *IAC Student,* reported a banquet of the Agricultural Society in September. As usual the committee asked Mr. Carver to take charge of decorating Professor Wilson's recitation room in Agriculture Hall, "and with the aid of some vines and autumn leaves he transformed the room beyond recognition." The quartet, including Mr. Carver, "filled the air with melodious sounds," and after the violin solo Mr. Carver followed "with a reading in which was depicted the simple beauty of an evening's scene on a farm. The calls of the shepherd boy and the caressing language of the milkmaids were imitated in a masterly manner."

On October 5, 1896, the town paper, the Ames *Intelligencer,* reported that Mr. Carver had left for Alabama. On his departure he had been presented with a superb microscope, complete with case, the gift of faculty and friends, "as he goes forth strong in the assurance that the best wishes of all follow him. We know of no one who failed to be won to friendship by his genial disposition, and we are not guilty of meaningless praise when we wish him Godspeed."

# CHAPTER X

## *"Let My People Go"*

It was an early June afternoon of 1881, just after dinner, and somnolence hung over the little Alabama town of Tuskegee. Booker T. Washington, a young man of twenty-three or thereabouts with a flowing mustache and with a neat and efficient mind made evident by his dress and manner, strode briskly up the mile-long hill from the station, his intelligent eyes noting every detail along the road. Small puffs of red dust rose and settled again languidly from the slow-lifting hoofs of an ox on its way round to the hitching racks back of the stores that lined the square. In the center of the fence-enclosed space stood the Macon County courthouse. A few Negroes lounged in the shade of the wide, curving stairs that led up to the second floor, or stretched themselves out on the drying grass beneath the quiet elms and magnolias. Across from the stately entrance on the north side of the square stood the general merchandise store of Campbell and Wright, in one corner of which was conducted the banking business of the county.

The young man whose purposeful air contrasted so strangely with the hot torpor that overlay the town entered, asked for Mr. George Campbell, and was directed to the back room and the gentleman with the long white beard. Neither Mr. Campbell nor his partner and brother-in-law, Captain W. H. Wright, had been expecting Booker Washington so soon. They were, however, pleased with his appearance and sent him across to the west side of the square to the tin and harness shop of Lewis Adams, who would explain to him all about the new school in which he was to teach.

This was the year 1881, when George Carver was struggling through the seventh grade in Minneapolis, Kansas, completely unaware that a daring experiment, though its full magnitude was not comprehended at the time, was about to take place in the heart of the black belt. Booker T. Washington, who himself had been climbing up from slavery for only nineteen years, was to try to emancipate his race from the adjuncts of slavery and instruct them how to live like free men.

In Macon County, as elsewhere in the deep South, were countless unschooled men and women, recently slaves, whom Emancipation had thrown on their own with no knowledge of anything except taking orders and laboring in the cotton fields. These children of the scarred back and branded breast suddenly had no food, no clothes, no homes, and had never been taught to provide such things for the morrow; they had never owned anything which had to be protected. Families had been torn apart by sales, marriage had been forbidden, and their women had been subject to the command of white masters; hence they were as lacking in morals as in stability. Their religion preached submission, but even the comfort of the hope of a better land hereafter they could enjoy only at night in the woods by "stealing away to Jesus." Thus spiritually crippled by white men, they were entering upon merciless competition with those same men, who were set in the determination to keep them without lands, without votes, without schools.

Laws against the education of slaves had been severe; some, who had secured a little surreptitiously, knew that real emancipation would come only when they could step out of the dark prison of ignorance into the bright light of knowledge. They tried to rush four million strong into that light, and it blinded some of them. Their numbers frightened white men, and the ex-slaves were whipped back into the dungeon. But the impulse still survived and would not let them rest. Scattered individuals and groups continued to creep out unobtrusively and fearfully from time to time, accustoming themselves gradually to a brilliance with which the eyes of any white child were familiar from birth.

The Negro Reconstruction Government of Alabama was resolved that its people should have education as a stepping stone to power. As one of its first provisions it initiated a free public-school system, from which the whites benefited also. But the later Constitution of '75, under white direction, ordered separate schools for the two races, thus curtailing Negro opportunities for higher education. Nevertheless, the young were eager and bounding with hope—all things would be possible to them once they had mastered the secret meaning of words and figures. The old prayed that they might learn to read the Bible before they died. In the little struggling schools which were springing up everywhere during the '70s, young colored men and women were trying to teach, even though they themselves barely knew the rudiments of the three *R*'s.

Most Southerners agreed that a little black boy was as bright as a little white boy up to a certain age. The argument developed from there on along the lines of medieval scholarship, such as the question of how many angels could dance on the point of a needle. With Southern savants it was the age at which the black boy stopped developing; was it twelve, thirteen, or fifteen? At least they agreed that after one or the other of these ages he could not progress, but could merely copy what he saw about him; it was therefore manifestly useless to try to educate him. The corollary to this dictum was slightly inconsistent—if he were educated he would be dangerous; he would think too much. He would try to step out of his place. "He was born for our use and our abuse, and in that place in which we have placed him he must and shall remain."

A few discerning white men of Tuskegee held a minority opinion. They believed that danger lay in ignorance and that safety lay in developing intelligence and thus increasing usefulness. Their more enlightened attitude was understandable; Tuskegee, founded in 1832 and named for a Creek chief, was a town of two thousand, half of whom were colored. Though it lay on the highway between Montgomery, forty miles to the west, which was for a brief time the Confederate capital, and Atlanta, one hundred and forty miles to the east, it had been spared the agonies of the latter. Many of its young men had gone to war, and the wealth of all had been reduced. The four miles of track of the little spur that connected the town with the main railroad at Chehaw had been torn up to make bullets. But E. T. Varner & Co. had laid the tracks again, and the heavy bales of cotton were now rolling on their way. Though its mansions were in need of paint they were unscarred by fire and still stood stiffly erect, wrapped in the dignity of many pillars. Though Union soldiers had passed that way, no special war hatreds had camped there, to leave a rubbish pile of bitterness.

Some owners had been indulgent in the matter of letting slaves learn to read if they wanted to. Some had found that the Negro could become an artisan, and certain youngsters who showed aptitude had been taught the skilled work of the plantation; large planters had shops in which the various necessary crafts of homemaking and farming were practiced —making the cooking utensils for the kitchen and dairy, constructing wagons and plows.

Lewis Adams had been one of these favored slaves. His white father had recognized him and given him advantages over some of the others. He was allowed to go where he pleased, and this freedom had increased his naturally superior intelligence. He had learned three trades well: he could make and repair shoes, could fashion harnesses and saddles, and was tinsmith for the town and the planters roundabout. He was a gunsmith also; in fact, he could turn his hand to almost anything. With a white partner named Lee, he now carried on these trades in a store which was patronized more by white people than by colored.

Adams was a gray-eyed, swift little man, inclined to be frisky; he had a manner which won him friends and a mind which earned him respect. Though he had little book learning, he was possessed of keen judgment and had made himself influential politically. Negroes had not yet been entirely disfranchised in 1880. Their votes as well as white men's could help send a candidate to the capital or keep him at home. And in the legislative halls the successful candidate sat voting yes or no jointly with a colored man whom only yesterday he could have ordered whipped.

To Adams came Colonel Wilbur F. Foster, publisher and editor of the local newspaper, the Macon *Mail,* and after the immemorial manner of politicians he asked what, if elected, he could do for the Negroes of the district. Mr. Adams had the answer ready: give them a state normal school. Though opinion was divided among the white townspeople as to the advisability of such a school—"where are we going to find servants, if the niggers are educated?"—nevertheless, with the help of the Negro vote, Colonel Foster reached the Senate safely and his partner, A. L. Brooks, landed in the House.

Since bills originated in the latter body, Brooks introduced a bill November 16, 1880, asking for an appropriation for two thousand dollars to be used as salaries in a school for training colored teachers; students would be admitted free on giving an obligation in writing that they would teach in the free public schools for two years after being qualified. This bill was endorsed by the Negro members of the Legislature and also by the chairman of the Committee on Education, Representative W. C. Thomas, who was another of the white men who believed the Negro would make a more useful citizen trained than ignorant. It passed the Senate and was approved by the governor February 12, 1881. There the matter rested for a bit, until the governor appointed George W. Campbell as chairman of the board of three commissioners, one of whom was Lewis Adams. Thus these two men joined forces—Adams the ex-slave with Campbell the ex-slave owner, who was also a planter, merchant, banker, and man of means.

But who was to teach the teachers to teach? The Federal

Government Freedmen's Bureau and the American Missionary Association between them had started several thousand schools, but Negro education was still so recent that the sources where anyone might be found with sufficient experience were few. Mr. Campbell wrote to three. Fisk University, Atlanta University, and Talladega College had no one to offer. He tried General Armstrong at Hampton Institute.

General Samuel Chapman Armstrong while commanding colored troops during the Civil War had become convinced that the Negro "had excellent qualities and capacities and deserved as good a chance as anyone," but not education in the so-called cultural subjects—mathematics, literature, history, and classical languages—which limited the educational practice of the day. He had at that time laid plans for a type of education that he believed would better fit the needs of Negroes—skill in manual labor which could equip them for self-support and at the same time build those virtues of providence, judgment, and foresight so deplorably lacking. As he said, teachers of great moral strength as well as mental culture were needed. After two years as Freedmen's Bureau officer at Hampton, Virginia, he had a chance to put his theories to work by starting the Hampton Normal and Industrial Institute, where the motto became, "Learn by doing."

When Mr. Campbell wrote asking for someone to open a normal school at Tuskegee, General Armstrong replied that he knew of no white man who would fill the requirements, but he did have a young colored man in whom he himself placed much confidence. The young man had worked hard for his education at Hampton, had graduated and taught for two years in a country school, and had returned to the staff of Hampton where he was in charge of seventy-five Indians newly admitted to the institute—one of the latest Americans acting as big brother to the earliest. General Armstrong had great faith in this young man and would like to suggest him for the post.

The sponsors of the school at Tuskegee did not hesitate; they telegraphed, "Booker T. Washington will suit us."

And so Booker Taliaferro Washington arrived in June 1881 and went to stay at the home of Lewis Adams on South Side Street, a quarter of a mile or so west of the square. He did not, however, spend much time there at first. As preparation for his work among unfamiliar people, for almost a month he traveled through the countryside talking with them, eating and sleeping with them. When he came back he knew something of the magnitude of his task and the utter inadequacy of the available facilities.

The two thousand dollars had been appropriated for salaries and could not be expended for buildings or equipment; these did not exist. Lewis Adams was superintendent of the Sunday school of the Methodist Episcopal Church, Butler Chapel, a little out beyond his house on pine-covered, red-clay Zion Hill. In this leaky, dilapidated structure another man had held school for a little while, but had left to study for the ministry, for he could see no future in the school. The building was again freely offered by the colored congregation to Booker Washington. This, together with the shanty hard by under a chinaberry tree, could serve as a place for instruction. On July 4, 1881, the State Normal School opened with thirty pupils, most of them older than their teacher.

Young Washington was burning to test in practice some of the ideas he had absorbed at Hampton. Furthermore, both he and the students wanted to eat, if it could be managed. Very soon a plantation which began a mile north of town came on the market. It certainly did not look promising.

Years before, a wandering Indian chief had been so pleased with the lush fertility of the new land he had encountered that he had called it Alabama, "Here we rest." But since that time King Cotton had held despotic sway and despoiled the land of its fertility. This little corner of his kingdom, stretching as far as the main line of the railroad, was known deservedly as Big Hungry. The eye could see only shifting sands and gullied landscape with here and there a few small tufts of yucca and cactus. Beyond were pine woods that must be cleared. The plantation house had burned, but four small buildings remained—the cabin which had been used as the dining room, the kitchen, a stable, and a hen house.

The price was high, five hundred dollars for a hundred wornout acres, some of which were worth no more than twenty-five cents; and nobody had any money whatever. However, the treasurer at Hampton lent enough for the first payment. The students cleaned out the residue of horses and chickens, whitewashed their new recitation rooms, and moved in.

Washington had a devoted helper in Olivia A. Davidson, graduate of Hampton and the Massachusetts State Normal School, later to become his second wife. She worked indefatigably as a teacher and at the less congenial task of securing funds to meet the payments on the property. White citizens gave festivals, and the colored townspeople came bringing presents according to their means—it might be a hog or only half-a-dozen eggs.

As a contribution toward the worthy object of procuring physical nourishment as well as mental, a friend gave one hundred dollars, stipulating it should be used to purchase a horse to work the land. Adams claims he stretched it to cover a "good" horse, a secondhand lumber wagon, a plow, harness, and a sack of corn to feed the horse. Standards differ. Washington has referred to that horse variously as blind, as lame, as broken down, and as worn out. But no horse ever went quite fast enough for Washington.

At least the horse enabled the students to start planting cabbages, watermelons, corn, sweet potatoes, and sorghum. This they did with enthusiasm, because it promised something to eat. Presumably the secondhand wagon did not last long, because another was soon needed and, there being no money to purchase it, they used the old hubs, found scrap iron to tire the wheels, fastening it on with wire and bent nails. In such a fashion the School Mechanical Department was started under an oak tree on the grounds.

A long-handled hoe and an ax made up the rest of the

equipment of the Agricultural Department. The ax raised a vital issue upon which the success or failure of this revolution in education depended, the great experiment in teaching without textbooks.

Enthusiasm for work stopped with the garden patch and did not extend to clearing land or learning how to farm. The students had worked hard as slaves. Why should they go to school to learn to work? "Education" to them automatically meant freedom from all effort and all hardship. They were not prepared to accept the idea that it constituted a step-by-step mastering of one thing surely before going on to the next. They desired in one seven-league leap to arrive straight in the Elysian Fields where there would be no more toil, but where they would bask forever in the radiance of the beneficent sun of learning. They cried out for Greek and Latin, they wanted to follow the Roman way to politics, which was synonymous with power. And, finally, they had a childlike desire to excite the wonder and envy of their unlettered fellows by conversing in polysyllables.

Opposition outside the school also was vocal. When they learned that the school required hard work instead of offering an easy path to learning, Negro preachers preached against it. And since one heritage of slave days was menial and personal service, the scholastic group severely condemned the Hampton-Tuskegee idea as tending to keep the Negro in subservient manual labor.

Nevertheless, Washington would not swerve from his conviction that higher education was not so important as some education; that those who could utilize higher education were exceptions and the exceptions would take care of themselves. The school was to turn out teachers, but teachers in the plantation districts. In his month of travel he had seen that most Southern Negroes had not the faintest notion of how to get along in their new-found freedom. He conceived the function of the graduates to be that of helping the "man farthest down," freeing him from the frightful burden of ignorance of the simplest and barest rules of how to live.

To show the pupils the dignity that lay in free labor, he himself shouldered the ax and led the way. And, if they grumbled, they could do no less than follow.

Furthermore, they flocked to the Institute in ever-increasing numbers. Washington was fond of the little whitewashed cabins, but something more was needed. When summer came he set them to digging for a new three-story building to accommodate the newcomers. They were not skilled carpenters, but in spite of mistakes the frame walls rose steadily, and in the room set aside to be used as a chapel the four teachers and one hundred and fifty students were able to hold their Thanksgiving service. A second service of thanksgiving was held at Christmas; the last payment had been made, and the land and all that was upon it belonged to them.

Not a student complained of winter discomfort and hardship, though many were frostbitten during the nights. Since the teachers had no blankets to give, they would make the rounds to give comfort instead.

Porter Hall was dedicated the next spring, 1883. But still the students came, and another building was necessary. This one, Washington decided, should be of brick. No bricks were manufactured in that part of the country, and it would be costly to ship them in. Therefore, they would make their own, and perhaps even be able to sell some locally and thus help knit the school and town together.

As he later wrote, "All the industries at Tuskegee have been started in natural and logical order growing out of our needs of a community settlement . . . asking for nothing which we could do for ourselves. Nothing has been bought that the students could produce."

A half mile out beyond Porter Hall they began digging clay for brick. No one knew how to construct a kiln, and one after the other failed until Washington finally pawned his watch to secure funds for a final effort. He never was able to redeem the watch, but he never regretted its loss. No amount of work was too arduous to make his dream come true. If his students worked hard, he worked twice as hard. He taught in the classroom, helped the boys clear the land, drove the horse, built fences, superintended the brickmaking, and planned the new four-story Alabama Hall. This experiment must not fail—and it did not.

When the four stories stood in all their noble splendor, the farmers and their families gathered from afar to see the wonder; colored folk had never before lived in a house made of brick which was their very own. Timidly as the newly dead entering Paradise they put out their hands, but it did not crumble before their touch. Its very solidity was a mystic symbol and a promise.

About a mile to the east of the grounds lived Felix Branum of the flowing white hair and little goatee who came to cook for the school and stayed to prove himself a friend indeed. Often and often when he walked over from his home in the early morning he would find not a dust of flour in the bin. The hungry crew would come in to dinner from driving fence posts or laying bricks or chopping wood only to be told, "No dinner. The groceries didn't come. Go back to work and I'll ring the bell when I'm ready." Then he would pick up the handles of his own wheelbarrow and trundle into town, buy a bag of rice from some merchant or, if he, too, lacked money, borrow some from Campbell and Wright on his own note and use it to buy a sack of meal.

On the good days they had "white meat" with boiled greens cooked in a big black iron pot out under the arborvitae and supplemented with corn bread, molasses, and tea. Wednesdays and Sundays they were supposed to have light bread, but wood was used for heating and for firing the kilns, which came first; there was not always enough left to cook the bread thoroughly and the center was often raw dough. Later they made a long oven of clay and at night set in it lighted Aladdin lamps a yard apart. This did a better job; in the morning Mr. Branum would withdraw more palatable food.

He was indeed an intimate and indispensable part of the

school, who had earned the right to state that "Me and Booker" were next going to do this or that. "Me and Booker" were partners in the financial responsibility and together had to study ways and means for getting along.

When Washington would "get in a tight" he could always turn to George Campbell, "from whom I have never sought anything in vain." More than once the Institute would have closed had it not been for this friend's financial aid, and at one time the indebtedness had mounted to sixty-five thousand dollars, with "nothing out yonder at the school" as security.

Washington had inspired a boundless faith in himself, and proved his venture to be a thing of promise. He made the townspeople feel that the school was dependent on the town, and the town on the school. And this trust was shared by the merchants of Montgomery.

Campbell and the other sponsors of the Institute saw to it that the Legislature appropriated another thousand dollars for salary, and in 1883 another invaluable person joined the staff, Warren Logan, also from Hampton. He came as treasurer, but was much more than that.

In those first raw beginnings, times were hard and friends were few. Though Washington bought on credit as long as possible, there was seldom enough for more than a few days ahead. If an unexpected emergency arose—and an unexpected emergency was always arising—you would have to give Mr. Logan a week to raise ten dollars.

Board had to be put at eight dollars a month, but that need keep no pupil away. The simple matter of finding room for new arrivals was sometimes insuperable, but lack of money barred none. Practically no background of education was necessary for registration. At best the students had previously had only three months of school out of the year and, with no reading at home to keep them up, inevitably they forgot from one term to another.

At Hampton, Washington had helped initiate a night school, and three years after his own institute opened he began the same practice there. When a penniless, friendless lad appeared, often without a change of clothes, he was told he could work for his education; he could "learn to earn," sign a contract to work for two or three years in the daytime, and go to night school. It might be at farming or in the sawmill, but the brickyard was the real test. Digging, molding, stoking kilns, and loading barrows were all backbreaking and monotonous, and if a boy could do these for ten hours a day and attend classes in arithmetic and geography for two hours in the evening, he really wanted to learn.

His payment for this labor was not in cash, but went toward food and a bed and clothes, and what was saved above these expenses was stored up to pay for day-school expenses later. The regulation to enforce perseverance was strict but necessary; if a student left, he forfeited his earnings. He might abandon the effort for a time, but as a rule he would soon say, "I believe I'll go back to school." Mr. Logan would make what concessions were possible. When summer vacation came, a student could draw a small amount. "You've worked hard all winter and a fellow has to have a dollar or so."

Washington had much sympathy with the neglected child, and strove to rescue him from an evil environment. Many of his students were still children, even though fully grown, who fought more readily than they worked. He never turned them away on this account. As punishment, instead of sending them home, he gave them extra work to keep them busy. If they became too unruly, he put them in the guardhouse until they had learned the new and gentler ways.

Dan was eighteen when he came to Tuskegee, and had already worked two years as a carpenter. When the instructor asked too peremptorily for his ax, he refused to give it up. A row followed, and the instructor called Dan a liar. Dan went at him with his knife in his hand, intent on murder. Dan was sent to the principal.

"You know you were very rude, don't you, Dan?" asked

Mr. Washington. "But I'll give you another chance if you'll beg Mr. B——'s pardon."

"No, he'll have to beg mine!"

"You're hot and angry," said Mr. Washington. "Go away and think it over and come back tomorrow."

Dan came back the next day, but he was in the same mood. So he was sent away to think it over for another day. He still wanted to cut the instructor's throat. This went on for four days, but still he was not sent away. Washington's patience, which was infinite, finally won. And his reward was great, because "Dan," after fifty years at the Institute, was still one of its most valued assets.

Teaching at Tuskegee had to go back to first principles. The students had to be taught how to care for their bodies, how to bathe, how to brush their teeth, and how to dress. The rising bell sounded at 5 A.M. and the retiring bell at 9:30 P.M. There were seventeen bells in all and every one meant something. At the first one each had to clean his room and then go to breakfast; and he had to eat everything on his plate. That depended, of course, on whether there was anything to eat.

Students were being trained to do things systematically; they had nothing like that at home. Coming as they did from plantation cabin life, they had to be taken care of all through the day, and the night, too, for that matter. Even at chapel, which was conducted each evening, the gospel of the toothbrush and the nightshirt was preached incessantly. No one could make them go to sleep, though they were usually tired enough to do so anyway, but quiet could be enforced, and was. A student officer would make the rounds in the dormitory and pull the covers back. John didn't have a nightshirt on! "I wrote to Mom, but she didn't send one yet," he would explain. Down would go John's name on a list, to be checked off only when the nightshirt had arrived and was in use.

For the purpose of instilling discipline, order, cleanliness —those virtues stressed in military drill—Washington had borrowed another idea from General Armstrong and instituted a military regime after the school had been going a few years. Guard duty at night by the more responsible students seemed particularly necessary.

On entering school, young men were required to purchase the uniform coat ($6.00) and cap ($1.35). "The pants ($4.50) may be procured later." These sums covered the bare cost of materials. Incidentally, making the uniforms provided work for the tailor shop. On Sundays and special occasions, as well as while drilling, all wore the coat of blue and the flat kepi patterned on that of the Union soldier; the officer of the day was distinguished by his long sash. A white major came from Fort McPherson to give instruction until some of the older students had been trained to take over. White people would not have tolerated the boys' being armed with rifles, so they drilled with sticks or umbrella handles, but the regulations of the commandant were strictly enforced.

Washington's presence was so forcefully commanding that self-restraint in his presence was automatic. When he walked into a room, he did not have to say, "Be quiet." Everybody just was. He was kind, but he had little time to joke and laugh, and few were really at ease in his company.

The time soon arrived when he had to spend many months away on the difficult and wearisome quest for funds to keep pace with his school, which he envisaged expanding out into infinity. He lectured incessantly about it, trying to make clear the necessities of his people and their potentialities; his own personality and achievements were his best argument. New England was his chief focus—New England which remembered something of the fervor of the Abolition spirit and had not, like most of the rest of the country, dismissed the Negro problem from mind, once the battle of slavery had been won. He approached possible friends with prospectus in hand, figures to show what he hoped could be accomplished in the way of making better human beings, given so many dollars and cents.

His responsibility was heavy indeed. So many people who

happened to hear of his experiment took it for granted that he could not succeed. If he failed, it would not be his personal failure alone, but the failure of four million others, who would be thrown back "where they belonged." Therefore, he never stopped, and that is how work became a tradition at Tuskegee.

The night guard would be the first to know when Mr. Washington had returned, because he would hear the galloping feet of the principal's horse long before that five-o'clock rising bell. Rain or shine, in rubber boots if need be, Mr. Washington would be out catching up on how things had been going in his absence. His tour of the grounds usually ended by hitching his horse, Dexter, to a post in front of the dining hall, where he would inspect the breakfast menu, the linen, the service, and the kitchen.

Was anything lagging? The principal carried a notebook and jotted down, "I notice a conduit is open," or the fact that a bridge had developed a loose plank, that repairs were needed on driveways or on buildings. Nothing escaped him. If he saw a boy walking across the lawn, he suggested, "Here at Tuskegee we try not to do things like that." When he gave vesper talks on Sunday evenings, the subject might be "Keeping in repair" or "Teamwork." With a vigilant eye he watched the students marching out of chapel, and if a button were off or a spot showing, he would take them out of line. This was neither criticism nor command, but a plea to keep up the standards. Though it might run counter to inbred habits of the students, nobody could resist it. Negroes had to prove themselves, and this was their proving ground. Most other large schools had white teachers to give them a hand up, but at Tuskegee they were on their own.

He had a multiplicity of details to look after, but he also had his long-range program, and they fitted in together.

Booker T. Washington's name did not begin to assume national proportions until 1895, when the committee of the Atlanta Cotton States and International Exposition decided to permit a Negro to speak at the opening. The decision occasioned violent discussion and serious misgivings among white people; if a Negro were to stand on the same platform with President Cleveland, he would be raised above them! At Tuskegee, while he was composing his speech, the faculty hung on every word. So much depended on it.

Northern newspapers covered the exposition because it was to signalize the fact that King Cotton was firmly re-established on the throne from which the Civil War had dislodged him. And Northern mills had a vital financial interest in the re-establishment. But the newspapermen were captivated by the immediate drama, and reported that rather than the exposition. James Creelman of the New York *World* thus described the Negro protagonist: "There was a remarkable figure; tall, bony, straight as a Sioux chief, high forehead, straight nose, heavy jaws, and strong, determined mouth with big white teeth, piercing eyes, and a commanding manner."

It is hard now to realize the impression such a break with tradition could mean in the South. The Atlanta *Constitution* said prophetically the next day, "That man's speech is the beginning of a moral revolution in America." The moral revolution was slow to come about, but certainly it did receive a tremendous impetus under Washington's direction.

Frederick Douglass, who had piloted the Negro out of slavery, had just died, and his mantle of leadership was now bestowed on Washington. Washington's trusted secretary for many years, Emmet J. Scott, has said that when Mr. Washington was first called the leader of his race he was at a loss to know what was expected of him in that capacity, but the tasks came so fast he was not left long in doubt.

Though the scope of his usefulness had broadened, the channel through which he worked remained Tuskegee Institute. One immediate advantage was its expansion and the opportunity to organize it into nine recognized departments. To each student who came to the school he aimed to impart the practical knowledge of some one industry "together with the spirit of industry, thrift, and economy, that they would be sure of knowing how to make a living after they left us." Everybody, boys and girls alike, had to work. They had to study actual things instead of mere books alone. The aim was mental, moral, and manual training, all three in equal amounts. Washington was still convinced that manual training was of vast importance.

Placed as Superintendent of Industries was his older brother, John H. Washington, who had helped him go to Hampton and had in turn been helped to receive his own education there later. Mr. Adams had joined the Institute in 1890. He could conduct his business on the grounds and at the same time give instruction in harness making, shoe repairing, and tinsmithing. When Horace White, editor of the New York *Evening Post,* had visited the school he wrote: "All the trades that can be carried on by hand or without much machinery are taught here, such as blacksmithing, carpentry, brickmaking, foundry work, dairy work, cooking, tinsmithing, dressmaking, laundry work, wagon making, saddlery, shoemaking, tailoring, etc. . . . I was informed that the demand for their wagons and carriages in the country round about is largely in excess of their ability to supply." The same could be said of the brooms the girls made from longleaf pine and of their mattresses, and the foundry could never keep up with the demand for hand-wrought andirons.

From the first, Washington had resolved to make the school an integral part of the community. His aim being not merely to build a good school where individuals could receive instruction, but, through them, to improve the conditions of his people, he must fit his students to be teachers who would return to the districts from which they came, taking back their knowledge with them for the benefit of all. The farmers, who were too old to go to school, must also be given aid.

The first Farmers' Conference had been called in 1892, and five hundred eager men and their wives had assembled to see more of the wonders of this school and listen to the gospel of "Live at home." They were made to feel welcome and at the same time were admonished to try to improve their status. One way for the women would be not to wrap their hair in strings, and to wear a dark-colored sailor hat to take the place of the red bandanna, and neat calico or gingham to take the place of homespun. Having no money to pay for these items, they were urged to plant a garden, grow fruit, raise hens, keep a pig and a cow, and take a load of produce to town for exchange.

Agriculture was the main dependence of the colored people in the Gulf states; it was estimated that 85 per cent were farmers, and the Board of Trustees of the Institute concluded that they would probably remain so. This meant that special emphasis must be placed on the Agricultural Department, and that an expert in agricultural science was needed to teach the mysteries of the soil and its mastery.

In the fall of 1896 the school weekly announced that the newly organized department would be in charge of Mr. Carver from Iowa.

## CHAPTER XI

# *"My Knees Got Acquainted with the Hillsides too"*

THE BOY FROM THE INSTITUTE pulled up his horse outside the small station of Chehaw. He was late, and the train had come and gone, but Mr. Carver from Iowa, who was waiting by the side of the tracks, did not seem to be impatient; he was bending over a bush, examining it intently. The boy gazed with only a small degree of interest at the new teacher, though he was odd, not like the people round there, with his gold-inlaid, celluloid watch chain, his flowing, soft tie and gray suit, a bit too tight, only the top button of his jacket fastened, a pert pink rose in the lapel. There seemed nothing extraordinary about the handlebar mustaches, nor the beak of a nose, rather Semitic, jutting from between deep, burning eyes. When the tall figure straightened up at the sound of the approaching carriage, it did not straighten completely; Mr. Carver was a little stooped, and looked rather like a question mark, though he had filled out somewhat during his two years on a salary.

He climbed into the surrey and started a companionable conversation. Holding out some twigs and leaves in his remarkable hands, he asked, "Can you tell me what this plant is?" But the boy stared and shook his head; he didn't know.

This was Mr. Carver's first sight of his new surroundings, and his eyes were intent on every aspect of the rolling Alabama landscape through which he was traveling—what he could see of it through the rusty clouds of dust sent whirling by the trotting horse. From time to time his view was cut off by the high banks of red and yellow clay that swallowed the road; the soils of Missouri, Kansas, and Iowa had never shown him such vivid colors. But beyond the road, lined with broom sedge and tufts of wild briar, and beyond the eroded cut banks, much of the land was abandoned to scrub pine, and yucca lifted spiny, parched heads from heaps of dry sand. He sadly observed the reason for the desolate scene: fields of coppery stalks flaunting balls of white stretching to right and left.

By early October, Alabama was beginning to take a few grateful breaths after the scorching summer heat. But it was also the time for the hardest work. Bent backs rose a little above the cotton rows—the backs of the very young and the very old as well as the sturdier ones of the years in between, who were better fitted for the toil. Black hands, small and large, reached rhythmically for the puffs of cotton.

Now and again the surrey passed a saddleback cabin of logs or rough pine slabs with three-inch gaps between, whipped into monotonous gray by sun and wind, the wooden shutter of the one window and the wooden door swinging open, chimney propped up by sticks, rickety and forlorn. Two poles with a few boards nailed on served as a ladder to the garret where the older boys slept with the rats. It had four sides, it had a roof, but these were so inadequate that they invited rain and cold to enter and dwell within.

The bare black feet of the lately emancipated had beaten the door yard hard. No tree, no bush, no flower bloomed there. A pigpen reeked at the very door, and down the hill was the open well where the filth was certain to drain into it. Lean, mangy hounds skulked about with flies sucking at their festering sores—flies which had flown straight from the place in the bushes which served as an outhouse. How could anyone keep well or have any ambition who lived in such a place?

The trio of man, boy, and horse skirted the town of Tuskegee, peaceful and white-painted, more prosperous than many similar towns of the South because of the business brought by the Institute; they followed the Atlanta–Montgomery highway for a mile and turned right onto the busy campus.

Cassedy Hall and Thrasher Hall had now been built and were occupied. From the long, low building which housed the foundry, the wheelwright, and blacksmith shops issued bangs and crashes, and from the sawmill rose a vibrant hum.

Mr. Carver's long legs, and feet which seemed overlarge for so slight a frame, had covered thousands of miles during his thirty and some years of life. Almost immediately he put them to their accustomed use in order to survey the place which was to be his home for many years to come. He started walking northward, being particularly eager to see the site of the new agricultural building.

John F. Slater, a wealthy cotton manufacturer of Norwich, Connecticut, had left a million-dollar fund, the interest of which was to go to helping Negroes. This fund, through its administrators, was one of the best friends Tuskegee Institute ever had. The board of the Slater Foundation, with J. L. M. Curry as chairman, had allocated five thousand dollars toward a building for the exclusive use of the Agricultural Department, and Morris K. Jesup, treasurer, as an individual had given another five thousand. This ten thousand was to cover the cost of materials which must be purchased outside. Clay for brick and at least part of the wood and the actual construction were available on the spot by student labor. The materials would be hauled on carts made in the wheelwright's division by mules raised at Tuskegee. The Slater-Armstrong Building, when finished, was to be the finest of any school in the South.

The campus, as Mr. Carver soon discovered, was still in a primitive state. It was hard to keep things tidy with so little money, especially when that little money was needed for the incessant construction. The roads were lighted by oil lamps, and a boy earned his board by making the rounds and keeping the wicks trimmed; a storm or a strong wind put out the lights, leaving the campus dark.

The roads were deep in dust now, and water had to be drawn from the springs to settle it. This meant they would be deep in mud during the rains, especially round the open wells when the sun was not too fierce to dry the surface, wet from the splashings. The unmarried teachers had a bathhouse under the hill, but those with families living in homes of their own had to carry up water. There was no sewerage. Refuse from the kitchen in Alabama Hall went down in a ditch, and turkey buzzards hovered about with evil beaks, curved and sharp for vicious tearing. The slow, heavy vultures alighted in such numbers that, while work was going on near by, a boy was kept busy chunking stones at the bright targets of wattles.

Wherever Mr. Carver's steps led him he plucked leaves and stems and asked a passerby, "Can you tell me what this plant is?"

"I don't know."

He was to repeat the question many times in the next few days; he was so taken with the strange plants. His books had not yet come, but he thought if he knew the common names he could trace most of them. However, the answers were all the same, "I don't know," and the accompanying stare implied that he was not quite right in the head to be wanting to know anything so unimportant as the name of a weed.

But "weeds" to Mr. Carver had hidden within them as great potentialities for usefulness as the strawberry patch from which he could look down into the bottom on the truck farm of cabbages and turnips and collard greens, or the nursery which was just being started there.

Across the highway spread the parade ground, where the boys drilled in the early mornings and late afternoons, and beside it stood the wide, low-roofed Pavilion. In order that Hard-Shell Baptist should not war with Primitive Baptist or Methodist either with them or the teachers from the North—who might very easily be Episcopalians—the school was non-denominational. Chapel had at first been held in Porter Hall, but as the Institute expanded a larger meeting place was needed, and this rude structure of unplaned boards had been erected. The floor consisted of the earth, and the backless benches had been made by spiking planks onto posts driven into the ground. Originally intended to be only temporary, it was forced to serve many purposes for many years.

Its function as a house of worship for all religions was soon to be abandoned. The earnestly philanthropic Stokes family of New York had given Washington money for a new chapel, and ground had been broken in the spring of '96.

It was logical that the agricultural building should be out to the north on the fringe of the campus where the farm proper began, but some thought the new chapel, just across the way from it, should not be so far from the center of things as a quarter of a mile. Washington knew, however, that something had been started which could not stop. The school was going to grow, and it had to grow in that direction; there was no other.

From this hillock on which the Slater-Armstrong Building was soon to stand the ground receded in a long, graceful sweep, pretty to look at but complicating the problem of erosion. And beyond were the piny woods of Big Hungry, deep within which roamed the Institute's thirty razorback hogs that looked as though they had been built for speed instead of for the table. There was no such thing as fattening these wild hazel-splitters; they would be lean no matter what you did.

With the exception of the small industrial nucleus, the campus was in reality a farm of two thousand acres, standing on ground a little higher than the surrounding country. The land was better, but only by comparison; it, too, was riddled with wash gulleys. The water had to get out somehow, and it took what topsoil it could along with it. You could drop a two-horse wagon into one valley, and it would be completely hidden.

In 1819, when Alabama had become a state, thirty-three million acres were chiefly virgin forests with some grassland. It was blessed with fertile soil, a long growing season, and abundant rainfall. These natural advantages were shared by the other Southern states, and helped bring about their downfall. Unlike New England, where every stone had to be laboriously dragged from the earth, everything in the South was too easy, and where life becomes too easy the moral fiber is likely to disintegrate.

Cotton was the seed from which had flowered both the ease and the downfall.

Cotton was grown and manufactured into cloth 2500 years ago. It was growing on this continent before the adventitious arrival of Columbus. The Virginians tried their hand at its cultivation; in 1764 eight small bags were exported to Liverpool, and less than thirty years later the amount had increased to nine thousand bales. The healthy baby of commerce had been born, but no one had the wisdom to foretell that it was to develop into a devouring monster, one of the greatest forces for the progress of mankind the earth has ever seen, and at the same time, by misuse, a powerful force for evil.

The process of manufacture still remained as costly as that for woolens, silks, and linens, and the world was still awaiting a cheap textile twelve years after the United States had won its freedom. Then a young man just out of Yale, Eli Whitney, went on vacation to Savannah and, as a result, in 1794 was granted a patent on a gin. Some say he caught the idea from a slave whose fingers had been busy separating the staple from the seed at the rate of a pound a day but who had a head for machinery. Since slaves could not take out patents, this tradition could never be substantiated.

The result of the invention was an almost fantastic increase in production. Out of New Orleans, Mobile, Savannah, Charleston, up the gangplank and into the hold went bale after heavy bale wrapped in sacking and fastened with iron, bound for distant ports. Cotton had set in motion the spinning wheels of industry in England and New England, and these crescendoed to a roar. Thus was launched the industrial revolution, which initiated the modern machine age.

Somebody had to suffer from the resulting monstrous growth of individual fortunes. The millworkers in both countries were exploited, but a more serious behind-the-scenes tragedy was being enacted, in the form of slavery. No long-fingered machine which could pluck the locks from the bursting bolls had yet been invented. Each boll matured at a slightly different time within the two months' span. Strong back muscles were required and a directing and selecting brain. The slave trade battened on this vast need for human labor.

Long after England had led the way among European nations to abolish slave trading and slavery itself in the colonies, illicit traders could find an avid market in the Southern states of the United States.

The journey began in Africa: slaves were branded with the merchant's initials by means of hot irons, their heads were shaved, and they were stripped naked, men and women alike. To the clanking of their leg irons they were stowed away. According to Captain Theodore Canot, buccaneering trader of the early nineteenth century, "The second mate and boatswain descend into the hold, whip in hand, and range slaves in their regular places; those on the right side of the vessel facing forward and lying in each other's lap, while those on the left are similarly stowed with their faces toward the stern. . . . The taller being selected for the greatest breadth of the vessel, while the shorter and younger are lodged near the bows." If a slave attempted voluntary starvation, "his appetite is stimulated by the medical antidote of a cat." Hundreds of thousands died on the long voyages; many cast themselves into the sea. Only one out of six, captured in Africa, arrived in the New World.

The journey ended on the slave block of those same eight states which, in consequence, became the chief cotton-producing community in the world. King Cotton spread out on his huge throne. His scepter was the lash, which he wielded over an army of controlled labor. Production had risen to five million bales in the year of secession, and Southern planters had grown fat. It was a strictly physical world—physical labor on one side and physical well-being on the other, brought about by good food, gracious surroundings, and perfect service. Planters had time to raise beautiful horses and build beautiful homes—things they could touch—but they had little time for thinking.

Cotton altered the physical geography of the South as well as its social forms. The army of slave labor was not in use except during the cotton season. To pay for its keep during the winter it was put to work clearing the forests to make new fields to plant more cotton. Trees were felled or killed by girdling and then left to rot. The destruction was finished by burning. What flames had not been deliberately set, occurred accidentally. Millions of acres of longleaf pine vanished.

Once the trees were demolished, the rolling topography of Alabama and its open winters allowed the valuable topsoil to be washed away. There were no deep freezes to hold the soil, and moisture fell not in the form of snow, which would melt gradually into the earth, but as heavy rains. Four out of five acres were now eroded; some were entirely gone—and eroded soil is gone forever. Millions of tons of plant food were being dumped into the ocean every year, which must be replaced by commercial fertilizers—potash, nitrogen, and phosphoric acid—at enormous expense.

The cotton plant itself, which is a heavy feeder, grown year after year, continued the work of exhausting the soil nutrients that were left. It was easier to move than to preserve old land. The old man was not joking when he said, "Son, I know a lot more about farming than you do; I've worn out three farms in my lifetime." Thus he continued to wear out farm land, move on to more fertile fields, and wear those out, too, until finally there were no more fertile acres to exhaust. Cotton in its greed had drained the earth of sustenance, leaving endless acres of waste land.

The dangers of the one-crop system from an economic as well as an agricultural point of view had been denounced for years. No balanced economy was possible under such extremes of wealth and degradation. The wealth had not been earned. The value of the cotton crop in 1860 was $200,000,

000, but Southern banks held less than one sixth of this capital, the rest came from the North. The one-crop system was hastening toward its own ruin when the cotton barons and the industrial barons, each with an eye on the expansion of the West, met, and the former were vanquished. But, unfortunately for the South, it was able to turn this conflict into a scapegoat; it laid the burden of its failure on the war and on the Yankees.

The world was still clamoring for cotton in such unbelievable quantities that, compared with the dislocation caused by war in times past, its restoration was remarkably rapid. Prosperity in the South could never be the same again, but its inhabitants would not admit that, and tried to rebuild on the same insecure footing, adhering to the one-crop system and the forms of slavery regardless of ever-diminishing returns. Although they increased the wealth of the world by millions of dollars, they became the most impoverished and backward of any large group of producers in the United States. And this despite the fact that the South could grow any crop that could be grown anywhere else in the country. Since ante-bellum wealth for the fortunate few had been based on cotton, that same few, now less fortunate, were determined to maintain the status quo—continue to glut the world market with cotton and keep Negro labor in the state of peonage.

The Negro had stumbled into the dawn of his new day with a consuming desire for education and the right to own his own land; he had believed these would naturally attend upon freedom. Emancipation had proclaimed, "You can go where you will." He had emerged and looked about and found there was no place for him to go save back to prison. After a few brief, wild, riotous years he had been fettered again by the Southern economic system which stubbornly persisted in throwing itself under the wheels of the car in which rode the Juggernaut, Cotton.

Negroes had worked the land for two hundred and fifty

years, and their work had been the basis of prosperity for both North and South, but neither the land nor its fruits were their own. The aggregate mass in the South was like a troubled sea, and the dark waters heaved and shifted continuously, usually from poor acres to worse; they moved uneasily from east to west and north to the cities and some few back again to the farms. They were at last free to travel, but they knew not whither.

Sixty-five per cent of the farmers of Alabama were now nominally tenants, and the one-crop system left the tenant at the mercy of the weather, both friend and foe of the farmer, with no reserve to outwit that weather during such years as it might feel an enmity. Food crops matured at the same time as the cotton, but he had no time for them, even if he had been allowed to plant; so long as he did not own his own land he had to raise what the landlord dictated, and this was the cash crop—cotton. If he planted corn, he might carry some of it away; if he raised hogs on shares and some died, he might say, "Those were yours that died. Mine lived." But he couldn't carry off a five-hundred-pound bale. The entire system was geared to cotton, including the banks, and he had no means of disposing of a diversified crop.

Being paid for nothing except the cotton he produced, he planted up to the cabin door, leaving only room for a bit of corn and cane, and went in debt to the landlord's commissary for the rest of his food. He was not a farmer as the word is used elsewhere in the country. He had no farm machinery, few pigs, no chickens, no garden. He simply did not know anything about vegetables; only occasionally did he even have shallots and collards.

His diet of meat, meal, and molasses left him without health; tenancy left him without ambition. Tenants had no legal claim on any repairs they might make; by improving the property they were increasing its value and thereby inviting the landlords to raise their rent. The charge of "improvidence," "laziness," "shiftlessness" was the result of the system rather than the cause of the poverty. Negroes were the first victims of the system, but eventually planters and poor whites suffered also.

A miasma of fear drifted over the pleasant land of honeysuckle and jessamine. The war had left a residue of fear in the white man: first, fear of Negro political domination, which he combated with disfranchisement; second, fear of economic competition. At first, Emancipation had seemed to offer the poor white a chance of becoming a planter, but by the beginning of the twentieth century this hope had vanished and he had to admit he was still in the laboring class. But he would not become a fellow laborer with the Negro. He had once proved that he was superior to someone else by being an overseer of slaves. In order to maintain his advantage he, too, would subscribe to the status quo, even though it kept him from making any progress himself.

Booker Washington looked for a great renascence in the South when the white men had recovered from their resentment and his people had mastered trades that would be useful to industry. "You can't keep a man in the ditch," he used to say, "unless you are willing to stay there with him." Wise as he was, he could not foresee for how long a time far too many white men would be willing to keep at least one foot in the ditch—on the neck of the Negro.

Alfred Adler in his *Individual Psychology* refers to the "ideal of superiority found to an exaggerated degree among the nervous." Such persons have recourse to the oppression, the minimizing, and the undervaluation of others. In the case of fearful Southern whites any person who was marked by a different color of skin and different texture of hair was the object of these attitudes.

The third fear was a subtle, subconscious expectation of retribution. A powerful social class that imposes its will upon and degrades a helpless minority looks uneasily over its shoulder as it walks abroad by day, and it trembles by night.

The Negro state of serfdom was insured by innumerable local laws—some of which were in direct violation of the

Fourteenth and Fifteenth Amendments to the Constitution that had been drawn and ratified by the states to protect the Negro in his civil rights, and a network of "customs" to bulwark the barrier of caste. Caste taboos among primitive peoples center chiefly about eating and sex. These Southerners reasoned that if the taboo against eating with a Negro were broken, it followed that he would seek to rape their sisters. One young white woman of the town of Tuskegee would not come out to the campus unless accompanied by her husband or brother, and even then would not dare descend from her carriage.

Negroes had no more desire for racial amalgamation than the whites; the vast amount that had taken place had been forced upon them. The admixture of white blood into African occurred in the offspring of white masters and slave girls, but breaking the taboo against a union which reversed the sexes was punishable by death.

To teach the dignity of human labor and to bring about a better understanding between white and colored peoples, Washington gradually gathered a faculty inspired with ideals similar to his own. He drew largely on Hampton Institute, but he kept in touch with other schools, seeking the best minds he could find for each department. One, who came from a New England college, was expecting to be an Episcopal priest; he had no particular liking for teaching and expected to stay a year at Tuskegee. But in three or four months he had glimpsed the scope and beauty of Washington's dream. All thoughts of being a priest left him; his calling was at Tuskegee, and there he was content to spend the rest of his life.

Dropped between the Negro and the white world was a curtain which consisted of the very fact that he was a Negro; it was like a second personality of which he was always conscious because it was forever thwarting his free operation as a human being. One of the first requirements of each new teacher was adjustment to the customs of his white neighbors.

With the exception of a few colored families with whom

Mr. Carver had lived as a youngster, he had spent all his life among white people. Now he was to take his place among members of his own race. But he was soon made aware of the vast differences between being a Negro and being a Negro in the deep South. He had been there only a little while and had not learned the ins and outs of the system. The food at the Institute did not seem to agree with him, so he wandered forth in search of something that would rest more easily on his stomach. At the bottom of the hill just below Cassedy Hall was a tiny restaurant and he turned in there.

Next morning at breakfast someone asked, "Where were you last night? You didn't come to supper."

"I went to a restaurant."

"What restaurant?"

"A little restaurant down under the hill on the way to town—a colored restaurant."

"You don't need to tell me it was colored. If you ate there, I know it was colored. You needn't have put that in."

This was the sort of thing Mr. Carver had already accustomed himself to, though he found it shockingly greater in degree in Alabama, because of the intensity of feeling behind it. He did not, at first, comprehend this intensity; nevertheless, he did not come into open conflict because he lacked any semblance of belligerence. He obeyed the dictates as he encountered them.

The dictates were multitudinous. In a town, a Negro did not walk to the right on the sidewalk but on the gutter side, right or left, so that he could be shoved off quickly where he belonged. He must not stir out on the streets after dark. He must stand uncovered while talking to a white man, whether he were a college president or the lowliest tenant, without regard for the fact that in the matter of education and social status as much disparity existed among Negroes as among whites; they must all be squeezed into the established picture of being servants. He must not address any member of his own race as Mr. or Mrs. or Miss; as inferior beings they were not entitled to such titles of respect. A student once referred to a teacher as Mr. Blank, and a white citizen who overheard him came blustering out to the Institute with a shotgun to correct the impudence. A white man seldom even called a Negro by his surname; Washington was "Booker" to the townspeople. And if a little gray were showing, he or she was addressed simply as "Uncle" or "Auntie." By some queer quirk in the white mind a concession could be made to one of the higher ranking teachers; he might be called Professor or Doctor.

These were all social customs which had been added to the more familiar segregation, or "Jim Crowism."

Some of the teachers from Northern universities bumped into trouble at first through ignorance of these "social customs." One who had recently arrived went into Montgomery to buy a tie. He looked through the rack and saw none that quite suited.

"You don't like them?" asked the white store proprietor ominously.

"No."

His fellow faculty member warned him hastily in a whisper, "They expect you to say, 'Yes sir.' "

But the warning came too late. An altercation arose. The proprietor grabbed a knife and stabbed the teacher, narrowly missing his heart.

Many of the teachers were thin-skinned and nervous, but they had some reason to be. Any infringement of the caste system was likely to be punished by the mob, and the Negro could not count on protection by law.

Another consideration ranked far higher in importance than this personal one; the existence of the school depended on white good will, and many were the bitter sacrifices made for it. The Institute people had to learn to suppress rigidly any show of resentment against injustice. A teacher was shoved in the gutter; he wanted to fight back, but he had to accept the outrage in silence. Constantly he heard a voice, "You can't do that. It would jeopardize the school."

Better not subject yourself to such indignities any more

than could be avoided. Better sit in your study and philosophize. Better stay on the campus as much as possible, in that oasis of freedom where courtesy and breeding were the natural order of things, and you could devote your attention to fostering the development of useful citizens.

The ignorant colored farmer cringed and grinned and mouthed his "Yas suh! Yas suh!" The Southern white man pointed to the almost constant grin and boasted, "See how happy he is? That's because we know how to treat 'em." But the smile on the face of the Negro was not necessarily the reflection of a happy spirit. It was his defense. He thus armored himself in the interests of self-preservation. The smile was the Negro's pretense that he was not afraid of the ferocity of the white man, who could take away his means of living, who could take away his freedom and put him in prison for no just cause, who could take away his life.

Countee Cullen's lines to Paul Lawrence Dunbar might have been penned of many another Negro poet who never wrote a poem:

*Born of the sorrowful of heart*
*Mirth was a crown upon his head;*
*Pride kept his twisted lips apart*
*In jest, to hide a heart that bled.*

Set one of the old people to talking about the days before surrender, one who was once a slave, and in the course of his reminiscing he would surely relate how he or one of his fellow slaves would not endure being whipped and ran away, no matter how violent the punishment was to be. Though it might be deeply buried, that spirit was still alive.

But energy and ambition had been drained from them by the one-crop system, which offered no hope of change or progress. The Negro was left out of that American conception that any man could be rich in free America if he wanted to. He might be free and twenty-one, but he was not white. As a result of this insult to their dignity as human beings, many sank into sullen serfdom.

In many places this young man from the West found the weight of apathy lying heavily. Unfortunately, he sometimes thought, too many interpreted the meaning of Alabama, "Here we rest," as that of doing just as little as possible to eke out the miserable existence in which they found themselves one year after the other. Cotton could stand a lot of abuse; "if you don't feel like it, don't work today. Just loaf and stay out of the rain." They just borrowed in the spring and paid back in the fall. Nobody knew anything else. Settlement time came a little before Christmas, and if they received any money at all it went into purchasing a few bottles of nepenthe, in the form of explosive whisky.

Few were eager to be reformed. Most were ruled by superstition. One would assert positively, "Chickens hatched in May sleep themselves away." Another would look at a miserable stand and mourn, "I guess the moon wasn't right when I planted that seed." Not a two-horse plow could be found in the county. They had a definite prejudice against deep plowing; they claimed that the land would all wash away.

As Mr. Carver looked at these farmers, the lines of Edwin Markham came to him:

*Bowed by the weight of centuries he leans*
*Upon his hoe and gazes on the ground,*
*The emptiness of ages in his face,*

. . . . .

*A thing that grieves not and that never hopes.*

This, he insisted to himself, need not be. Always to be encountered here and there were a few souls eager and anxious to learn, or else no progress would ever be made in this world. He found some who needed only intelligent direction. It was these few who gave him patience and led him to plead for understanding. "The white people must have infinite patience, infinite patience in helping my people on. Remember their heritage. They need a lot of help."

The wasted lands and wasted lives Mr. Carver saw everywhere about the countryside cried for assistance. "The virgin fertility of our Southern soils and the vast amount of unskilled labor have been a curse rather than a blessing to agriculture. This exhaustive system of cultivation, the destruction of forests, the rapid and almost constant decomposition of organic matter, together with the problems of nitrification and denitrification, the multitudinous insects and fungus diseases which are ever increasing with marvelous rapidity year by year make our agricultural problem one requiring more brains than that of the North, East, or West."

The way toward rehabilitation would be long and painful, but the goal could be reached. The different methods worked out at Tuskegee were interdependent and all acted helpfully upon each other. The one-crop system being at the root of the matter, some substitute for it should be found, and the best way to find it would be through an experiment station.

Accordingly, his most immediate task was to draw up plans for one. He submitted them to Mr. Washington, who submitted them to the School Board of Trustees. One of its members drafted a bill which was introduced into the 1896–97 session of the State Legislature. On February 18 the bill was passed, "to establish a branch Agricultural Experiment Station for the colored race and to make appropriations therefor—to be located at Tuskegee and run in connection with the Normal and Industrial Institute."

The Board of Control—consisting of the president of the Alabama Polytechnic Institute at Auburn and the director of the Experiment Station there, the State Commissioner for Agriculture, and members of the Institute Board of Trustees who lived in Tuskegee—was charged to "cause such experiments to be made at said Station as will advance the interests of scientific agriculture and to cause such chemical analyses to be made as are deemed necessary." Fifteen hundred dollars out of the agriculture fund was appropriated for equipment and improvement, Tuskegee to furnish all necessary lands and buildings for use of the said Station and school. Mr. G. W. Carver was named Director and Consulting Chemist.

He could not state explicitly what the Station would do, but the Legislature could be assured that no time nor expense would be spared to make the work of direct benefit to the Alabama farmer. He formulated a plan of attack: education in soil conservation, diversification of crops, "live at home," finding new uses for farm crops, utilization of native crops.

Tuskegee stressed the value of community service. The students came in the first place because they wanted to get learning, but during the many years they spent at Tuskegee —and these were indeed many because most progressed through the academic courses via the night school—they were continually reminded that the educational plant was not solely for their individual enrichment, but to lead the race forward. It might take six, eight, ten years to reach the point of graduation, and during all that time in the field, the shop, the classroom, they were subject to the gentle yet constant pressure of duty. They were the trustees of knowledge, and had an administrative duty to spread that knowledge among the less fortunate who could not go to school; they were to help others of the dreary poor toward a happier and more healthful way of life. When they finally emerged as graduates, many had in their shining eyes dreams of building another Tuskegee. They, like their teachers, were consecrated.

Commencement time came around in May, the close of the sixteenth year. As in all times and ages parents yearned to see the result of their sacrifices and experience a sense of pride and of thankfulness that their children would have a better future than they. Many came from thirty or forty miles away, starting on Tuesday, camping by the wayside, and creaking and rattling in early Wednesday morning, some before daylight. They took possession of the grounds, which became one vast hitching post. They crowded classrooms and shops to touch the strange machinery. They heard their children's voices, saw battalion drill, and applauded the brass band. A place in the bottom land had been set aside where they could sit and eat. It took five hundred loaves of bread, an ox, and a hundred gallons of coffee to feed them.

Washington's commencement addresses were unlike those of more orthodox schools, which stressed "success." Instead, he urged, "Go back to the place where you came from and work. Don't waste too much time looking for a paying job. If you can't get pay, ask for the privilege of working for nothing."

In that spirit many left Tuskegee, the nourishing mother of schools, and started offshoots on the old plantations. You found a little Tuskegee cropping up at a small settlement, at a crossroads, in a shanty, an abandoned farm, a country store. These educational outposts of an idea appeared in South Carolina, Georgia, Mississippi, all the way from Virginia to Texas. And they began to leaven the economic life of the South.

Though classroom duties ceased during the summer, Mr. Carver was not idle. By way of vacation, he co-operated with the Alabama Polytechnic Institute in a monograph of the fungi of the state. The first issue contained 44 families, 349 genera, and 1110 species; he hoped to double these the next year. He collaborated with the Division of Agrostology of the Department of Agriculture at Washington, which was endeavoring to secure specimens of all grasses in the United States; for this collection he sent over a hundred specimens.

He also collaborated with the Smithsonian Institution in connection with the Pan-American Medical Congress. Its members realized that many of the old reliable vegetable drugs were becoming scarce, thus giving rise to many synthetic substitutes of questionable value, and they were endeavoring to bring together and catalogue with notes all available data on the medicinal flora of the United States. In this study Mr. Carver discovered a large number of official drug plants, and an equally large number of nonofficial, which were recognized only as household remedies.

He believed, however, that many of these would become official as soon as their medicinal properties had been proved.

In a letter to Ames, August 2, 1897, he reported on his activities and concluded,

> These and my other duties have kept me very busy, and take me in amongst the lizards, frogs, snakes, ticks, mosquitoes, and "chiggars," of which there is always a superabundance. But these are all of minor moment to the objects in view. I bid you adieu, hoping to visit you at some convenient time.
>
> Respectfully yours,
> G. W. CARVER.

James G. Wilson had said in a letter to a Negro college that if young Carver were to go South to teach "I will follow to see what I can learn from you people and consult with him about the building up of your institution." Since then, in March, he had been called to Washington as Secretary of Agriculture, and had already initiated the most comprehensive and far-reaching agricultural program the United States had known.

When Mr. Carver went to Washington in connection with his summer research work, he asked his former teacher to give notice to the country of his endorsement of the Tuskegee efforts by coming down to dedicate the new agricultural building in the fall. Indeed, the Secretary would be only too glad to come.

The first hint to the school at large that its Professor Carver was anything out of the ordinary emerged when he received the formal letter of acceptance and asked little John, son of J. H. Washington and sole office boy, to "take this to your uncle." "Uncle's" face lit up with joy. And when it became generally known that the Honorable James G. Wilson, Secretary of Agriculture, was going to make the two-day journey to see the Institute and dedicate the Slater-Armstrong Building, at Professor Carver's invitation, the latter assumed a new importance.

A tremendous to-do followed, of cleaning and decorating and erecting arches laden with holly and evergreens and moss, of trimming the Pavilion with native grasses, draping it with bunting and flags. The boys whose duty it was to keep the street lamps trimmed and the chimneys clean polished furiously. It was almost Christmas and the fireworks traditional to the holiday season in the South were lavishly bought.

One evening in mid-December 1897 Mr. Washington and Professor Carver, behind a pair of the principal's swiftest horses, drove to Chehaw to meet the eight-twenty fast train from the East. This was the first time any representative of the Federal Government had taken official cognizance of the school, and the white dignitaries of the town were all on hand. About ten the carriages were heard approaching the campus. A boy whipped up the two black horses, and they swung under the triumphal arch—Mr. Washington and Professor Carver and Secretary Wilson in a tall silk hat, the only top hat that had ever been seen in those parts.

The band at the entrance under the arch crashed into "Hail to the Chief," and one of the professors sent up skyrockets. A thousand boys and girls lined the driveways, ablaze with dancing lights leaping up into the darkness. It was the time of year when they were bringing in the sugar; the girls waved cane stalks tipped with cotton balls dipped in oil, and the boys flourished pine fagots amid yells for "Our Booker." An enthusiastic student wrote: "Our choir! How it did sing! The ringing notes of the sopranos harmonized most beautifully with the tenor and bass voices. The visitors were struck to wonderment, and with mouths agape they allowed not one note of the warblers to escape being taken in."

The next day, though more sober in tone, had a deep significance. It marked the dedication of the first building ever erected for the purpose of teaching agriculture to colored people—scientific and practical in all its branches. Planters, professors, judges, two governors, the clergy, and the press were in the audience of five thousand, or sat in the decorated Pavilion to hear and deliver speeches.

These ended simply but effectively when Washington said that agriculture was not, to be sure, just beginning at Tuskegee, but it was beginning in a new way.

# CHAPTER XII

## *"We Are Climbing Jacob's Ladder"*

PROFESSOR CARVER'S TITLE was Director and Instructor in Scientific Agriculture and Dairy Science, and he had five assistants in farm management, stock raising, truck gardening, horticulture, and dairying, respectively. These were big-sounding terms, altogether too big for the work they had to do, which was to teach young men how to apply simple rules of science to farm problems.

Work had begun for Professor Carver on October 8, 1896, with only thirteen pupils and no systematized course of study. When school closed May 26, 1897, he had enrolled seventy-six pupils, three of them "ladies," and over thirty-six in the dairy. He also had a carefully prepared two-year course, similar to Iowa's but modified to suit the different conditions and state of scholarship.

He had spent much time designing the internal arrangement of the agricultural building. On the first floor were the classrooms and on the upper floor were lecture room, herbarium, and reading room. The dairy was no longer a churn under a sweet-gum tree, but had its own equipment in the basement.

Like the teachers who came from Eastern universities, such as Harvard and Brown, Professor Carver had to unlearn some things and learn many new ones; all had, themselves, to be re-educated. They could not use the methods by which they had been trained, because the material of the student body was not of the same quality. These boys and girls would not even understand the language in which their teachers' courses had been couched; it might sound fine, but would be incomprehensible. When Professor Carver presented the school with a separator, nobody knew how to put it together. So he did. Milking began at three-thirty in the morning. A little later he would go in and expostulate, "Now I told you not to put the cream back in there! That's a separator—keep it separate!"

Though the professor's classroom work was light, his other duties were not; he was busier than a hen with one duck. The faculty was small, and such an enormous amount had to be accomplished. Every little while something new that needed to be done would crop up and he would be told, "That's in your department." Seemingly, if no other place could be found, it went in the Agricultural Department. He had no idea he was in charge of so much, and at first he was a little bewildered. Two years had passed before he had the department organized so that he really knew what it included. But he willingly accepted every new task, even going into the laundry to show the girls how to turn a collar.

All the faculty had to do whatever was necessary. If a department head wanted an improvement, he had to draw up his own plans for it. Mr. Logan helped with the music, and Mr. T. Owens, Professor of Mathematics, taught the Logan children Latin, since it was not included in the curriculum. Tuskegee came first; even a teacher's family was secondary. The campus group was small and intimate—whatever anyone did loomed with tremendous importance. A spirit of friendly rivalry pervaded the grounds. Everybody was trying to do things, and each wanted to be as good as the other.

Professor Carver was kept hopping with outside activities. For some years he collaborated with the chief of the weather bureau in Montgomery, measuring rainfall, displaying red and white weather flags on a pole, and sending daily observations.

The problem of keeping the little community in good health was no small matter, and much of this responsibility was turned over to him. Sanitary plumbing and the typhoid carrier were equally unknown in those days, and epidemics were a constant menace. As chairman of the Sanitary Committee, he analyzed samples of water from wells all over the county. In report after report he announced finding bacillus coli, and either condemned the wells or recommended that pump and windlass be installed; the rope or chain method insured that everyone was practically washing his hands in the well when he drew a bucket of water.

The table scraps from Alabama Hall were dumped by a trough into a wagon and carted away to the woods, where they were left for the pigs. But once, when the cattle coming back from these woods were counted, a heifer was missing. Professor Carver went out on a search and discovered it in the stream, dead. He analyzed the reservoir and found typhoid, but deduced that carelessness on the part of students had killed the heifer; they had thrown dishwater in with the scraps, and the alkali in the soap had affected its intestines.

However, the typhoid sent him to his desk in a hurry; he wrote the Surgeon General in Washington, and a public-health expert came down at once. Other people who lacked Professor Carver's scientific attitude were not in the habit of taking such things seriously, and it's a wonder they hadn't all died in consequence.

Before the coming of Professor Carver the stock also suffered under the threat of disaster. Once several head of cattle had been turned into a pasture in which peach trees had been pruned and the dying foliage left on the ground. His speed in identifying the hydrocyanic-acid poisoning saved the herd.

The veterinary advice he had to impart was considerable. Because Washington so loved fast horses, W. E. D. Stokes had made him a present of a fine Napoleon gray named Dexter. One night the student guard heard a noise in the stable and came around the corner on the run. Being a lumber-headed creature, he blazed away with his shotgun. Only, instead of any marauder, it was the saddle horse he hit, spattering its face and neck with shot.

BOOKER T. WASHINGTON
at the time he founded Tuskegee Institute, 1881

GEORGE W. CARVER
at Tuskegee Institute, 1896

Mr. Washington sent immediately for Professor Carver and anxiously asked for an opinion. To the professor's way of thinking, since the shot were only bird shot and just under the skin, it was not necessary to take them out; the damage was not serious; the animal would soon recover.

However, Dexter was valuable and Mr. Washington was very much attached to it. Furthermore, he was not certain just how much Professor Carver might know about the matter. Accordingly, he sent into town and asked Dr. Ludie Johnson, the white M.D., to come out and prescribe treatment. Not being a veterinarian, Dr. Johnson sought Professor Carver in consultation to find out what *he* thought. Then he went to Mr. Washington and reported, "Just leave the shot alone and the horse will recover. Your new man knows what he's talking about. Better do as he says."

This happening spread all over town, that a colored man from the West had prescribed the same treatment as Dr. Johnson, and confidence in Professor Carver began to mount.

A few, however, were still heard to murmur that they wouldn't trust that Yankee. John H. Washington, "J. H.," as he was called, had protested in the first place against his brother's decision to import a man of science. The mind of the superintendent of industries had been made up beforehand that a scientific agriculturist was unnecessary, and he wasn't going to change it.

One morning Professor Carver was told that the students were having difficulty getting butter to form.

"What's the matter with it?" asked J. H.

"I don't know," returned Professor Carver mildly. "But here's a bulletin on making butter."

"I've read it."

"Here, let me have the churn, and I'll try."

Professor Carver worked the churn, and all that resulted was a heap of foam—no butter. He was puzzled. "I'll go up to the barn and see if I can find out what the trouble is."

"Why go to the barn?" demanded J. H. "The trouble's

right here. If you know so much, why don't you know what's the matter with the butter?"

Professor Carver was growing irritated at this type of obstruction. "If you want me to find out, I'll have to go to the barn. Have you any objection?"

And away he marched to the barn.

Presently he marched back again. He was smiling a little over the picture of himself as a little boy playing tricks with Aunt Sue Carver's churn so he could go fishing. "I want some boiling-hot water," he stated. This sounded crazy, but when it was produced and the churn had been heated, behold, there was the butter. Then he explained the reason. "You'll have to stop feeding the cows so much cottonseed meal," he said, "if you want butter to form. Even if it is the cheapest feed. Cottonseed is rich in stearin, which has a high melting point. You can't get butter by churning in a normal atmosphere if you have an excess of fatty acids."

But J. H. was unconvinced and told his brother, "We don't need what they call a scientific agriculturist. We need a dairyman."

J. H. had been foreman of railroad construction at Hampton, and he had little understanding of the man of science, nor did he wish to get understanding. Being psychologically antipathetic to the Carver type of mind, he could not admit there was any good in it, and developed a personal antipathy toward the individual whose methods he could not comprehend.

Pretty soon his wrath rose again. The sheep developed scabs, and Professor Carver directed the boys to put the animals through an Australian dip. He gave them the proportions of rock lime and water to use, told them to let it stand and then dip, and went back to his botany class.

But in a short time the storm broke. J. H. was angry. "We don't need an 'expert'! All we need is a man who knows his business!"

"What's the matter?"

"Matter? You told the boys to put the sheep through a

dip and twelve of the ewes have died. That's what's the matter!"

Professor Carver was not given to speaking until he had his facts marshaled. Silently he went to investigate.

The boys had used unslaked lime, and the water had shot up to the boiling point. Without waiting for it to cool they had immediately plunged in the sheep and, after burning the first one, had not had sense enough to stop, but put through a dozen. Professor Carver was unused to such utter ignorance; he had not taken sufficient account of it and their inability to follow directions.

But J. H. went away muttering, "That man Carver doesn't know what he's doing." He protested to his brother, "You ought to fire him."

Washington knew better than to argue with a man who would not listen to reasonable argument. "Suppose I did," he returned. "Everyone would criticize me for having made a mistake. No. I think we'll keep him."

He knew what a valuable person he had. Professor Carver had been at Tuskegee less than a year when Washington gave a talk at Ames. The local paper stated, "Our only colored graduate, now three years an alumnus, has already achieved distinction in his line of work and has won the esteem and reverence of all with whom he has come in contact." This was essentially true, and its truth was confirmed by Washington, who called him "one of the greatest men God ever made. We wish we had half-a-dozen more just like him."

The rock on which the school was built was "service"; its quality magnetized the air, and few who breathed it could escape thereafter. Tuskegee alumni in business for themselves regularly sent money back. This spirit fitted in with Professor Carver's own psychology, and he with the spirit. Washington would sit at the council table and tell how these little sums came in. A graduate might have been able to save only five dollars by the end of the year, but he would dispatch it back to Tuskegee. Or he would deny himself pleasures, if need be, to make his offering. "If they can do without," thought Professor Carver, "why can't I?"

The first requirement of a scientist was a laboratory, and a scientific agriculturist was no exception. The school was very poor. One department might be allowed five dollars, another ten dollars, or even twenty-five, but these sums did not stretch far. Professor Carver had to make what he wanted for his laboratory.

He fretted over what he was to do for sandpaper, and while he was worrying he lay down and fell asleep. In his dream he entered a big wagon shop, where a man was putting a tire on a wagon wheel. He walked up to the wheelwright and asked, "Do you know how to make sandpaper?" The man answered, "Yes," but did not offer the explanation; he merely continued to stand there working. Finally Professor Carver said cannily, "I'll tell you how I do it." And he went through a process as he guessed it might be. "You did all right," replied the wheelwright, "except you didn't boil the sand." Professor Carver woke up and went to his laboratory, boiled the sand, and the sandpaper was as it should be.

Professor Carver liked to make things; he was born that way. But the students didn't know what to do. "There's no need to whine, 'Oh, if I only had so-and-so!' " he instructed. "Do it anyhow; use what you find about you." Then he took them out with him to scour rubbish heaps for bottles, jars, wires, rubber, string, glass. "Equipment is not all in the laboratory, but partly in the head of the man running it."

His equipment was a strange conglomeration, garnered chiefly out of junk piles. From nothing you must build slowly; when he saw a chance to get any new piece, he seized it. His classroom bell was a horseshoe mounted on an iron standard made for him in the foundry. He had a lamp, which helped to warm his hands when they grew too stiff from cold. It also reflected light on his microscope, and it had to do duty as a Bunsen burner. For graders he punched holes in a piece of tin, reeds could be made to serve as pipettes, a broken bottle could be cut clean-edged with a piece of string. A cracked china bowl served as a mortar, and he used a flatiron to pulverize his material. Zinc sulphate was costly, so he picked up the discarded zinc tops of fruit jars. He never had to buy a pencil; when one he had rescued was worn so he could not grasp it in his hand, he made a holder and gave it more service, down to the last half inch.

He was ridiculed, of course, and accused of living out of trash boxes, but he didn't care. Small memoranda are still in existence: "Professor Carver, please let me have seventy-five dollars to be returned at earliest convenience. (*Signed*) BOOKER WASHINGTON." The professor would not have had that seventy-five dollars to lend if he had not practiced conservation. Saving the things that others threw away became not merely an expedient, but a real matter of teaching conservation by example.

Saving, however, in itself was not enough; you must have order also. He went a step farther. He showed his pupils a box of string, saved, to be sure, but muddled and snarled. "That," he said, "is ignorance. And this"—holding out a box in which each piece was neatly tied or rolled into balls—"is intelligence."

The laboratory work was simple, so that it could be easily understood by the students and they could manage the technique of analyzing soils to learn which of the fourteen plant elements might be lacking, of testing fertilizers and feeds to see what made muscular tissue, fat, or milk. In clear language he taught the trinity of relationship between the soil, the plant growing on it, and the human being or animal consuming the plant.

"A thorough mastery of the soil is necessary in order to keep all of the mineral elements there in proper quantity and form to supply the needs of that particular crop.

"A thorough mastery of economic plant life is equally important in order that its composition will be all it should be.

"The human and animal body must be studied also in order that the food eaten will give 100 per cent nourishment at the minimum cost."

Farming had been generally unpopular at Tuskegee; other teachers would punish students by making them work at it. It wasn't a trade or a profession, just what they had always done. White people knew trades, but Negroes had always farmed, and they wanted to escape from that class.

In 1899 there arrived at the gates of Tuskegee a big, powerful young man who had walked from his home in Georgia. He had lied and he had stolen to get there, because get there he must. The registrar asked Tom Campbell what he would like to do to earn his way. How about farming? More places were open in that department than anywhere else. Tom emphatically said, "No!" He had just come off a plantation and was trying to get away from it. "Then how about agriculture?" "I'd like that fine," said Tom.

By this simple stratagem Thomas C. Campbell was assigned to Professor Carver, and Professor Carver made a type of labor the lad had once hated seem attractive. He was able to arouse in his students a desire for knowledge of what agriculture means—keep them interested and delighted and at the same time give them useful information. He possessed the two essentials of a good teacher—a thorough knowledge of his subject and an intuitive sense of how to instill it. One of his later assistants said that he had graduated at Cornell but had been educated under Carver.

To all who were not simply clods he was able to impart in varying degrees some of his own motivating compulsion, "I don't know, but I'll find out."

"You can't teach people anything," the professor once remarked. "You can only draw out what is in them." Though hardly a pupil in his classes, with the notable exception of young Campbell, had more than average intelligence, he brought out the best points of each, made each feel proud of his ability and want to extend it.

No permit, however, was given them to stop and preen themselves at any stage of their advancement. He made a parable of the little brown sparrow who borrowed plumage from the lyrebird, from the peacock, and from the egret and exclaimed, "How fine I am!" "Now you know," said the professor, "he was not entitled to those feathers. Underneath he was still the same little brown sparrow."

A natural genius, Mother Necessity, and an unflagging grind had produced the Carver phenomenon. He could not transfer the first two, but he could help what gifts there might be in his students by urging on them the third—industry. This he was able to do, even though the lackadaisical attitude of many of these boys who had grown up in an atmosphere of Southern sloth ran directly counter to his own quick habits. He stirred them to action by mild scoldings. "Get the drones off you! Remember," he was wont to say, "the more ignorant we are the less use God has for us."

He was thoroughly impatient with dabblers. Each student must complete what he had started. "I will help you as long as you are making progress, but once you decide to quit, I will not waste my own time further. And don't take up any of my time with a frivolous excuse. All I want is the thing done."

He had no patience with "about." "There are only two ways: one is right and the other is wrong. About is always wrong. Don't tell me it's *about* right. If it's only *about* right, then it's wrong. If you come to a stream five feet wide and jump four and a half feet you fall in and get drowned. You might just as well have tumbled in from the other side and saved yourself the exertion of the jump." In botany class he held up a sketch of a man's hand and then a leaf showing the similarity of the human venous system and the plant's. Each boy and girl also was asked to draw a leaf. If it was wrong, "Tear it up," he ordered, and the student would have to stand and draw that leaf on the blackboard until it was perfect.

His methods were not those of the other teachers, but his classes were entertaining. One of his characteristic pastimes was teaching his boys how to train the wrinkles in their foreheads. "Always lengthwise in a smile," he directed, "never up and down in a frown. Unless, of course, something should come to your notice which ought to be frowned upon. Then don't hesitate."

It was generally accepted that Professor Carver could identify any plant they brought in, whether he had seen it before or not, but his entomology class once rashly tried to hoodwink him. They produced a bug neatly pinned to a piece of cardboard and laid it on his desk.

"We just found this strange bug, Professor. What is it?"

He looked long at the curious creature. It had the head of a large ant, the body of a beetle, the legs of a spider, the antennae of a moth, all ingeniously put together. Finally he delivered his pronouncement, "Well, this, I think, is what we would call a humbug."

He liked pupils to do such things, and was delighted with the imagination that had fathered the hoax.

He never had to call the roll in botany classes, because everybody would be there with hands full of specimens. He was at odds, however, with current methods of teaching the subject, and with current botanies, which he considered were made for botanists, not for students. He himself would not give ten cents for the usual course, and the average student hated botany, just hated it. It was too voluminous, befuddling rather than illuminating, and created a heterogeneous confusion in the mind. He himself had been confused when he was studying alone, so he knew what he was talking about. At Ames he had tried, unsuccessfully, to argue his point with Dr. Pammell. The object was to know plants, or why study it? Instead the student was given a lot of technical terms, and when he had learned those he did not really know plants, he could not classify them.

Watch a child, he used to say. Don't coach it but let it alone. It would think in groups, showing that was the natural way for the human mind to work. And by following this natural working you were saved mystification. If you held a close communion with plants, they would speak to you and tell you what you wanted to know. If you observed them with sufficient attention, you would find that their distinguishing characteristics automatically grouped themselves. You would know the difference between one group and another as naturally as a child who saw a couple coming down the street knew which was the man and which the woman. The child would also see a complexion difference. An Indian would go into the dark group, but his straight hair would be different from the African's. This same type of familiarity through observation would distinguish plants also.

Suppose the agricultural student had to stop after learning the Latin names of a plant. According to the curriculum, entomology did not come until next year, and histology the year after. He still did not know how to deal with the pest that attacked his peach trees. He should not have to wait for the "ologies" but be given the group all in one bite so he would know how to grow a peach tree and, at the same time, protect it from disease by being familiar with the fungi or the pests that were attracted to the peach. In reverse, if he were familiar enough with a certain insect, he would know what plant it fed upon.

And why discourage a child by the physical make-up of a book? Existing ones lacked bodily proportion; they were much too thick for their length and breadth, and most of them were an ugly brick red in the bargain. Alongside a child was placed a stack of books almost as tall as he was. In time he had read all the books and received a degree, but he had only hazy ideas about a great number of things. Teaching should be in keeping with the books, infinitely simpler.

In fact, all education should be simplified; the extent was too great and the intent too small. The large grass family, to which nearly 75 per cent of our food plants belong, was supposed to be troublesome. But, according to Professor Carver, identification was easy and simple. Every known grass had a long bladelike leaf attached to a sheath encircling a jointed stem; if a plant had those three things it belonged in the family.

After finding out by observation the characteristics of a

great family, the student could find with comparative ease the names of different members of each particular group by an association of resemblances and distinct differences. In other words, he put them into the great family by common characteristics and subdivided into the smaller groups by distinct differences.

Occasionally, Professor Carver lectured on this subject: "I say 'tree' to you. The tree being one of several thousand members of the vegetable kingdom, you have no idea what I mean; you are more confused than before I spoke the word. The extent is too great. I say oak tree, and immediately thousands are shut out. You are now getting information; before, the word was just a generality.

"But you still don't know what I mean. Why call it oak? It has certain qualities; it belongs to the genus Quercus and contains the glucoside quercitrin. All oaks contain that, and you can split it up and have stains and dyes. Now you are beginning to get somewhere; you have more information.

"But the extent is still too large. I narrow to white oak. There are a hundred or more varieties of oak, but we are now down to two; there are only two white oaks. What is the difference? They grow in different localities—one upland and one bottom. The upland is exceedingly tough and makes the best vehicles because of its unusual strength and elasticity. In the bottom, the cells are large, loose, and open, because they must take in plenty of water. The wood is black and fairly tears up in ribbons for making wickerwork and baskets. All this time we have been getting more information by decreasing the extent and increasing the intent."

Though funds were lacking for publication, Professor Carver started work on a new type of botany with the proposed title, *An Outline for the Study of Economic Plant Life of Use in Agricultural Classes.* It would have one fascicle for trees, another for shrubs, another for the orchard, and another for the farm. Technical terminology would be omitted as much as possible. He himself seldom used the botanical term without the common name; in fact, that would come first, so the student would not have to be always turning to the glossary and so interrupt the train of investigation. He did not propose to reject the current system of education but give suggestions which educators might adapt and use. Ecology, mycology, entomology—the whole scientific category that had to do with plant life might be treated the same way. He did not care who did it, Peter Parker or Susan Smith, but merely wanted to start the movement on its way.

Practical demonstration allied itself to theory in the mind of Professor Carver. The space immediately about the Institute buildings being almost treeless, before visitors were due, teachers and pupils used to go into the woods and cut pine branches to stick in the ground. After commencement these would die down and present a sorry sight. With the advent of an expert, the time had come for landscaping. Professor Carver was in charge of the grounds, and his first winter had set about converting the unsightly campus into a park, grading and terracing, and in the spring was ready for planting shade trees, shrubs, flowers, grass.

The grass was a constant source of trouble to him. Being an artist on the ground as well as on canvas, he would lay out the paths with an eye to the most harmonious arrangement and with due observance of the mathematical perspective effects of landscaping. And then students and faculty, instead of walking where they were supposed to, would dive straight at their objective regardless of the thin, delicate blades of young grass.

He was growing upset and peevish over this, so he delivered one of his lectures to himself. "Why waste time getting perturbed and accomplishing nothing? People are going to travel in a way that is logical, if they are to get there." Then he sat down and watched the way they walked naturally, and he put his paths under their feet. Thereafter, he observed with content, they stayed in them.

## CHAPTER XIII

# *"Way Over Yonder in the Harvest Fields"*

PROFESSOR CARVER had come South to be of service to the farmers. That was the big thing, and whatever he accomplished was an outgrowth of that impulse and somehow must return to it again. The Experiment Station at Tuskegee Institute was the pivotal point around which Southern agriculture, insofar as it affected Negroes, revolved. And Negroes, though they could not control policy, made up nearly half the population. Training students who could go forth and spread the word was a vital means toward this end, and meanwhile knowledge, so desperately needed, could be scattered through the miles which lay immediately about Tuskegee.

That demonstration is the purest form of teaching was a principle completely adhered to by this particular school. The results of the experimentation were to be published, as the need for them arose, in bulletin form. But bulletins were of no value to those who could not read. It was no good putting the fodder up too high so that the people could not reach it. Points must be illustrated from real objects they could see and touch. Farmers were urged to send samples of soils, fertilizers, and insects, and, most important of all, to visit the Station. It was to be an object lesson on view at all times.

The experimentation would be to no purpose unless the Station made a practice of doing things under conditions similar to those of the farmer. The start was certainly in accordance with conditions similar to those of the farmer. About twenty acres were set aside, out beyond the agricultural building. The land was so poor that a one-horse wagon could carry the entire crop of cowpea vines produced by half of it. The school had previously tried to grow crops on this land and had netted, instead of a profit, a loss of $16.50 an acre.

The Legislative appropriation for the Station being insufficient for the work that had to be done, Mr. Washington wrote to a big firm asking whether it would donate several hundred pounds of fertilizer for this worthy purpose. The company replied, "We sympathize with your desire for experimentation on Southern soils, but we want to be frank with you: we are convinced there is only one colored man who is capable of conducting such a scientific experiment, and he, unfortunately, is in Iowa."

Mr. Washington responded triumphantly, "We have him right here, and he is to conduct the experiment." The Station received the fertilizer.

The twenty acres were divided into plots, and crops were planted. The students did the work, but Professor Carver spent much of his time there overseeing every movement, having them measure carefully, teaching them to follow directions precisely, and watching progress with anxious care. Up and down Betsy the rhythmic ox plodded, with the boys trudging after her. "Plow deep," he directed, "plow deeper. Plow deep while the sluggards sleep."

Professor Carver looked at the light gray, sandy, upland soil underlined with red and yellow clay which outcropped. "In spite of its hopeless appearance," he decided, "this soil can be redeemed." He placed it among the most responsive in the United States, the fertility of which could be maintained with little or no cash outlay, simply by curbing waste. Still there was no money for fertilizer, and the Station could not continue to depend on donations. Nor could the farmer. In any event, the principle was wrong. The waste of animals constituted excellent fertilizer, but these farmers had so few animals. Organic waste of some sort, however, was available to all.

While on one of his tours of trash heaps, to see what he might salvage for his laboratory, Professor Carver discovered a splendid pumpkin vine having seven runners thirty-seven feet long by actual measurement, and loaded with fine pumpkins, growing from the center of what appeared to be tin cans. This was the campus dumping ground, because the terrain was so badly washed it seemed useful only as the source of an occasional load of sand when one was needed for plastering.

A pumpkin seed had found its way into this pile of what is generally regarded as worthless rubbish, and Professor Carver immediately seized upon this as a perfect object lesson on the value of organic waste as fertilizer. The piece of land was plowed, harrowed, leveled up, and planted in white silver-skin onions, cantaloupes, watermelons, Irish potatoes, and corn. Then he waited to see how they grew.

At the same time and for the same purpose a compost pile was started. He had a pen built, and in it was piled all the organic waste from the campus in the form of paper, leaves, rags, grass, weeds, street sweepings—anything, in fact, that would decay quickly. This layer was covered over with rich earth from the woods and swamps, and when the whole was properly rotted it was applied to the wasted acres.

Another means of enriching the soil was to plant Leguminosae, the second largest family of seed plants—four hundred and twenty genera with seven thousand species. The weak stems and butterflylike flowers of these pod bearers made them seem particularly decorative, but ineffectual. Actually they were about the hardest-working plants. All others fed upon the nitrogen in the soil, which cost the farmer who could pay for it seventeen cents a pound to replace. But the pod bearers, such as vetch, peas, beans, clovers, and peanuts, had the power, unique among plants, to make the soil richer, by reason of their growth upon it, rather than poorer.

They could extract nitrogen from the air and impart it to the soil. The roots were studded with little swellings called nodules, the cells of which contained bacteria that could, by a process of symbiosis (the more or less permanent united life of certain animal and vegetable organisms rendering mutual service to each other) fix air nitrogen to make it available as plant food. From the roots, fixed nitrogen was released into the soil ready for the next hungry plant.

Certain of these Leguminosae would also afford valuable additions to the animal dietary. In the desire for something new and novel in the way of forage plants Professor Carver started experimentation with various members of this family.

In '96 there was no crimson clover anywhere in the county, nor for many counties roundabout. He planted this and the cowpea and hairy vetch. In '97 he secured a pint of velvet-bean seed which yielded fully three pecks. He experimented with the peanut, which was no more considered a farm crop than was parsley; the children liked to eat peanuts, so a few families had a few vines.

Developing agriculture means keeping an eye out for new things. The soja pea, now known as the soybean (*Glycine soya*), the little honorable plant and the main dependence of China for its food supply, was said to have been brought back by Commodore Matthew C. Perry, but nothing had been done about it in this country. This, too, Professor Carver planted.

He might exert every effort to educate away from the one-crop system, but the efforts of one man could make little headway against the Southern economic system and the complex of social institutions bound up in it. Farmers were in business and, theoretically, should be able to make a profit, as did any other businessmen. The immediate need for cash outweighed the long-time need for conservation. They simply had to keep on growing cotton.

The best the professor could do was persuade as many as came within his orbit to include a subsistence crop with their cash crop in order to lift their general living standards. To better his domestic economy and the health of his family, the farmer should have a more balanced farm—grow a vegetable garden, raise livestock and chickens for his own use, perhaps have some left over for sale.

Meanwhile, Professor Carver could help increase the farmers' income a little by showing them how to raise better cotton as their cash crop; they need not keep on producing two-bolls-to-a-stalk, bumblebee cotton—a bumblebee had hardly to lift his wings to reach the big pink blossoms.

It was not enough for Professor Carver to grow good cotton, he must always be making experiments, and crossbreeding was his specialty. By 1909 he had developed four new varieties—two types of long-staple upland, one wilt-resistant, and another especially prolific with a medium staple, all particularly adapted to the light, sandy soils of Macon County. He dispensed packets of seed to farmers who wanted it and issued leaflet No. 16, instructing them how to cross and fertilize by hand, using the recently developed Russell's Big Boll (male) and long-staple Sea Island (female), the hairs of which were easily detached from the seed.

One of the most remarkable features of the Station was a crop of cotton originated and improved by Professor Carver, the yield being considerably more than a bale an acre. One bush would carry 275 bolls of enormous size, frequently four at one joint on an ordinary stalk. All without the use of a single pound of commercial fertilizer.

Almost any agriculturist coming that way sought him and his advice. The Colonial Secretary of the German Empire, accompanied by a cotton expert of his department, spent several days at Tuskegee to observe the Carver hybrid, and asked for three graduates to go to the African West Coast to introduce it. And a man from Queensland, Australia, took back some seed which he passed on to his government. In 1906 he wrote Professor Carver that it was being successfully grown all over his country.

The puzzled local farmers could not understand how Professor Carver, who had never seen cotton growing before, could beat them raising it when they had spent their lives in the fields. Patiently he explained that the principles of plant growth were the same always. This plant that he was looking at needed certain things; the soil he was looking at had certain physical and chemical constituents. Very well, he would make the right adjustment between them.

Professor Carver found it practically impossible for the Station to tell with any degree of accuracy just what demands would be made upon short or no notice at all. For this reason he kept open house, as it were, and held himself in readiness to give advice. If the farmers could not come themselves, they sent in their samples:

> Mr. G. W. Carver. Dear Sir, You will find the inclosed packages the soil of diffrent farms whom desire to have their soil anelized. We send it this way for convient to each other. yours Affectninate.

Another would read:

> PROF. G. W. CARVER,
>
> I am today mailing you one quart of water from my well. Please analyze this water for me considering first the health of my family and then the wealth of it.
>
> I am also sending you one pint of earth from the well (No. 1), Number two that creek land and number three hill land.
>
> Please advise me what kind of fertilizer to use on numbers two and three.
>
> I am yours obligingly,
>
> P.S. I am also enclosing a little bag of coal, supposed to be coal which came out of the well. Remember I am the one that brought you a rock last year that came out of the well.

He would reply with the results of the Meisch and permanganate tests on the water, directions for cleaning the well, advise compost for the land or give the proportions of commercial fertilizer, and state that the coal, though varying in its purity, was a fairly good sample of cannel.

If the farmers were unable to write, he encouraged them to come in and bring their problems. He reported to the principal: "Yesterday a man rode five miles in the cold, drizzling rain and called me out of church to prescribe for his ox that was at home 'very sick.' A few days before, a man brought his horse six miles here for treatment. Last summer a lady rode twelve miles twice a week in order to take lessons on buttermaking and the care of milk."

Advice to individuals was important, because individuals made up the group, but the larger the group that could be reached the better. The Station had been established early in '97 and the plots planted in the spring. By fall a new project was ready to begin operation. The farmer and his wife were to have their day in school, and it was to be called the Farmers' Institute.

Thereafter, farmers from fifteen or twenty miles distant, but chiefly from Macon County, attended the Farmers' Institute every third Tuesday in the month, all the year round. There were usually about seventy-five in all—not, perhaps, a very large number speaking in terms of population, but each constituted a little nucleus of better farming in his own neighborhood. If one grew taller corn than another, his neighbor would want to know why, and they also would try to follow the practices learned at Tuskegee.

First came short and simple talks in the agricultural building, couched in language these unlettered folk could understand. The professor explained the need for rotation of crops: no two plants feed exactly alike; some are deep feeders, some shallow; some heavy, some light. Two deep or two heavy should not follow each other. To demonstrate his meaning he had cut sections partly away from bamboo canes and filled them with different types of soils which the farmers could see for themselves.

"In the South we are sinning against the land," he said. "We are letting it go unnourished from the waste of washouts and erosions and are not protecting it. In return it is punishing us." Then he took the farmers to show them a gully cut twenty-five feet into the earth, just from the drip of a barn.

After the lesson in dairying or poultry keeping they all walked in a body to the Station plots where they could examine simple produce actually growing out of the same kind of soil as theirs. No matter how scientific the investigation may have been, the discussion was practical. Professor Carver bent down and picked up a handful of soil; he opened his hand and the earth fell apart. "You see," he said, "when it's like that, it's all right to cultivate it. But if it sticks to the plow, then it's too wet. The air can't get in, and the plant won't have anything to feed on unless it gets air."

He lifted up the root of the cowpea to show how it was studded with nodules, like a string of beads. Of the experimental legumes, at the end of the first two years the cowpea had stood the test best; its relation to the soil physically, mechanically, and chemically was the most satisfactory. The roots penetrated deeply, thus loosening the soil. They decayed rapidly and formed valuable absorbents, in which upland soils were deficient. The cowpea would return twenty-five dollars' worth of nitrogen to each acre, and it was an excellent food for man and beast. Vigorously he advocated that every farmer grow some and prepared a bulletin containing eighteen ways of cooking them.

March was the season of forest fires, when the sky was illuminated by night and the brightness of the sun was obscured by day. Preparatory to April planting the farmers burned the weeds and dried stalks of the year before, and, through carelessness, fires spread to forests. Thus the chain of desolation was lengthened.

Professor Carver pointed off across the fields toward the haze of drifting smoke. "Look," he said. "There goes destruction riding the wind—millions of dollars going up in smoke. These poor soils need as much humus as they can get, and a great deal more. The habit of burning off the fields and wood lots is one of the greatest curses that has ever come to the Southern farmer. Our forests and swamps should be cherished. If you burn your fields you are burning your fertilizer and will have to buy it. Turn it under instead. Don't continue to follow this foolish practice any more than you would burn off the outside bills of a roll of greenbacks."

There before the farmers was the proof of the professor's

preaching: the land that had been used for dumping proved to be one of the show places on the ground. There before them was a twenty-pound cabbage and the biggest onion that had ever been grown. Many of the onions measured seven inches in diameter. The watermelons and cantaloupes were of a fine, marketable size, abundant and very prolific; the vines remained green and continued to bear longer than in any other place. The Irish potatoes grew large and smooth with an enormous yield.

The loss from the Station the first year was $2.50 an acre. The next year also the ledger read $2.50, but in black instead of red. In seven years, with no commercial fertilizer whatever, it profited $75 an acre. Production jumped rapidly from 40 to 266 bushels of sweet potatoes an acre, and from about a third of a bale of cotton to the acre to a bale and a quarter an acre.

The minutes of a near-by Farmers' Institute meeting testified to the heartfelt interest and progress being made. May 27, 1904, opened with singing "Father, I Stretch My Hands to Thee." There followed a Scripture lesson, prayer, and another song, "Alas! and Did My Saviour Bleed." Then came a little talk on "How and why we grow cowpeas." One farmer said why he grew them was: first, because they are good for man; second, good for stock; third, good for rebuilding and enriching the land where grown. He said further that he could pay his teacher better.

After another religious folk song, "We Are Climbing Jacob's Ladder," the Reverend Huggins of Rising Star community reported meetings held regularly from two to four times a month; vegetables were now grown plentifully from January to January. Mrs. Susan Johnson reported for the mothers and children. Besides discussing conditions, etc., they were taught how to sew, cook, and make shuck hats.

Mrs. Tatum of Liberty Hill said that the women were ahead of the men; they had in the treasury $6.25 for summer school; for her part she had sold $4.00 worth of rutabagas. Mr. Hunt brought some fine onions; he said that he worked his garden mostly on moonshine nights while it was cold. Mr. Philpot of Baptist Cluster said that a good bit of his cotton was affected by the cold. Professor G. W. Carver of the Experiment Station advised all to observe their crops closely and, if not in good condition now, replant or plow up the entire crop and plant over as he had done.

Mr. Howard of Oak Grove reported that they had a two-acre school farm planted, had already supplemented one month to their school after government term was out, and were going to supplement two for this summer. Mrs. Susie Howard said that they had paid $10.10 out of their mothers' treasury and decided that their teacher should not go unpaid, neither should she work for less than other teachers.

Pinkston Crossroad was going to build a schoolhouse this summer. Oak Grove had a nice sweet-potato patch and was planning to buy a cooking stove by next term. Hickory Grove Club assisted mothers in buying three wall lamps and nine shades. This club also worked the cotton patch and had raised $2.58. The club from Solomon's Chapel was composed of school children and had $1.00 in the treasury.

After singing "Let the Heaven Shine on Me" the meeting adjourned, to be called again the third Tuesday of the following month.

To bring together the accomplishments of the farmers and show what progress was being made, gradually there evolved the idea of a fair. The first of these was held in '98 in a corner of the Pavilion, called by courtesy the Macon County Fair, because the produce was brought chiefly by the farmers of Macon County who had attended the Farmers' Institute.

The fair started from small beginnings. At first the entire thing could have been carried in a two-horse wagon, except for one white ox, two milch cows, a few hogs, two mules, and three horses, which made up the exhibit of livestock. But each fall of the year thereafter they gathered in the old battalion ground, farmers with samples of their crops, and the women with quilts and canned goods, needlework and home-cured meat. The town whites began to take part, at least as much because it was good business as through neighborliness. The Macon County fairs grew and they grew until the school was asked to join the state fairs at Montgomery. In 1903 crowds gathered about the booth in the capitol under the stairway to the right where Professor Carver had his exhibit of dried foods and soja peas and demonstrated the value of sweet potatoes and cowpeas.

The Farmers' Institute meetings rose to a mighty crescendo in February at the time of the Farmers' Annual Conference. To call them together word was sent through the county, though all were welcome from wherever they might come. On oxcarts and mule wagons, stretching out a quarter of a mile, they rode in the night before and during the early morning—handkerchief-headed aunties and gingham-gowned young women; old men smoking their corncobs, young men in their best, though often their coats were many-patched; excited children with big eyes gleaming from their dark little faces. At such times the roads leading to Tuskegee were never empty and the dust never settled.

A delicious aroma of roast pig drifting on the campus air met them, and light glowed red from the barbecue pit, where student cooks performed all night at the savory task of basting. In the battalion ground many of the farmers, too, were employed all night twining paper ribbons on the spokes of their wagon wheels, setting candy-striped poles in the corners, fastening on their tallest stalks of corn, whitewashing a paled sty in which would ride a majestic hog.

In the morning they gathered outside the Pavilion, which had been freshly sprinkled with sawdust from the mill and decorated with branches of longleaf pine, partly to enliven the bare, drab boards and also to fulfill the purely practical purpose of keeping out the weather, February weather being uncertain. From the smooth needles rain slid quickly and soundlessly to fall with a soft plunk to the earth.

And then came the parade, ending at the chapel.

The new chapel, just across the way from the Slater-Armstrong Building, had taken a long time in the building. Over a million bricks had to be fired, the oak floor sawed, and the pews and cornices designed and carved from the trees on the place. The students had laid it off with a level they had made themselves—boys from sixteen to twenty, the youngest, not even the best in the school. If the carpenter asked for skilled labor the principal would say, "I believe you can do it yourselves," and with that faith they went ahead.

Tuskegee was not like Hampton, where instruction by white experts was available; the people of Tuskegee had to train themselves to train each other. Washington wanted no outside help on the chapel; it was to be a living thing expressing the spiritual fervor and material accomplishment of the school. To have it a beacon in the county a dynamo was installed by the students—their own little plant, which made it the first building to be electrically lighted. The whole campus loved that chapel, and to the country folk it was the New Jerusalem.

Washington would mount the platform and give a talk: own your own land, rotate your crops, improve your stock; I notice too many razorbacks; get rid of those. He told them about "Old Jim Hill," who used to grow two bolls on a cotton stalk; now he grew fourteen, and his neighbors accorded him the automatic respect of addressing him as Mr. James Hill.

Then he stopped and called on the farmers to tell what they were doing to better their land and their homes and, in the process, themselves. "What about you, Mr. Jones? You have been coming to the Institute regularly. What have you accomplished this year?"

Mr. Jones stood up. The type of farmer he represented was, by ordinary, a serious even a solemn individual. His face was set Indianlike in vertical lines, and he seldom smiled. He was imbued with evangelistic zeal and earnestly tried to fulfill the school behest: when you learn one thing you must pass it on; the strong must help the weak. He had "hardly words to express" himself, but he longed to try: if he had ever mortgaged anything, then Jonah had swallowed the whale; his wife had never greased her mouth with a piece of mortgaged meat since they were married.

At twelve came recess and dinner, and the barbecued oxen and hogs and sheep were washed down with gallons of coffee and red lemonade. Mr. Washington presided in a paternal fashion, though he could only look on at the feast. His digestion had become uncertain, the result of the usual bad dietary in youth coupled with the present nervous strain of an excess of work and responsibility.

In the afternoon the guests traipsed about the campus. They flocked around the stand Professor Carver had set up. There on the spot he was cooking tomatoes, offering them for his audience to taste and eating some himself to prove they were not poisonous. Before interested housewives he demonstrated the eighteen different ways of cooking cowpeas, all of which they could carry out themselves, to a running accompaniment of words. "In painting the artist attempts to produce pleasing effects through the proper blending of colors. The cook also must blend her food in such a manner as to produce dishes which are attractive, wholesome, and appetizing. Harmony in food is just as important as harmony in colors."

The visitors wandered in and out of the buildings and through the Experiment Station grounds, inevitably creating a certain amount of havoc. But though they overran his young lawns and bruised his infant shrubs, Professor Carver did not flinch. "The place belongs to the people, and not to us," said Washington, and the professor concurred. "This is the only time they are allowed freedom to do as they please and have a good time. Let them tear up the campus if they want to."

They did, and it took a week to clean up afterward, but, as Samuel Johnson said, "Gratitude is the fruit of great cultivation; you do not find it among gross people." The Negro farmers of Macon County showed their gratitude in words of praise and wonder, and in deed also. Though they crowded in numbers of eight or nine thousand, and no restraints of any sort were imposed upon their merrymaking, not one instance of disorderly conduct occurred.

At seven or eight in the evening all climbed into their carts and wagons and buggies again and started, many of them on another all-night ride, for home, the children curled up around their feet like puppies, the little ones in their mothers' laps.

At Commencement people from the North would be invited down and would be taken on a Sunday tour through the countryside. They had a stake in Negro progress or would, it was hoped, have a stake if they could see for what purpose their money, if they gave it, would be spent—observe what money could accomplish in the way of salvaging human waste.

Naturally Washington wanted his people to appear at their best, so he sent out advance couriers. "If you can't paint, whitewash; if you don't have whitewash, we will supply it; if you are pressed for time and can't whitewash all your house, whitewash the front." In politics you would call it pump priming, but it was a start in the direction of beautifying because, in the fervor of getting ready, some little residue would be left and carry the people through to the next time. The place looked so much better when it was cleaned up that they would make an effort to keep it so.

Washington was a showman. Faculty and guests rode in style with a driver to each carriage, and he had relays of horses stationed along the route. This was well planned for the dash, allowing only time to stop briefly at the churches and schools where hundreds were gathered with their eggs and hams and canned goods already out on display.

When automobiles first came in the roads were still unpaved and tires were always blowing out. Professor Carver, though riding in the first car, had to be dusted off before he could speak. He carried an extra supply of collars in a little bag and would go round back of the church and pull out a clean one before he made his appearance.

May Commencement was, in many respects, similar to the Farmers' Conference, though its emphasis was concentrated more on school activities.

They were alike in another way—the crowds became so great they could not spread out over the grounds; both school and farm had to be brought to the spectators. The principle of visual demonstration was applied to every aspect.

Commencement dramatized education. It was not something academic and far away, but close to the parents' own daily life. On the platform of the chapel they could see a miniature engine to which steam had been piped, or a piece of a brick wall being laid. A cow was led up onto the platform and milked there; a horse was shod and its teeth filed. An emergency case was carried in for treatment by a student nurse. Students went through the process of making a loaf of bread, as though it were in slow motion; the dough was mixed, kneaded, and put in the oven, and another was taken out, brown and smelling richly. One girl cut out a dress, fitted it on a model, sewed it up, and the model walked off wearing the dress.

At the 1905 Commencement the big news was that the biggest celebration of all would be held next October. President Theodore Roosevelt was going to visit the Institute.

President McKinley and all his cabinet except one had paid a call in 1898 on their way to Atlanta to celebrate the Peace Jubilee at the end of the Spanish-American War. The school had prepared floats drawn by horses, mules, and oxen showing its past and present, triumphal arches of flags and fruits of the fields had been erected, and students again waved stalks of sugar cane tipped with open bolls of cotton. But somehow that event did not have the same significance, because President Roosevelt was an acknowledged well-wisher of Negroes and would extend himself to the utmost to help them on their upward way.

His friendship with Booker Washington had begun some time before the assassination of McKinley in September

1901, which had hoisted him into the presidency. He had immediately wished to consult with Washington regarding the appointment of Negroes to office and, since he could not leave, had asked Washington to the White House—two simple men meeting to talk over common problems at the place and time most convenient to both. The storm of protest over a Negro dining in the White House had been startling to both, and Washington's life had been threatened because he had dared to "step out of his place." At the Institute the older men stayed up at night and the guards were doubled. The children were aware of the excitement in the air, but faculty parents made it a point never to discuss the race question where they could overhear it. All that had been tacitly forgotten now, and the town was agog over the President's contemplated visit.

His time would be short and, since he could not possibly cover the grounds, it was decided to put the school on wheels and let it pass in panorama before him on the reviewing stand. A boy stood at the gate whipping the horses to make them go by the stand at a run; if they should happen to tip over they could just stay tipped over.

Riding the floats were students carrying on the school activities just as they would do in the classroom or at the farm: girls and boys ginning and baling cotton and making butter by old and new methods; girls fashioning brooms and baskets, stuffing mattresses and upholstering furniture, dressing chickens, or sewing uniform hats, girdles, and collars of "Alice blue" silk to honor their guest; boys treating a cow, spraying fruit trees and pruning, fitting valves and unions for steampipes, or setting type and operating a printing press; tailors sitting cross-legged stitching uniforms.

Afterward Roosevelt walked to the principal's house through the grounds which, due to Professor Carver's untiring efforts, were beginning to show considerable improvement. The lawns were covered with Bermuda grass, the foliage had grown up before the chapel, and here and there were soft, rich masses of pansies and verbenas. Just before he left, the President telephoned Mrs. Roosevelt to thank her for his birthday message—and how was Quentin?

Both Lewis Adams, the ex-slave, and George Campbell, the ex-slaveowner, the two who might almost be called the founding fathers of Tuskegee Institute, died the same year, 1905, but many other friends had come to carry on the work they had initiated.

Negro literacy at the time of the Civil War was about 3 per cent; by 1910 it was nearly 70 per cent, but this was not enough. The Southern states lacking both money and the desire to provide adequate educational facilities for rural colored children, Washington himself wanted to build experimental schools that would teach the little ones not only their A B Cs, but also how to live.

Rising Star, a few miles from Tuskegee, had become such a model school. It was the well-kept home of the teachers, and recitations were held in the living room. By spending the day in such surroundings, the children learned the lessons of everyday life, including cleanliness, and these lessons they carried to their own frustrated homes.

Anna T. Jeanes, a Quaker of Philadelphia, gave Washington money to establish more schools, and even the impersonal but invaluable General Education Board of the Rockefeller Foundation grew out of this movement which had its inception at Tuskegee.

Washington had early interested Julius Rosenwald in the subject of Negro education. Rosenwald once said he had simply fallen into a business that had money-making possibilities, and he modestly attributed his enormous success with the house of Sears, Roebuck and Company to luck and not to ability. It became his function to give, and thereby receive, happiness from this money. Having seen the miracle that education had performed in the person of Booker T. Washington, he wanted to do what he could to help the Negro, as a race, out of the ditch.

Some five thousand schoolhouses now stand as a monument to this endeavor and provide educational facilities for

40 per cent of the Negro school children in the country districts of the South. Toward these white-painted beacons with trim windows and tidy furnishings, standing out startlingly against a succession of weathered shacks, the mother must start early in the morning and hurry the children to get them on yonder to the teacher. A school bus carrying the white children clatters by, but the little Negro children, barefoot or clumping in some adult's castoff shoes, must trudge the many miles to and fro on foot. At least they are on their way, and the goal of most is Tuskegee Institute.

The local press took cognizance of the Institute whenever notables arrived, and they had a battery in 1906: President Charles W. Eliot of Harvard; William Howard Taft, Secretary of War; Andrew Carnegie, for whom the shoemaking department made a pair of golf shoes, a token exchange for the white-pillared library he had given the school a few years before; Paul Lawrence Dunbar, who contributed the Tuskegee song which was set to music by N. Clark Smith, the musical director of the Institute.

That same year also came J. E. Kwegyir Aggrey of Africa. Aggrey was greatly impressed with the work being accomplished at Tuskegee and talked about establishing such a school in Africa. He longed to take Professor Carver with him. "A man like him, with ample facilities, could work wonders in Africa. Verily my people are sleeping on acres of diamonds." Professor Carver could not leave his chosen sphere, but Aggrey did eventually carry out his ideas in the Achimoto University College in the Gold Coast Colony.

Like Washington, Aggrey sought not an amalgamation of, but co-operation between, the races. "You can play a tune of sorts on the white keys," said he, "and you can play a tune of sorts on the black keys, but for harmony you must use both the black and the white."

# CHAPTER XIV

## *"Go Tell It on the Mountain"*

CLOPPING ALONG the dusty Alabama roads went a light wagon piled high with tools and boxes and jars and drawn by a mule with leisurely flopping ears. It was Friday evening when classwork was done, and Professor Carver had boxed up demonstration material and started out to hold his customary meeting of farmers way out in the sticks. Sometimes teachers from other departments begged to be allowed to go; it was a new experience for them to visit the desolate places in the swamps.

They jogged along through the loblolly pines, fording the branches; often the only drinking water was from these muddy streams. The dwarf forests of dry sticks which marked last year's cotton fields could not hold together the nourishing topsoil, and winter storms had taken their toll—washing, eroding, leaching, laying bare the subsoil, which might have significance to the geologist but could not feed the farmer's family. In an occasional hollow a bit of cane flashed startlingly green—cane for sweetener which would make up one of that diet-restricting triumvirate of "meat, meal, and molasses."

One way to quiet the indeterminate migration of Southern Negroes was to build up again their fundamentally sound desire to own their own homes. The advisability of thus becoming stockholders in the body corporate was constantly held up before the families with whom Professor Carver came in contact: they should not buy buggies until they had bought land. They should save five cents each working day and put it where they couldn't get it again until a year was up; then they would have $15.50, enough for three acres and a nest egg of fifty cents for the next year. In 1907, when cotton was fifteen cents a pound and going higher, he urged them to use the extra money to buy land. The effect of ownership was immediate and striking in creating self-respect and stability.

One home in Reeltown stood out in marked contrast to most of the rickety, forlorn cabins; though not beautiful, it had a vegetable garden. Anyone could tell that this farmer was an owner, not a tenant. Professor Carver pulled up the mule and swung his long legs to the ground. "Good evening, Mr. Baker."

"Lawd 'ave mercy! Look here, Sally. It's Perfesser Carver come with his black box to hunt yarbs. Come right in, Perfesser, and sit a piece. Rest yo' hat?"

The professor made everybody his friend. Some said if Jesus Christ was coming it was "just like Perfesser Carver coming; he was a real lovin' man."

"Did you plant cotton again this year, Mr. Baker?"

"No, Perfesser, only twenty-five acres. Yo' said it wa'n't good fer de lan' to grow jes' one t'ing all de time. De res' Ah got in co'n an' oats an' a li'l bitta rye an' sweet 'taters an' peanuts. Now Ah'll tell yo' de truf. When Ah come to dis cummunity white fo'ks tol' me Ah cain't make a livin'. But Ah plowed deep an' went in de woods an' raked up oak leaves an' swamp muck—mah ol' marster knew about barnyard manure an' leaves an' muck lak yo' do. An' when mah co'n come knee high, it was de purtiest color. Ah done jus' lak yo' tol' me. Now what's dat t'ing yo' got dere?"

"It's a wire chicken coop. I brought it for you to keep, but at the meeting tomorrow I'll show everybody how to set hens and have good luck with them."

"Ah tol' all de folks yo' was comin' to mah house and make talk about how we ought to live. Ef dey do lak yo' say dey'll benefit by it. Some say yo' know more'n God does."

With great pride Mr. Henry C. Baker, born a slave, took

their guest out-of-doors to prove how he and his wife had themselves benefited by the professor's teaching. He was always urging the people to drink more water; this was a problem because usually their source of supply was so far away it was tiresome to haul it to the cabins. But the Bakers had their own well. When they peered in to see how deep it was, he suggested they let down their bucket of milk to keep it cool. They looked at the garden house, where Mrs. Baker exhibited with pride her jars of Hopping John—black-eyed peas and rice already prepared to bring them luck on New Year's Day. For his supper she brought out meat she had pickled according to his instructions and a jar of jelly sealed with white of egg.

The South was more abundantly blessed with native fruits than any other section of the country, and nearly any fruit that grew in either the temperate or subtropical climates could be raised in Alabama. Southern farmers, once they knew how to utilize this advantage, could have fresh vegetables of some kind all the year round. Long before any save advanced members of the medical profession, Professor Carver advocated fruit twice a day, raw if possible, issuing bulletins on such matters as how to utilize wild plums.

Secretary Wilson, after his visit, had sent down thousands of packets of seeds to be dispensed. Parkman Brown, let us call him, gave a glowing report. He had planted parsnips, and when they were so high he had taken them in to the old woman. "How did you cook them, Mrs. Brown?"

"Cut de tops an' biled 'em. Dey suteny made de purtiest soup."

"What did you do with the roots?"

"Th'ow'd 'em away."

It was no use teaching the farmers to raise vegetables when their wives did not know what to do with them afterward. On his sorties into the country Professor Carver therefore carried along jars and showed them how to pickle, can, and preserve. The housewives, too, must learn how to arm themselves against the winter months—those long, lean hounds which prowled wolf-like round the door.

Eating habits being the most nearly fixed of any social customs, if a new dietary were to be added to the present one, it must be palatable and it must be demonstrated as being palatable; farm families would not improve their diet unless it tasted good to them. The apex of Professor Carver's triangle of soil, plant, and animal was the use of the resulting food in the human body. He had always been greatly interested, not merely in the value of foods, but in their preparation. A good cook should know the different constituents and what they were for. Though he had not had access to foreign delicacies and garnishings, in dealing with the foods that had come within his range he had become an artist at blending subtle tastes and making the most simple and inexpensive fare both nutritious and delicious.

From time immemorial the custom had been to postpone hog killing until freezing weather. Though the hogs matured in the summer and the farmer was put to the expense of caring for them after that and running the risk of cholera the longer he kept them, the practice had seemed necessary to avoid having the meat spoil in the heat. At the country meetings Professor Carver told them how to cure it and how to keep it during the hot summers—how to make scrapple and liver puddings.

Occasionally one of the houses Professor Carver visited had two rooms with a dog trot in between, and in such a one he might stop overnight, if they knew him well enough to feel safe; if they knew he would not act above them and make fun. For his part, he enjoyed hearing their talk, believing you could get a good deal of wise information from simple people if you listened attentively.

He would stay with them to Sunday, eat with them as one of themselves, as happy as could be over the cakes and blackberry jam prepared especially for him. Once they became accustomed to him, they in turn liked his ways, his simplicity.

He was not haughty as some would be with so much learning, but would sit down and talk to them in homely words they could understand. They realized that he knew things and had their interests at heart.

In the very early days some white persons were always present at the week-end gatherings; they did not like any assembly of Negroes. Even when they knew its purpose, many plantations did not permit a meeting at all; the owners "didn't want their niggers getting notions in their heads."

The meetings were usually held on Saturday afternoons, but sometimes on Sundays. The church was the most important influence in the life of rural Negroes, and you could always find them in numbers at their little places of worship. Some kept their doors closed to strangers. They were afraid of being ridiculed, but Professor Carver never did that, and he was accorded a place in their hearts and confidence.

Though the slaves had been seized from many different parts of Africa, they had a common understanding in the sorrow of enslavement, and the white man's religion offered them a common release. Slaves could not sing in the fields, but had to slip out nights into the woods to hold prayer meeting and, this world being so unsatisfactory, hope for a better one "Where Sabbaths have no end."

The Negro had an indefinable quality of charm and sweetness that was seldom found so universally in any other race. Such was his strength of character that the cotton fields and levees had left him without bitterness. Nothing could destroy his humor or his song, which sprang in a perpetual, glittering fountain. No baton was needed in the tumble-down bottom churches to beat out his spirituals: "In this-a band we have sweet music" and, "We want no cowards in the band, we call for valiant-hearted men." The majesty of the Old Testament lived again in these religious folk songs—"Blow out de sun, turn de moon into blood," as they "Marched with spear in hand," or "Marched with the tallest angel." They injected a subtle poetry of their own into, "Dark midnight was my cry," or "De moon ran down in a purple stream." And always they sang of the obligation to fulfill their Master's bidding:

*"I know moon-rise, I know star-rise,*
*I work in de moonlight, I work in de starlight.*

*"Head got wet wid de mornin' dew,*
*What you goin' to do when your lamp burns down?*
*Mornin' star was a witness too,*
*What you goin' to do when your lamp burns down?"*

Coming home from the church at night they crossed muddy streams on logs, holding aloft a burning pine knot, to keep them from stepping on snakes. And they went to bed by the flickering light of a chimneyless lamp.

Every community had its own melodies, or its own variations of those melodies. For the Sunday-evening chapel service at the Institute, Washington would ask for one. The embarrassed pause lasted only a little while, then a voice from the student congregation would start a high, quaint melody heard in the cabin home or bottom church. Quick ears caught it and began humming, adding the words little by little until in a few moments a thousand voices were blending in nostalgic song which possessed a form and beauty unsurpassed in the world's musical literature. This was a rich way to mine the wealth of music in the Negro soul.

When Professor Carver conducted his country meetings, again and again he stressed the importance of "living at home" instead of buying from the plantation owners' commissariat. The aim was not merely to raise their own foodstuffs, but to start the slow climb out of debt by having eggs and chickens over and above their needs, which could be exchanged in the town shops. "A good garden is one of the best family physicians. Have a garden, a little place by the house, even if it is only big enough to throw a dipper over it. But if you cannot afford to put a fence around, don't have it where the chickens can get in. And if a hen does make trouble and you want to throw something at her, throw shelled corn. The laborer is worthy of her hire, and she is entitled to half of what she earns."

The farmers were likely to be careless with their stock, and little lessons in this respect also were needed. With unthinking cruelty they would tie the feet of their fowl together and carry them head down to market. "However short the distance," explained the professor, "this practice is wrong. Imagine yourself thus handled. Use a box to carry them," he begged, "and if it is hot, make the box large enough for them to lie down."

He had a story he used when he wanted to impress on the people the necessity for thoughtful care of their stock.

He himself had been riding along one scorching day and stopped at a number of cabins for a drink, watering his dusty horse at the same time. But at one house he became so interested in his conversation with the farmer that he forgot the mare and her need of refreshment. Shortly he drew up before another well. As he was swallowing a long, cool dipperful he heard the horse whinny; she, too, was thirsty. Without waiting for an invitation she walked up to the well, seized the bucket in her teeth, put her head in, and drank.

To encourage the independent farmers who were not tied to the plantation system, the professor sometimes varied his week-end procedure. He would walk into town on Saturday afternoons and talk with the groups of farmers bringing in their produce and gathering around the square. He would lift a turnip from the basket of one and carry it over to another to compare the little one with the bigger one, so they could see for themselves and discuss when each had planted, how much and what kind of fertilizer one had used to grow the larger turnip and have it mature earlier.

The white farmers lounging on the courthouse lawn were willing to profit also; if Negroes could accomplish more than whites, they wanted to find out how. Seeing his head bent in earnest consultation, they would call jovially, "Come here, Carver. Tell us what you were telling them niggers."

The professor was only too glad to oblige them; a person

who does not answer another's plea kills him in his heart. Furthermore, Professor Carver, taking the long view, knew that the Negro problem was only the Southern problem. They lacked the same things, and what would help one would help the other. If he persuaded one man to raise more, he had helped his neighbor too; it spread and spread, and that was the big thing in life. If the land were well worked, the merchant also prospered and the whole economy rose.

If the farmers were to reduce their cotton acreage they must raise other crops, and then a market for these must be found. The originally small, accidental root swellings on the wild member of the morning-glory family which was called the sweet potato had grown into valuable human nourishment. To be sure, they also yielded immense quantities of small culls with a woody fiber which could not be used as human food, but if the culls, vines, and peelings were supplemented with protein to make a balanced ration, they constituted an excellent stock feed.

Sweet potatoes could be easily cultivated; with care two crops could be grown a year—an absolute failure was unknown. More bushels could be raised per acre than with any other known farm crop, and with less injury to the soil. Professor Carver had increased the average yield of 37 bushels an acre to 266 bushels an acre. As a result of his experimentation during the first year of the Station he published a bulletin in 1898, followed with others in 1906 and 1910.

Though sweet potatoes were perishable, that handicap could be got around by removing sufficient water to inactivate the enzymes. His method of dehydrating was such as not too intelligent people living in the country could employ, just by drying them on the back of the stove or, in hot weather, spreading them out in the sun. Dried and then roasted and ground, they could be used as a coffee substitute; our ancestors had depended upon this during the starvation days of the Civil War. Even the American Indian had found that dyes and alcohol, and other useful by-products, could be developed from sweet potatoes.

With prophetic vision Professor Carver could see that sweet potatoes had potentially great commercial value, and native industries were the greatest lack in the South. At a 1905 Farmers' Conference he gave a lecture. "By the advance of civilization, the markets have become more fastidious; and he who puts such a product upon the market as it demands controls the market, regardless of color. . . . If every farmer could realize that plants are real, living things, and sunshine, air, food, and drink are as necessary for them as for animals, his problem would become intellectually enjoyable and practical at one and the same time. If you examine and pull to pieces the sweet potato, you find that for every hundred pounds the roots contain sixty-nine pounds of water, one of ash, and thirty of sugar, starch, plant cellulose, fat, etc. Sugar and starch and cellulose are composed of carbon, hydrogen, and oxygen. Water (hydrogen plus oxygen) comes from the air—hence we readily see that all except one of the hundred pounds of sweet-potato roots come from the air."

The sugar and starch could be converted into other things. He showed the farmers' wives how they could make laundry starch: remove the skin, grate the sweet potato, put it in a cheesecloth bag, and dip the bag in water; dip and squeeze as long as a milky juice comes out; let the water settle and pour off the clear top liquid; stir the paste up again with more water, again let it settle, and pour off. The result would be an excellent starch, and if the water washings were boiled down they would have a syrup of better quality than sorghum.

Professor Carver earnestly believed one of the fundamental laws of success to be the saving of small things. Farmers were at one time the most wasteful and the most poverty-stricken of all people. Enough grease, for example, was thrown away each year by each family to keep it in soap. Step by step with conserving the land marched conserving the human values. Such simple things as pine needles, burlap, and used string made into mats could brighten these wretched homes and thus improve the tone of the people living in them.

He was saddened by the waste he saw on every hand and by the meagerness of the farmers' lives. They had so little joy, so little comfort, so little beauty. But he did not waste his own time in idle sympathy. He believed that all things were put upon the earth for some useful purpose and that it was his function to discover as many of these as lay within his power.

An essential step in building pride of ownership was to inculcate pride in the appearance of the place itself. Rural housing was one of the most serious problems of the South. Its homes were the oldest, had the lowest value and the greatest need of repair of any farmhouses in the United States. And there were more than two million of them. All were in sad need of furbishing, but this cost money and the people had no money. Some way must be found to provide adornment at little or no cost.

It was a lifelong habit of Professor Carver's to rise at four and go into the woods. "Alone there with the things I love most, I gather my specimens and study the lessons Nature is so eager to teach us all. Nothing is more beautiful than the loveliness of the woods before sunrise. At no other time have I so sharp an understanding of what God means to do with me as in these hours of dawn. When other folk are still asleep, I hear God best and learn His plan."

As he looked across the rolling landscape he noted "vast deposits of multicolored clays, ranging from snow-white through many gradations to the richest sienna and Indian reds on the one hand, and from the deepest yellow-ocher to the palest cream tintings on the other."

Surely useful things could be made from this clay.

One of his favorite texts reads, "I will lift up mine eyes unto the hills from whence cometh my help." He explained it, "Now that doesn't mean just to look at the hills without seeing anything. It means to search. I took it to mean that I should try to see with every method at my command—with chemistry, with physics as well as with my eyes. And by so doing, the help came."

When the professor returned to his laboratory on Sunday night he carried along handfuls of clay, and when he went back through the countryside again he had a simple technique for making color washings with which the interiors of the drab little shacks could be made bright and clean. If freely applied, the lime could build up morale, save deterioration, and aid health in cellar, hen house, pigsty, stable, and barn.

"Take a few shovelfuls of white clay from the cut bank, like this. It has some sand in it, so we'll sift it through a gunny sack. Then we'll stir it into water in the big iron wash kettle and let it stand two minutes. Now let's see—the rest of the sand and gravel have sunk to the bottom and the water can be poured off. Next we put it in a flour sack and keep dipping it until all the clay is suspended in the water. And here is our whitewash!"

If by any rare chance a house or school were built of dressed lumber, sizing was necessary, but it might be made from a pound of rice or starch or flour or boiled skim milk. From rotten sweet potatoes Professor Carver extracted a water-soluble bluing, which could also be used for laundry purposes, and if this blue were added to natural yellow clay a soft green resulted. In all he created twenty-seven combinations of color washes.

The two years Professor Carver had allowed himself at Tuskegee were behind him, but he had relinquished any thought of leaving. The needs of colored people in the South had proved themselves so overwhelming that he had long since irrevocably abandoned a career as a painter; painting would only remain as a private escape and a joy, when he could find time for it. He would never, so long as he lived, forsake the duty which had been laid upon him of helping his fellow man.

He still pursued the pleasure of painting when he had shut himself up in his own rooms. In his new medium of clay he continued to paint some landscapes, but chiefly still lifes; one of peaches, done with his thumbs, has been sought by the Luxembourg galleries in Paris.

If anyone asked him whether the colors would last, he would point to the hills and say, "They have lasted there for thousands of years without fading. They will continue to last, even though I take them out and paint chrysanthemums with them."

Professor Carver had two eyes that burned deep in his head. And he had two kinds of vision. As a scientist he was aware that cobalt had been called the goblin of the mines because it was thought to be worthless ore, that clay owed its hue to iron compounds or decayed organic matter which had become carbonaceous, and that impurities determined the tone. As a painter who had mixed his own colors he knew that many pigments retained in their nomenclature a memory of the lands from which they had been dug: raw sienna, *Terra di Siena,* from the earth on which the Italian city had been built; umber from *Terre d'ombre,* the dark earth; terra cotta from baked earth. Ultramarine was lapis lazuli. One tradition said it had been brought from Afghanistan beyond the sea by Marco Polo in 1271 and ground into shining blue by the old masters.

His desire to be of service to all who could benefit by his knowledge, and his growing demand as a wellspring of wisdom among white men led indirectly to a remarkable discovery. Early in the spring of 1902 the professor was asked to inspect a herd of fine cows belonging to a neighboring planter. He set forth on his mission. Near Montgomery his roving eye caught sight of a red claybank. He stopped his horse, descended to inspect it, and dug up a pailful. After he had passed judgment on the cattle he returned with the clay and in his inconsiderable little laboratory began to experiment.

Long the professor labored; in this red clay he could detect blue, and when he had finished his intermittent oxidation he had that almost unique phenomenon—a new blue.

Dyestuffs are comparatively common, but pigments which can be used in paint are rare. Chemists were at this time seeking synthetic indigo as alchemists had sought gold. By a feat of chemical gymnastics Professor Carver had produced an unrivaled shade which could be used in water colors and in oil.

The land on which he had found the clay belonged to a group of Montgomery capitalists who had spent three hundred dollars to have its value determined and had found nothing of consequence. They had been ready to sell the tract for seven thousand dollars, but Professor Carver's discovery changed all that. They called off the negotiations and held it for development; now they would not sell at any price.

Rumor of Professor Carver's blue spread abroad. The *Iowa State Register* was moved to remember "our Mr. Carver," who had "manifested a high order of ability, and was bright and quick of comprehension, full of hope and courage, genial and gentlemanly in his manners, and obliging and kind to all with whom he was associated. To say that he was a favorite and that his departure was keenly regretted would be a simple statement of facts known to many at the time. Since going to Tuskegee Mr. Carver has not been much heard from by his Iowa friends, but recent reports show that he has not been idle, that he is associated with a remarkable body of men, and that he has won a place of great prominence and usefulness." It added the hope that he would return to Iowa with a well-earned fortune.

Simply because he was happy over his blue Professor Carver showed it at fairs along with the rest of his clay exhibit, and Northern manufacturers made inquiries. Technical experts accept nothing until it is proved, and a representative of one of the great paint companies made a trip to Tuskegee Institute to see the color for himself. In his long canvas apron Professor Carver wandered about his office. Against the light he held the glass which contained the powdered blue, cherishing it in his strong hands—strong yet capable of manipulating the most minute objects with delicate precision. He told how the Egyptians so loved this color that they had adorned their tombs with it in order to sleep with it in death.

"Dr. Carver," said the expert, "according to our observation this is seventy times bluer than blue. We would like to put it on the market."

"No, no, no!" exclaimed Professor Carver in alarm. "I don't want to commercialize it."

This was a rule to which he firmly adhered. He would not commercialize any of his products for his own profit. He was not personally interested in a "well-earned fortune." And he had no desire to help a rich corporation to grow richer.

The paint would have to sell at a high price, and he would not offer anything which required a labyrinth of machinery. Furthermore, he would not have his name exploited, then or ever, because it would obscure his fundamental purpose, which was to help the man furthest down.

He did attempt to protect the color with a patent, though the patent proved to be small protection. A year later the company advertised a "new and improved" blue. The burden of proof that it was his discovery rested on Professor Carver, which would have been costly and time-consuming. He had no time to bother with that. His interest lay in the thing itself, and his pleasure in making it come into being. Multiple oxides had no place in the lives of the poor farmers and householders; they needed a cheap paint to preserve their homes. In all his efforts he constantly asked himself, "How can this be adapted to the requirements of humble people?" They were the ones who were in the greatest need of assistance.

Professor Carver's assistance was most needed on his own home ground, or its spiritual equivalent. By 1904 sixteen Little Tuskegees were holding their own conferences, and he attended as many as he could as often as he could. Wherever Tuskegee graduates went the school reached out to help. Professor Carver did this personally with his agricultural graduates; where they went he went, too, and kept returning to see how they were getting along and to give them aid in their problems. Sometimes their homes were in distant lands where he could not follow, but they could keep in touch by mail. If one returned to Cuba he wrote back for advice and reported on his progress.

Thomas M. Campbell, Professor Carver's most promising student, had been at Tuskegee seven years when a signal honor came to him in 1906; the United States Department of Agriculture appointed him Agricultural Collaborator for Macon County. It was strange to see a Negro working for the government in the South. At first his duties were not clearly defined, but when he made his first visit through the state, visiting a series of schools in western Alabama, Professor Carver, like a father starting his son in business, went along to bolster him up.

That year marked another innovation also. There being at that time no demonstration home and farm agents, he had filled in, but more and more it seemed necessary for him to widen his scope. The field work had to go on, but it should become the task of younger men. He had designed a wagon to be specially equipped with demonstration materials to take the place of his old cart, and the money for it was donated by Morris K. Jesup.

The Jesup Wagon, a farmers' college on wheels, started its career May 24, 1906, its object being to metamorphose shiftless tenants into thrifty farmers. It "became the vehicle of the first Negro Demonstration Agent in Federal employ, and went forth from Tuskegee on a regular schedule to the surrounding communities." It would stop at a house to which all the neighbors had been summoned and give a demonstration in plowing and planting, and return at the appropriate times for cultivation and harvest. This was, in fact, the beginning of the Federal Government Service in the South for Negroes.

Mr. Campbell was placed in charge of the movement and by 1920 was directing the service in seven of the Southern states. The pioneering mule was long since dead, and the Jesup Wagon had given way to a huge automobile called

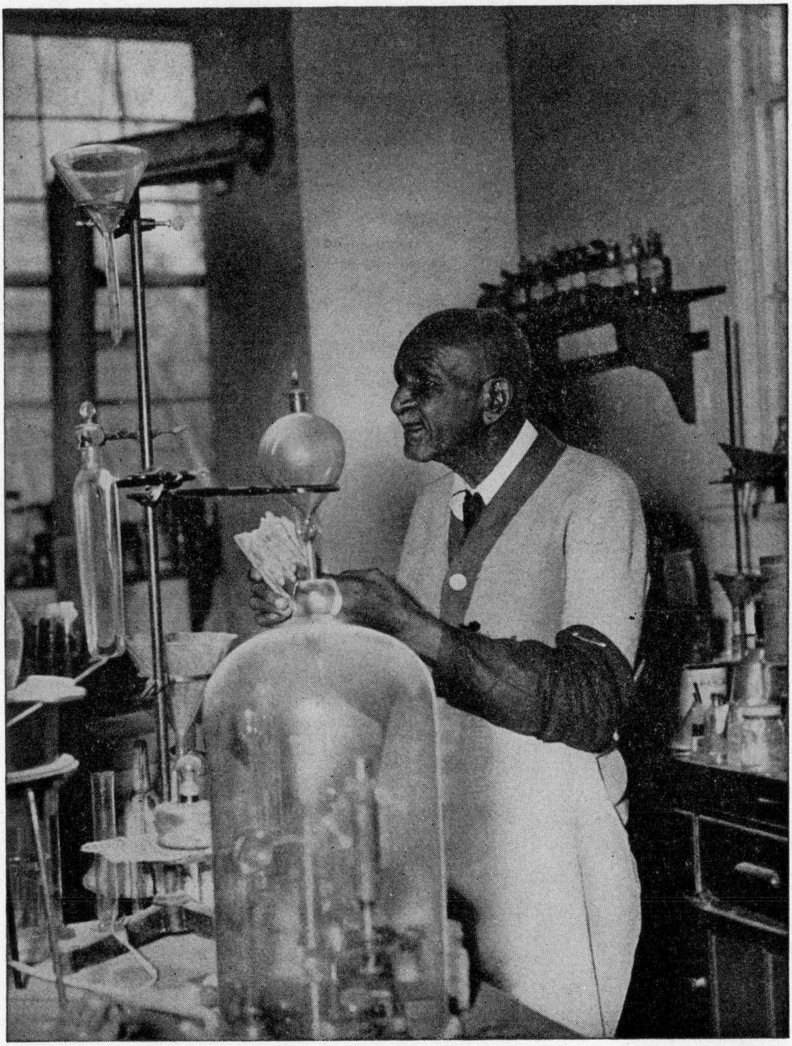

Dr. Carver in his laboratory

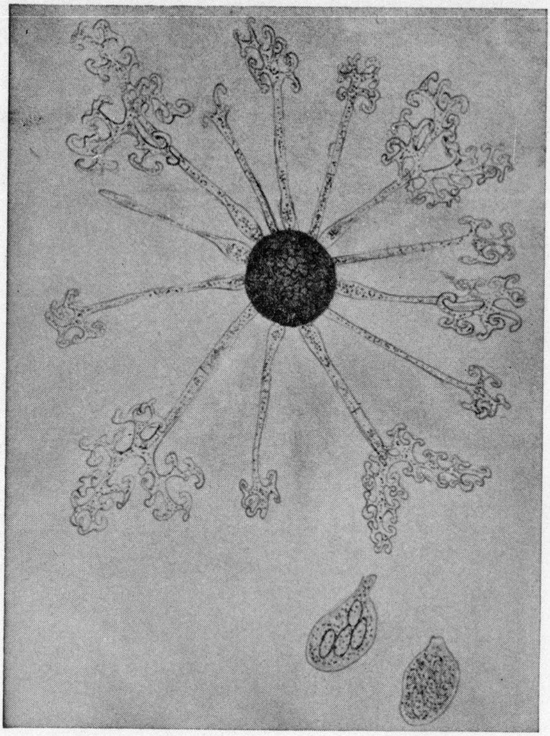

Mycological drawing by Dr. Carver

Professor Carver's design for demonstration wagon

the Movable School, planned to carry out, as Professor Carver's assistant, Austin W. Curtis, Jr., has said, the professor's "ideas on the potentialities of art and science through creative research, to turn the ugly into the beautiful, the waste into the useful, that even the poorest of God's creatures might be healthier, his home more comfortable, his surroundings more beautiful, his life more significant."

The idea of the Movable School spread to other countries and helped shape their educational policies with respect to retarded groups. A similar plan, adapted to local conditions, was put into operation in China, India, Macedonia, and Southern Rhodesia. It could not always be an automobile, nor even a wagon. In Albania, for instance, where roads were scarce, donkeys were loaded with demonstration materials and climbed the narrow mountain trails with their welcome gift of knowledge. But whatever the means of locomotion of the movable schools, they fulfilled the same purpose.

The Movable School of Tuskegee now travels over hundreds of miles, demonstrating as it goes home economics, a balanced diet, rotation of crops, and conservation of the soil, of lumber, and of other natural reserves. It tries to persuade the farmers of the Southern states to "gather the fragments that nothing be lost." And they flock to learn.

## CHAPTER XV

# *"Then Why Not Every Man?"*

FROM THE VERY BEGINNING "our Mr. Carver" was greatly in demand as a lecturer before colored audiences; the important duty of advancing the course of scientific agriculture could not be confined to Tuskegee and its environs alone. To fulfill this obligation he set forth on trips from time to time, speaking at the Congregational church in one town, the Baptist in another, at conferences and Negro schools everywhere. Several times he was called to Berea College, a biracial institution until Kentucky law decreed that white and colored young people must not be educated within twenty-five miles of each other.

He was sought, first, by virtue of his reputation and then, after he had once been heard, for his merry and inviting personality. His voice was still high pitched as a woman's in normal conversation; Will Rogers later said he was the only person he knew who could sing tenor while he was talking. But his voice also had the resonance of a singer and was as effective. In spite of giving the same lecture often in essence, he always varied it with his audience. Seldom did he prepare a talk beforehand; he would begin: "In the words of the preacher, I will now take my text. I will then depart from it never to return again." But he always did, and it was considered a rare treat when he was well launched, with audience and subject properly blended.

At a Hampton Conference in 1899 he read a paper in which he said: "The fitting of men to die and rest from their labors was almost the exclusive mission of education in its early history. Now it makes labor a source of pleasure and profit and knowledge, teaching us how to live properly, thus making Heaven less problematical."

Speaking before state and national teachers' conferences on the subject "Does Scientific Agriculture Pay?" he won many friends for Tuskegee's practical system of education, many converts to the application of science to agriculture, and encouraged young men to seek instruction in this field. At Nashville, Tennessee, he said: "The Honorable James Wilson writes me that chief among his needs are trained scientists to fill the increasing demand." And he quoted from a letter: " 'Have not half enough. Aside from the pressing needs of our own country they are drawing upon me from the governments of Cuba, Puerto Rico, the Philippines, and the last application comes from Ireland.' "

Professor Carver had been at Tuskegee only a few years when he was asked to speak at a small school some miles below Montgomery. On the same train rode a woman photographer from Washington who had taken pictures of the Institute and was going through the South seeking more views of some of the "Little Tuskegees."

The teacher of this particular one, young Mr. H., met the train late in the evening with horse and buggy, and all three rode off in a damp drizzle of rain, the photographer on the front seat with the tall and earnest Mr. H., talking busily about what he had accomplished and what more he hoped to be able to do. Professor Carver lent an attentive ear from the back seat, until they reached the local hotel and deposited the lady.

Mr. H. turned the horse toward the schoolhouse, where Professor Carver was to stay with him overnight, delivering his talk the next day.

Then Mr. H. abruptly disappeared. In this unfamiliar place Professor Carver waited and waited. He could hear the confused, uneasy sound of a crowd gathering, horses stamping, metallic rattlings, and low voices charged with an ominous quality. Through the gloom he could make out the big hats of the riders and catch the dull gleam of gun barrels.

He realized, as Mr. H. had already done, that one of the sacred social customs had been violated by having a white woman ride on the front seat with a Negro. He realized, further, that in height and outline he looked enough like Mr. H. to be mistaken for him. "I can't stay here," he thought to himself. "I must get away."

He blew out the light and softly opened the door, slipped through, and closed it behind him. A gust of rain hit him sharply in the face. It was strange and unknown territory, and he had only the vaguest idea which way the railroad lay. Behind him he could hear the mob all around the schoolhouse. The sound seemed to reach out and envelop him as well. When it seemed too near he hid in ditches. Once a shot went past him, but wide. He dared not stay on any road, but kept to the fields, slipping in the mud, stumbling into pools of water, walking and walking and carrying his suitcase. Every time he fell it jabbed into him.

All night long he plodded through the cold drizzle and in the early morning arrived, nearly exhausted, at a little railroad station he had never seen before. Eventually a train came, going north toward home, and he boarded it, still shivering.

This was what educational pioneering meant in the South.

Tuskegee Institute, or "The Booker Washington School," as it was known elsewhere in the country, was growing with astonishing rapidity; more acres were being added, and new buildings were going up on all sides—every year a little more and a little more. By the turn of the century the operating cost of the plant was eighty thousand dollars, sixty thousand of which had to be raised by the efforts of Washington alone. The faculty staff numbered eighty-six, and there were forty-two buildings on the grounds; by 1906 these figures had jumped to one hundred and fifty-six and eighty-three respectively—practically doubled—and the school had an endowment of over a million dollars.

Electric bulbs replaced the oil lamps on the campus in 1900, a feature to be proud of and one which even the town lacked. Washington always wanted to be neighbors with the town. A chance came when Congressman Charles W. Thompson was going to have a Northern committee visiting him. The students rigged up lights from their own plant to his house, so he could put on a show for a night. After that, month by month the citizens had their houses wired by the students. Whenever the Institute could serve the town it wanted to do so.

The town prospered as the school expanded. It became increasingly expensive to haul the large amount of supplies up from the station in the bottom, through the town, and out to the campus. A new station, therefore, was built nearer town on the Chehaw line, and a spur extended to the Institute.

In 1903 Rockefeller Hall, a boys' dormitory, was erected, and Professor Carver moved into the rooms on the ground floor he was to occupy for thirty-five years. In almost no time they became a combination of library, picture gallery, museum, and hothouse. Bookcases lined the wall space, and the gaps were filled with his paintings; laces were draped here and there; glass cases were crammed with a geological collection.

Whenever Professor Carver walked or drove abroad his eager eyes spied and his eager hands gathered up objects of all sorts—plant fossils, the tooth of a mastodon, the skeleton of a prehistoric lizard—until he had a collection of rare botanical, entomological, anatomical, and ornithological specimens. The grandmothers of the neighborhood could remember a great noise and a great light over by the pine trees; they dated the happenings in their children's lives as before or after the time when the stars fell on Alabama. Some thirty miles from Tuskegee Professor Carver found and lugged home a meteor, presumably one of these stars.

In his office were limbs of trees, moss, snakes; he picked up everything he saw. Students would bring in cocks, blackbirds, ducks, and together they practiced the taxidermist's craft and stuffed and mounted birds and barnyard fowl. The smaller children also brought their finds to the professor, who fostered their natural interest.

An eight-year-old presented him with a fluffy young wood thrush he had caught. The professor took the bird, soothed it, and with his long fingers stilled its feeble fluttering. Then he began to describe its habits, telling the lad how the bird lived, the things it ate, where it loved best to sit and sing, and softly whistled the song of the bird. "And now take it back and turn it loose, my boy; take it back to its mother. It's terrible when a young bird is taken from its mother."

Small children had none of the awe of him which possessed their elders. They merely accepted, quite simply, the fact that the professor could do anything, and laying his hand upon the heads of these smallest ones was a benediction. When Davidson Washington's pet goose fell sick, he thought he would take it to Professor Carver, but kept putting it off. One morning his father said, "It's too late now. Your goose is dead."

But Davidson replied, "I'll take him to the professor anyhow. He can make my goose well."

Belief in Professor Carver's infallibility spread, with certain distortions, to other members of the younger generation. A teacher who happened to be in Montgomery one day observed three urchins on the street. The two older boys were whipping the smallest one and he interposed. "Here! You mustn't do that! What's the matter, anyhow?"

"We don' like Jim—he's no good. Y'all know dat man out at Tuskegee? Ef yo' sen' 'im yo' blood he kin tell 'ow much colored y'are. We did—yas, we did too!—an' he said Ah'm one haf and Jake's two thirds, but dis 'ere low-down Jim's two an' a haf pa'ts niggah!"

In practicing his advocacy of "no waste," Professor Carver practically never threw anything out; almost certainly he could convert it into something useful or beautiful. In racks were ranged his lacemaking needles constructed from a can opener, a toothbrush handle, an umbrella rib, a paintbrush, a conductor's baton, a spoke from his mother's spinning wheel.

In the summer of 1908 he went back to his birthplace in Missouri. He wanted to see the old folks once more, and this would probably be his last chance. Aunt Mariah Watkins lived in the same house in Neosho, and the schoolhouse he had first attended was still standing. He visited again the cave on the Baynham place where he had once been afraid of bears, and found instead crinoids, brachiopods, bivalves, and corals. Aunt Sue and the old home were gone from Diamond, but Moses Carver still survived, a patriarchal gentleman getting on for one hundred and pretty much enfeebled. For the last time George Carver bade farewell to Uncle Mose and received as a parting gift his mother Mary's spinning wheel.

As time passed the professor's rooms became more and more crammed with his accumulation until they were stuffed to bursting and there was hardly room for himself. "I'm just a little crowded here," he would remark with his charming smile as he moved a pile of books and pamphlets from a chair to make room for a guest to be seated.

Here he passed his evenings at work; even when he was talking to a visitor his hands were engaged on some task or other, perhaps polishing rough stones until they gleamed like marble. Once when a Frenchman, a son of a member of the Chamber of Deputies, came to call, he was creating a lace design. The man from the land of lacemakers pronounced it a pure gem; nothing he had ever seen could compare with it; the French people would go mad over some of these pieces!

Ordinarily, Professor Carver shrank from showing his paintings except to those with whom he felt a kinship; he would be revealing himself. With a few people of his own generation he felt really at ease, and one of these was Mrs. Logan. They used to hold long conversations in the rockers on the porch of the Logan home. Mrs. Logan believed the paintings should be on view, but he required much persuasion. Under pressure, he consented to have two or three exhibits in the auditorium on the top floor of the Huntington Building, the academic building in those days. People actually had more appreciation of these than of his laboratory work. A picture was something concrete they could see. Nobody knew what he was doing in his laboratory; it was so remote, and nobody knew what it was all about anyhow.

Professor Carver joined very little in the purely social affairs of the campus. He had slight interest in parties as such, and when he was accused of being selfish by not associating with other people he could always plead the pressure of work. His non-attendance he further explained as due to embarrassment over an ineradicable inability to remember names. He could remember the names of an infinitude of plants because of the association of resemblances, but this rule did not hold good for human beings. More likely his remaining aloof on such occasions was due to the shyness he had never conquered. The impact of trivialities distressed him; but quiet was the great restorer, and he withdrew from the chatter of inconsequential matters to his own room, whence passers-by might sometimes hear him singing, or the soft sound of a piano. Many criticized him because he was hard to know; he was so different from their familiar world of petty affairs—he seemed to be one who was set apart from others.

If anyone had the temerity to ask Professor Carver why he did not marry, he merely replied, "I never had time." A rumor persisted among the older folk that when he was comparatively new to Tuskegee he had once viewed with a warmer than friendly eye a young woman on the campus. But in the course of time it developed that she had little sympathy with his absorption in weeds and clay, nor could she grasp the spiritual significance of these things in the upbuilding of the race. No basis for a true marriage could exist here. He had retired again to his ivory tower and the state of being alone, for which he had apparently been destined.

Though Professor Carver seldom sought companionship, when he was thrown with fellow faculty members he was sociable enough. He was a jolly, friendly dining companion, full of jokes, once remarking, however, that the table was a place for free speech but little thought. This was intended as a merry sort of irony and accepted as such. He himself read the daily papers faithfully, as well as his own field of literature, and kept himself informed of what was going on in the world. Never did he gossip about his neighbors; never did he utter a harsh word or an unkind word. He seldom grieved or mourned, or at least never let anyone see him, but remained cheerful and lively in mood. He would have nothing to do with anything that meant unrest or meanness, but responded immediately to anything that meant joy or happiness.

"Some people," Professor Carver used to say, "don't get much fun out of life. They don't know how much fun it can be." Most of his joy he derived from his contacts with young people. His youthfulness both in mind and in action met their blithe spirits on equal ground while, after work hours, he played and tussled with the boys under his care as though they were puppies or his own children. Withal, he was always kind and always wise. Consequently, they did not transcend the bounds of decorum nor overstep the mark of deference. If he inquired, apparently of space, "Has the tipping of hats to ladies gone out of fashion?" they hastened to correct that carelessness.

A visitor once observing the manners of a small group of boys remarked to one of the teachers that they seemed to be the best-behaved on the campus.

"Well, just see who they work for—Professor Carver."

Professor Carver held that training of the young should be based on natural inclination. This theory he followed also when parents wished a child to follow one of the arts for which it lacked talent. A girl at the school who was studying harmony made an arrangement of "Swing Low, Sweet Chariot," and her mother inquired with some pride what the professor thought of it.

"I'm sorry you asked," he replied, "because now I'll have to tell you. No child is capable of arranging a spiritual. That song had harmony before she was born, and she will never understand it because the time and occasion for understanding are past. It was born in the souls of those who suffered, and her arrangement is sheer effrontery."

He could not bear to hear piano plunkers perform gymnastics, and when the parents of children who were merely expert at arpeggios sought his advice he replied in the words that had been spoken to him at Simpson about his own art. "Unless they have unusual gifts, they had better learn something at which they can make a living."

But, by the same token, he had the utmost sympathy for the young people at Tuskegee whom he saw hungering as he had hungered, both for education and for bread, though the latter seemed of the lesser importance. From time to time, when something was needed to bring happiness in their recreational hours, he would come to the rescue, giving the girls a piano for their dormitory and, a little later, another to the boys, or lending four or five hundred dollars for the establishment of a boys' camp, which was never repaid.

No one knows the number of students he assisted—both boys and girls—because he handled these charities himself. Whenever either Mrs. Washington or Mrs. Logan would say to him, "I know of a girl who wants to go to school, but she has no shoes," always the shoes mysteriously appeared and the girl could go to school.

Some years after he had left Ames behind him he sent an unsolicited donation to the Alumni Association of Iowa State College. "The demands are unusually great this year; people are suffering in the school and out of it, and my little surplus goes to help them. I have a boy also that I am educating. But my beloved alma mater grows dearer to me all the time."

The boy he was educating was a young fellow he had taken from a reformatory, assuming all obligations, to fill the place of the son he would never have. But reclamation came too late for this particular bit of human waste; he defied all upbuilding effort. His feet rested upon a foundation of quicksand. As fast as the professor tried to fill in one place he would sink in another. He could not be made to see the true meaning of the Institute and finally had to be rejected. With a heavy heart Professor Carver saw his foster son start for the railroad, suitcase in hand, only nineteen and supposedly just starting out in life, but headed in the wrong direction.

Over the years, hundreds of young men have gone from Tuskegee who, during their initiate, would make no important decision without first discussing it with the professor. They visited him in his office or in his sitting room, more often on Sundays when they were free of classwork, and he liked to have them come.

Though he was never sanctimonious and pulled no long faces, to the little groups that dropped in on Sunday afternoons his talks had a religious tone in keeping with the day, which he himself devoted to spiritual matters. For Professor Carver no conflict existed between religion and science; science confirmed the Scriptures rather than opposed them, and God and the spiritual world were closely united to the natural world.

Finally, the boys asked the professor to have a regular Bible class. This he did. It was held between suppertime and chapel, first in Rockefeller Hall, but as the attendance grew and grew they moved to larger and larger rooms, and still people were standing. By 1911 the class had about one hundred steady attendants, and eventually three hundred tried to crowd into the assembly room of the Carnegie Library.

As his audience was wedging itself in, Professor Carver stood with watch in hand, and somebody would begin the reading on the stroke of six. The aim was not merely to become familiar with the Bible but, by example and demonstration, to turn the scriptural stories from mythical tales into something vivid and immediate. When they were coming to passages that could be illustrated, he would have apparatus which would bring them from the far away and long ago to the very real here and now.

Did science and the Genesis story of the creation conflict? No exact record could be obtained because the truths upon which science was built naturally did not trace back to that time. Nevertheless, the corresponding facts of evolution had been proved, and the professor traced the evolution of the earth from its gaseous to its present stage and the creatures that lived upon it from a single protoplasmic cell to man.

The Institute at this time maintained a Bible school, and one of its teachers protested to Mr. Washington that Professor Carver's method of teaching the Bible was not in accord with orthodox theology.

Said the principal, "Is this class optional, and free to anyone who wishes to attend?"

"Yes."

"Do many students and teachers avail themselves of this opportunity?"

"It's always crowded."

"How long has it been running?"

"More than three years."

"Well, if anyone at this institution can have a class in the Bible which is not compulsory and well attended for three years, I advise you to say nothing and not in any way disturb it, because we have to compel students to attend most such classes."

That ended the theologian's criticism, and Professor Carver continued, in such subjects as, "God, the Father of Science," to knit trees, birds, rocks, and rivers with religion; to explain the affinity of water and salt and the atmospheric conditions of the valley, in describing the parable of the lingering of Lot's wife. While the discussion of Sodom and Gomorrah was proceeding Professor Carver was fiddling with something on the table before him. "And what happened to these wicked cities?" he asked. The answer came in a sudden burst of flames and fumes shooting up from the table, and the Bible students choked and coughed and fled.

Though the class period was short, it ended on the minute, because he as well as the students must be in place promptly for chapel. Whenever he was on the grounds he was in his seat at the proper time for morning and evening service.

To those young people who were blessed with imagination, walking or talking with Professor Carver was like reading an exciting story. He was a universal magnet, and when he stepped out through the door they fell in with him, on the chance that he would pick up an ordinary rock or stick and begin to tell of its mysteries. And boy or girl, man or woman, counted himself fortunate to be permitted to spend a few hours with him in his rooms.

Professor Carver had his own lighting system; different-colored glass—yellow, blue, green, and white—could be adjusted to his taste. "I like the various colors," he explained. "I find that one suits me at one time and another at another. One is more restful than another, one more stimulating, and another gives a steady glow for writing."

Some of the time set aside for writing was taken up by his *Economic Botany,* some with a *Nature Study Chemistry for Boy Scouts,* some with complying with the requests of magazines for articles—the *Review of Reviews,* the *Cornell Countryman*—or his job as collaborator on the *Nature Study Review* published by Teachers College of Columbia University. He had published fourteen bulletins by 1908, and their form was already being copied elsewhere. Hours and hours were devoted to his column, called *Professor Carver's Advice.* Through this medium he was able to warn farmers in advance of hazards which were just around the corner, such as hog cholera, or he would caution stockmen against the rattlebox (*Crotalaria*). He would publish a minute description of the weed and its habits, and explain that animals were not particularly fond of it and an occasional branch here and there did little harm, but where the pasture was thin and green food scarce the stock might eat enough to produce harmful results. This he followed with detailed symptoms and the remedy for the animals, and precautions to be taken in the fields, particularly along the fences which remained unplowed.

Unceasingly he continued his mycological contributions:

*New or Noteworthy Alabama Fungi,* published in 1897.

Anthostomella sphaerotheca sp. nov.

Stroma thin, black, crustlike, containing 1–6 or 8, prominent, subconic perithecia, perithecial wall poorly developed, ostiolum very short-papillate: asci nearly orbicular, about 20×18μ, aparaphysate, very thin and delicate, soon deliquescing and liberating the spores: sporidia oval or spindle-shaped, often inequalateral, ends acute, light fuliginous but transparent, the center usually occupied by a large oval vacuole, 16–18×5–6μ.

On dead petioles of *Sabal Adansoni,* Tuskegee, Ala., Jan. 20, 1897. G. W. Carver (no. 101).

Externally this clearly resembles *A. minor* E. & M., but the asci in that species are cylindrical, and the spores only 7–8 long. The quickly evanescent asci are often hard to detect, a hasty examination giving the impression of a *Sphaeropsis.* The black, thin, crustlike stroma and imperfectly developed perithecia suggest the Dothidiales, and it is possible that the species may ultimately be placed in *Auerswaldia.*

The job of the mycologist consists not merely in identifying the disease, but in looking ahead and preparing to combat the danger, though it may be fifty years away. The *Journal of Agricultural Research* of May 1928, issued by the Department of Agriculture, contains a historical account of frog leaf spot caused by *Cercospora diazu miura,* which had lately attacked the soybean. "In 1901 Carver noted the occurrence of a fungus, which he designated as *Cercospora canescens* E. & M., on soybean and several other unrelated hosts. This appears to be the earliest reported occurrence of a Cercospora on soybean in America." It was not recorded again in the United States until 1924.

A 1941 issue of the *Journal* of the Washington Academy of Sciences reads: "Since Carver appears to have been the first to observe the asci of this species of Taphrina (on red and silver maple, 1897) it seems particularly fitting that it be named in his honor. It is therefore named *T. carveri.*" As their discoverer, more and more were named for him: *Colletotrichum carveri, Metasphaeria carveri,* and a host of others.

Professor Carver had many "firsts" to his credit. Once he received a package from the West, and on the cord with which it was wrapped he noticed a peculiar fungus. This he incubated and, when traced, it was discovered to have come from old twine imported from Great Britain. Here was one of the many ways in which the public's food supply and pocketbook were protected by the mycologist.

Some of Professor Carver's possessions, including the mycological collection, were unique, many were valuable, and he would take no chances on an uninformed person's making a mistake or being careless in handling them. Consequently, no one could get in to clean his rooms. He, himself, took care of his things and kept them put away and protected from rats and moths and deterioration. His first clock still says Standard Time in letters as brightly gold as when new.

His insistence on being on time was considered an idiosyncrasy by some of the more indolent members of the faculty. With the normal human distrust of the nonconformist they were disturbed by his habits. He was so utterly different from everybody else. He was not orthodox. Once he was even waited on, half jokingly, by a small group because he carried water to his own rooms and scrubbed them himself. A Teacher shouldn't do that. All the others had a boy to carry their water and another to scrub and keep the rooms tidy. But it was not in the professor's nature to sit around and have someone wait on him. They pointed out that Teachers didn't scrub. It wasn't dignified.

"I always have and I expect to keep it up," he asserted stubbornly. Then he produced what to him was an unanswerable argument; the only way he could learn was by doing things himself. He would say, "What's the reason I can't do that?" This applied to scrubbing floors as well as to a chemical experiment. "Can't I improve on the way it has been done before? The way to find out is to do it, then I don't have to accept the conclusion of somebody else. When I scrub, I am using soap I have made myself. If I have the actual experience of using it in the manner I eventually want it to be used, I am finding out something, then I can tell others how it works."

They were baffled by his argument and had no rebuttal, but continued to be uneasy. In other ways also he was charged with a lack of dignity; he never could be made to conform in dress. Some of the faculty shared the farmers' lack of thrift, and they poked fun at Professor Carver's economies. "There goes the great Professor Carver. He looks like a ragamuffin!" He wore shabby, baggy work clothes most of the time. "You must change on Sunday," they insisted, and he would, but no one could tell the difference. A person could buy a good serge suit in those days for twenty dollars; Professor Carver would buy a hand-me-down for eight. Or, from season to season, he would just put away in trunks the suits he already had and then bring them out again, year after year, wrinkled and with sleeves too short, smelling of moth balls and becoming more and more out of shape as his figure became more stooped.

He repaired and mended them himself and sewed on his own buttons. He wore a flowing scarf; any person with dignity wore a four-in-hand. In an effort to reform him somebody once sent him fifteen ties all at once. Probably he was presented with at least a hundred, but he just gave them away. To determine what dyes would best stand the strain of wearing, he preferred to make his own ties and scarves, and dye them with plant juices.

He had a quick answer for exasperated inquiries. "Professor, why in the world did you have your picture taken with that checked collar?"

"I had the collar on."

When he was starting for Washington everyone was horrified. "Aren't you going to get a new suit?"

"No, I'm not going to show my clothes. I'm going to have a conference with the Secretary of Agriculture."

"Professor, aren't you going to change that suit for the parents' meeting?"

"I thought they invited me. If they want to see suits they can come to my room and I'll show them two or three."

The little ones at the Children's House were provided with their own bits of ground, and parents and friends were invited at intervals to admire the work and the children themselves, all attired in sailor hats and starched white dresses. These gardens were planned as co-operatives, and contracts were drawn up:

> We agree to (1) raise vegetables on one of the plots set apart to us for a garden; (2) follow as best we can the directions of our teacher; (3) share equally in the expense, labor, and profit of the garden.

This was signed by four witnesses.

Thus the children were made to understand what a contract meant, how binding it was, and how each shared any loss, regardless of excuses.

The way to keep the young person at home, according to Professor Carver, was to make him a part of that home with a share in its responsibilities—give him his own garden spot, a calf or a pig or a chicken for his own, which he must learn to take care of.

The Division of Nature Study and Children's Gardens was designed to put the youngsters' natural instinct for making mud pies to use in teaching them what those mud pies could do. Not a single person was ever too young. "In the kindergarten the child should receive its first logical and practical awakening to the wonders and glories of Nature, which will clothe each fact with beauty and enlarge his vision until he reaches the laboratory."

In his *Progressive and Correlative Nature Study* Professor Carver offered a suggestion to teachers: "Students want to discuss the topic rather than give a direct answer. This is not permissible. Nothing is more to be deplored in the classroom than to hear pupils giving their opinions regarding such matters as the intellectual world has recognized as fact decades ago."

He advised that the children walk briskly out-of-doors for twenty minutes, then tell what they saw, the object being to train their minds to comprehend at a glance what passed before their eyes. Conversely, they were to stand before a plot of ground ten feet square, study it for ten minutes, and then write the result of their observations.

The publication of this *Nature Study* in the spring of 1902 was probably the direct inspiration for Professor Carver's being invited to Knoxville to conduct a nature-study course the following summer. The *Aurora* called him a "genius who lives in the closest touch with Nature. An encyclopaedia, though modest in telling his information." He took his classes on excursions to the woods and hills and boat riding on the Tennessee River. These views of a type of countryside new to him gave him fresh subjects for paintings, which he treasured up in a mind that never forgot a scene; he could transfer them to canvas when he was back in the more scenically monotonous Tuskegee. He ended the course with a lecture on art, using some of his own paintings to illustrate his points.

Every inch of window space in his rooms was filled with plants. Professor Carver, it seemed, could take a leaf or sprig and put it in a pot and it would bloom radiantly, just as he could wear a posy in his buttonhole on the hottest days without its wilting. Chiefly these plants consisted of amaryllis, which he never stopped breeding. He had developed one that was ten inches in diameter, and another that was pure white, and was working on one that would bloom twice a year.

With all his activity the professor could never forget the flowers that meant so much to him. In 1900, in the midst of replying to queries about soils and crops, he announced he would take pleasure in answering any questions about floriculture. It was a real pleasure and not a figure of speech.

"One bright branch growing against the wall is grace." He assumed the sight was soothing and restful to other tired brains and bodies, as well as his own. He had an unselfish interest in making others happy by spreading the spirit of love flowers represented to him and the spirit of the beauty inherent in Nature, and inspiring in others something of his own appreciation.

Shortly after he arrived in Tuskegee he was going along one day with his botany can under his arm, looking for mycological specimens. A lady passed what she thought was a harmless, shabby colored man carrying a strange-looking box. She stopped him and asked if he were a peddler. In his invariably pleasant manner he explained that he was seeking plant diseases and insect enemies. She was delighted and immediately asked him to come and look at her roses, which were badly diseased. He told her what to do for them; in fact, he sat down and wrote out the directions.

Through friendly gossip, word of his infallibility was noised about. Once a dispute arose downtown about the name of a plant. Finally one man said they had a teacher out at the normal school by the name of Carver who could name any plant, tree, bird, or stone in the world. And if he did not know there was no use to look any further. Another man was put on a horse and the plant brought to Professor Carver. He named it and sent it back.

After that, his laboratory was never free from specimens of some kind. People began calling upon him for advice, and he was so gracious with his information that they felt quite free to do so. Then they fell into the habit of dropping in at the Institute to bring him little presents of bulbs or seeds, or just to see his flowers. He always had time for anyone who was genuinely interested, as when a local hairdresser brought some visitors out, and he showed her how the root of the yucca could be used as soap.

Packets of native seed were constantly streaming out of his office to other schools or organizations. In mailing one package of lantana, vinca, French mulberry, and magnolia grandiflora, he wrote, "It is such a little contribution that it is hardly worth mentioning, but I am so very fond of flowers and pretty things of all kinds that I like to contribute anything that may give pleasure to others, even though it may be small."

And the school returned gratefully that the opportunity of adding something beautiful to other homes was not a small thing. Since he put only a moderate amount of seed in each envelope hundreds of people shared the kindly gift, which would grow in ever-widening circles. Thus some of the brightness of Alabama was sent to almost every state west of the Mississippi, and many east of it.

In another respect also this giving was not a small thing, because it contributed immeasurably to happier relations between the races. No one could scorn the donor of such simple and lovely presents.

A measure of the worth of a man is not merely the degree of fame he achieves, but how the "folks back home" feel about him. As Professor Carver walked through the streets of Tuskegee he would see a particularly charming garden and compliment the gardener. Immediately racial barriers were down and they would fall into a brisk discussion of her particular problems.

He could do more than any other one man to create a pleasant atmosphere among the adjacent white people simply by being a friendly person who loved flowers.

## CHAPTER XVI

# *"The Dungeon Shook and the Chains Fell Off"*

BOTH Washington and Carver, so dissimilar in many respects, had fundamentally the same viewpoint and the same aim, however widely their techniques might differ. In their thinking, both were robust, nonconformist, and reverent. Both had positive programs with which they were dealing vigorously, and so were spared the bitterness that comes of frustration. Both were "successful" men, insofar as success is measured in proportion to the study or devotion given to one task.

The hard years that had passed since Washington first came to Tuskegee had altered him, even in appearance; from the swift arrow he had become the heavy hammer. But he did not permit the responsibility of guiding an entire race and the vision of the ultimate goal of that race to obscure the details. Away from Tuskegee he was the great Booker T. Washington, who was to dine with presidents and kings, but at the little Alabama town he was "the principal."

He found his greatest relaxation in hunting. But as he went through the country on Dexter's back, pursuing this avocation, he never for a moment in his pleasure forgot his people and his relation to them. If he found a destitute family, he had immediately to hand the means of relieving their distress; included in the Institute budget was a small fund for just such purposes.

There goes a story, perhaps apocryphal, that once when President Theodore Roosevelt was in Louisiana he wanted to hunt bear in the bayous. A colored man in the neighborhood was rumored to have good bear dogs, and a secret-service man was dispatched to the man's home to ask whether they could be borrowed. He firmly declined. The secret-service man protested, "Don't you understand it's the President of the United States who's asking for your dogs?"

The owner was still firm. "He can't have 'em. Can't nobody have 'em. Not even if he was Booker T. Washington himself."

If Washington had a few minutes' respite from his duties he would take a small book of verse out of his pocket and study it, or hoe in his own garden. He was good at gardening; he raised large and succulent and juicy onions. And Professor Carver coveted them for himself. Returning once from an early-morning walk, he dropped in to see how the principal's garden was coming along. Mr. Washington was presumably at his office. He swiped three and was just leaving with his booty when he beheld Mr. Washington entering the gate. "I didn't mean for you to see me," he grinned, and received an answering grin. As a matter of fact, he had a fair exchange to offer, because he had been out gathering choice wild vegetables for his friend, whose dietary was limited.

It had long been proved that these two men understood each other very well, though they differed immeasurably in personality. Washington was the leader of an uptreading race, it was on its way, in the spring of the year as far as the modern civilized world was concerned. That world and what they would make of it lay ahead. His favorite spiritual was, "We are climbing Jacob's ladder, every rung goes higher, higher." He exulted in the challenge and met it with zest. Professor Carver was a quiet man, a scientist, wrapped in laboratory problems. But when these problems were resolved they would be achieving the same end.

Both were pioneers, and there is always something to adjust in pioneering. Washington was positive about what he wanted; Professor Carver was equally positive about his way. And they respected that positiveness in each other. Once Mr. Washington told the professor someone had said he was all wrong about something or other, and he replied,

"Mr. Washington, I might be wrong in this instance or that one, but not in *all*. That isn't possible. I wouldn't believe it if I had said it myself."

If the point that had arisen were one of school policy, Professor Carver, though he might disagree, would not interfere. But, by the same token, he would brook no interference in his own province, which he knew better than any outsider possibly could.

A typical row arose regarding a sweet-potato bulletin. Professor Carver had written it and turned it over to Mr. Washington for approval. When he went to see the principal about it, Mr. Washington was seated at his desk. He picked up his pen.

"I see you say that nobody knows where the sweet potato originated."

"That's right."

"Nobody knows?"

"Nobody knows."

"Then let's say it was Macon County."

He dipped his pen into the inkwell and started to insert "Macon County."

But Professor Carver quickly interrupted him. "Mr. Washington, you can't do that. Such things must be known and classified. If you want to sign that bulletin, all right, but if you want me to sign it you'll have to leave it alone. I can't let it go out under my name."

"Why not? Let's give the sweet potato a home."

"But anybody with any knowledge at all would know that it couldn't have originated here. The plant series doesn't warrant it. You can't just arbitrarily put it anywhere you choose."

He could not let Mr. Washington make himself ridiculous, and so he delivered a body blow to the altercation. "I don't believe the Institute is in any position to withstand the fire that will be directed toward it if that is published."

"Well, all right. If that's the way you take it."

"It isn't the way I take it. It's just the way things are!"

Washington could appreciate that attitude, and there the matter ended.

These were the disagreements of two honest and intelligent men. They could argue like anything without for a moment losing the respect and deep sense of fellowship existing unspoken between them.

Sometimes at one o'clock in the morning Professor Carver would be awakened by a knock on his door. "Mr. Washington would like to know if you——" But the guard did not have to explain further.

Professor Carver would reply instantly, "Of course. Tell Mr. Washington I'll be right out." And he would dress hurriedly and go out to join the older man, who was walking up and down, and back and forth—waiting. Plagued and harassed as he was by his infinitude of problems, he found, not necessarily a solution, but peace, with his friend. They would walk and talk about various things; sometimes they talked very little. Eventually they would be back at Rockefeller Hall.

"Good night, Professor."

"Good night, Mr. Washington."

And both would go to bed refreshed in spirit.

As in any small community, the word of any unusual happening spread; the guard would tell his girl, she would tell another girl, and the dean would hear of it. Some of the smaller souls on the campus could not understand. Someone at table the next day would say to the professor, "Why don't you tell him you won't do it? Interrupting your sleep like that!"

Should this occur, Professor Carver was stern in his reproof. "Whenever Mr. Washington calls, I shall be ready. I consider it an honor and a privilege. And another thing. I'm never going to tell my boss I'm not going to do anything, and then accept money from him. Before I say that, my resignation will already be on his desk. As long as there is no interference with fundamental principles, I'm going to do what the Institute asks me to do as well as I am able to.

That's my position—always has been and always will be!"

Washington, too, had suffered painful experiences, and confessed he had frequently been tempted to join in the denunciation of race evils, but always was saved in time by the realization that it would do harm rather than good, and that better ways could be found to handle the situation. His "better way" is engraved on the base of his statue at Tuskegee: "I will let no man drag me down so low as to make me hate him."

He had one such experience when he was giving a talk somewhere in Florida. There had been a lynching the night before. A sheet was hung between the white and colored sections of his audience, and the grim-faced white men sitting in the front rows held pistols in their laps. With no sign of perturbation Washington started to tell stories and continued until the muscles of their trigger fingers relaxed and the muscles of their faces softened in laughter. Then he was able to get over the point of his speech.

His success in like emergencies led him to testify to the innate honesty and good will of the white man, which would prove itself in the South as soon as that part of the country had recovered from its long-range, sullen resentment against Negroes who were competing in the labor fields, and against Northern "foreigners" or "aliens" whom it suspected of trying to force it to do something it did not want to do.

Washington's interest in politics and race relations was as foreign to Professor Carver as his love of hunting, but the latter could not possibly avoid considering the question of the advancement of the race. Nor did he wish to, since helping to mold the race from raw material into useful citizens was one of the things for which he had been placed upon the earth.

Both put this squarely up to the Negroes themselves. Professor Carver wanted it to take concrete form and not dissipate itself in announcing what they would someday do. He would advise a colored audience, "Stop talking so much. You never saw a heavy thinker with his mouth open."

The summer of 1900 Professor Carver had made a trip back to Iowa. Having time to spare in St. Louis between trains, he utilized it by going through the Edison plant, and interpreted what he observed as a lesson to Negroes. When he saw only white workers at the machinery, he asked himself, "Where are the colored men?" He found them down in the boiler room, shoveling out ashes and shoveling in coal. He longed to get them upstairs. It was high time they were trained to be producers instead of consumers. If the eight million Negro population should be wiped out, he warned, the country would continue to move on; if the white population should be wiped out, the country would have to take a backward step to accommodate itself to Negro capabilities. Negroes could not legitimately object to Jim Crowism in Atlanta streetcars while they did not own a wheel nor a rail. "We can never amount to much," he ended, "so long as our only possession is our own labor, and that the very cheapest kind of labor."

In order to refute the common attitude that Negroes were figures of fun, he advised his boys to stop clowning and bend their energies toward enriching the sum of life. He once remarked to a young white friend, "A good many biting things are said about our colored people, and these frequently irritate Tuskegee boys and make them angry. They are inclined to deny these and make hot comments on their critics. But I tell them, 'You get nowhere that way. If fault is found with us, no matter how rudely, we should try to think to what extent it may be well based, and then correct our shortcomings as far as we are able. Even the most unfriendly criticism may be a help if you take it right.' "

Washington, not content with having students erect the chapel, wanted them to go on and prove themselves again and again in bigger and better ways. Accordingly he projected an enormous dining hall, asking the trustees only to approve the building. "I'll get the money," he promised, and he did. He was perfectly aware that even colored people had never expected they could carry through such a huge undertaking alone, so it was necessary to convince them as well as white people that they were capable.

It took a long time. The boys sweated for months raising the huge timbers, and for many more months the structure was open to the winds. But eventually it stood complete—a stately edifice, red brick, white-pillared, and graceful, for all its impressive size. They strung electric bulbs around the white dome so it would burst into light on the night of the opening celebration—a shining halo to crown their achievement.

White people were astonished at the marvel; they were not accustomed to Negroes' owning anything, and a shrill cry rose above the continuous dull mutter of animosity. The dome seemed a particularly flagrant piece of presumption, and the cry found words, "That Washington is trying to start a nigger capitol!"

Some dark nights rocks were thrown onto the campus, but the threats did not materialize; for the most part the animosity remained intangible and eventually died down because no resistance was opposed.

With Washington, Professor Carver had to endure the hardships attendant on any pioneering. When these were purely physical, he had no complaint, but when they stemmed from base human emotions, he was made bitterly unhappy. Once when he made his morning rounds of the Station plots he found his grain had been eaten off and his young plants trampled. Cow and mule tracks indicated the nature of the culprits—but the gate was closed. They were, therefore, innocent agents of destruction; some human hand had been at work. The gate had been opened at night, the stock let in and then removed early in the morning, and the gate shut behind.

Morning after morning the same thing recurred. Finally a student came to him, hesitant and fearful that it might not become him to say this, but he hated to see the havoc. "If you'll come down to the Station before four tomorrow morning or after ten at night you'll know whose stock is doing the damage."

This the professor did, and immediately identified the teacher who owned the animals. Until then he had not known that any of his own people could be like that. It was a new experience, and not a happy one. He recalled a talk he had heard given by another Negro, who had also tasted bitterness: "We are like crabs in a hamper. All lie quietly for a long time. Finally one takes a notion to move around and, growing bolder, starts to climb up the sides. Don't worry, he'll never get out! He struggles while the others watch him. As soon as he gets ready to put one foot over the side, all rush to pull him back. Don't worry, he'll never get out!"

Being a man of rare tenacity, Professor Carver's work came before his personal griefs. He could stick it and did. He only wanted to be let alone to accomplish what he had to do.

In some minds he remained a foreigner, and hence an object of distrust. They, too, had been through educational institutions and they could not do the things he was doing. In fact, they could not conceive of anybody being able to do them. They felt they must, somehow, prove he was wrong.

The United States Department of Agriculture recognized Professor Carver as an authority on soils and plant life, and his assistants, no matter how well grounded themselves in these matters, looked up to him as an unfailing and strictly accurate source of information. One of these would sometimes get lost on a plant disease; he could not diagnose it, but Professor Carver could, and could give the remedy and cure. Or perhaps he found a plant in the woods which he could not trace in any book. He showed it to Professor Carver. The explanation required only a brief study. "This does not belong among wild plants; it has escaped from domestication." If someone sent the professor no more than a seed from the tropics, he could couple its common name with its

Dr. Carver investigating plant diseases

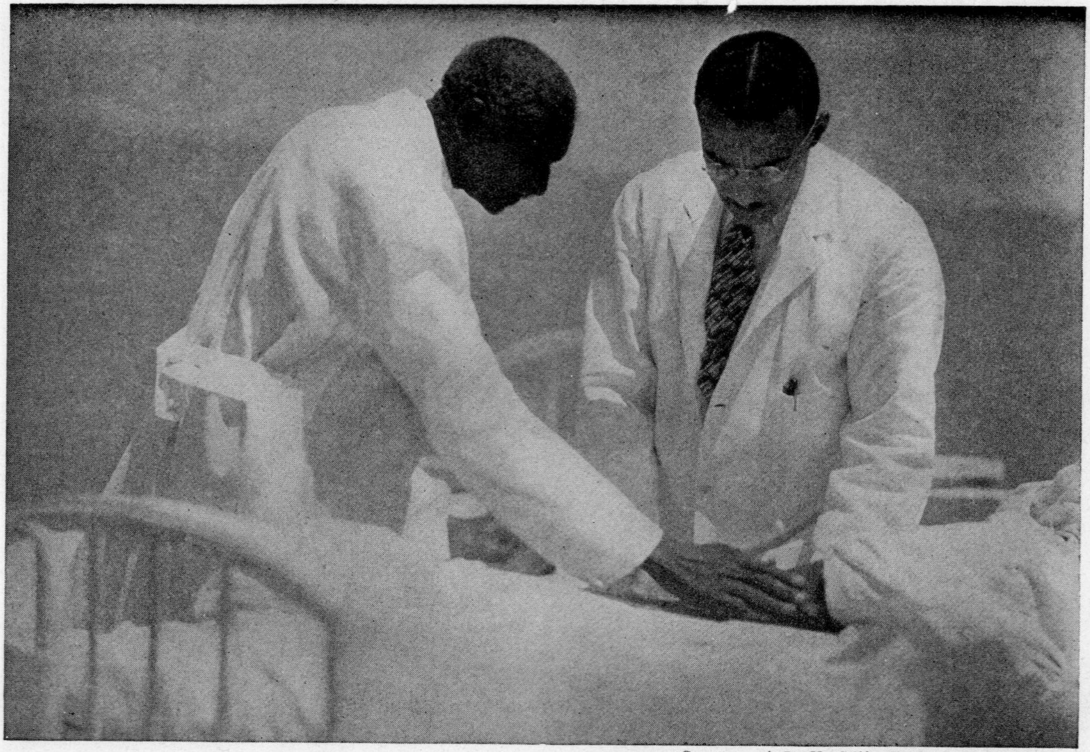

*Courtesy of P. H. Polk, Tuskegee Inst., Ala.*

Dr. Carver with Dr. John M. Chenault and infantile paralysis patient

botanical characteristics and get the answer. He was always right.

It was commonly accepted that a Negro failing was to use words that were too big for him. Professor Carver also used big words, but they were necessary in his business. Plants must be called according to their proper classifications, because such names indicated both their potentialities and possible dangers. Scientific exactitude was not merely his habit but was highly essential, for instance in the matter of knowing how to distinguish poisonous properties. He included the common name also wherever possible to aid the layman in identification.

Some people on the campus, who were not accustomed to scientific terminology, were sensitive. Granted, the professor was always going off to Washington about something or other. But that didn't mean much right here at home. And they had no means of knowing just how important he was, because he kept so much to himself, intent on his work and not on his reputation.

To those, fortunately very few, who were inimical he was nothing but a lot of big-sounding words that meant nothing and they, personally, were convinced Carver didn't know what he was talking about. They said as much to the principal.

"You have no proof of that," replied Mr. Washington. "You'll have to produce some proof; you can't just make such a statement."

So they made a plan between themselves and, with exceeding great rashness, tried to discredit him on, of all things, botany.

The table in the council room was in the shape of a T, with each person's name on a brass plate. The principal sat in the middle of the T, his secretary on his left, Professor Carver on his right, and the other members ranged down the table.

One of the three conspirators came into the council room with a handful of plants. He was to project the movement.

Another had a list of the common names of these plants, and the last a textbook which referred to them by their botanical names.

The first singled out one of the bunch of plants and held it up. "Can you tell me what this is, Professor?"

Professor Carver looked up from the report he was reading. "That? It's *Datura stramonium*. It's what is called Jimson weed." And he returned to his report.

A low-voiced consultation took place, while references were sought in the textbooks to check the statement.

Then he heard, "And what's this, Professor?"

Again he tore his attention from his papers. "That's *Asarum canadense*—wild ginger." And again his eyes sought his papers.

Another pause ensued, as the leaves of textbooks were turned.

Once more he was shown a plant and asked the same question. He was slightly impatient; he didn't want to be bothered just then. "Here," he exclaimed, "give me those!" and he reached for the pile of plants. "This is *Ambrosia artemisiifolia*—ragweed." He tossed it down. "This is *Oenothera biennis*—evening primrose; *Marrubium vulgare*—horehound." They were scrambling about among the books, but he went so fast they could not possibly keep up with him and in a few moments were thoroughly confused and mixed up. They couldn't follow him at all. "*Dioscorea villosa*—wild yam; *Sarracenia purpurea*—pitcherplant."

He peeled them off and cast them down until he had finished the pile. "There, that's the end of it!" He hoped he had finished with what seemed to him just fooling around, which did not have any point at that time and place when other things were more important. It never crossed his mind that this was a carefully laid trap to expose him before the rest of the council.

The conspirators had given up and closed their books. To Professor Carver's utter amazement they sheepishly explained what they had been trying to do. But the attempt had failed. They guessed he did know what he was talking about, after all.

That particular question had finally been settled by ocular demonstration, the only kind they could understand. In some quarters, however, it did not allay the conviction that Professor Carver was only a theorist, not a practical man.

Throughout the ages there have arisen individuals who lived beyond their day and generation. And it often takes half a century for the mass of people to catch up with them. He was constantly committing the unpardonable crime against the herd of being "different." His ideas were those of a crazy man; he was too far ahead, and people can't see far ahead.

There existed a general vagueness among many of the people at Tuskegee. They had glimpsed the transcendent idea of self-abnegation in a general way, but could not go all the way. They did not fully comprehend, and human frailties entered in. They lacked that feeling of being secure in their abilities which makes for well-poised efficiency, and which would enable them to carry through every detail of their work and personal relationships. They had thrust their heads and shoulders through the crust of postwar slavery, but they were not giants. And it took a giant to keep his footing on this insecure land they trod. All around them lay quaking mires, and they could be sucked back in without warning, without having committed any offense, and a hideous death might be the result. Safety for all peoples at all times has lain in banding together, and this people needed some measure of safety more than any other.

Professor Carver had a more certain sense of his destiny. He could bear to be alone, except for his God. He could not have come through these painful times without the help he received from a Power Divine to whom he constantly turned for guidance to keep his spirit free from rancor, and to give his spirit peace.

More and more he sought his laboratory where his own peculiar genius could find its best outlet. His equipment, poor as it was, held a fascination which the extensive business of organizing half the school in farm activities could not hold.

When he was about to make an experiment he was up at three in the morning, the door locked, ready for the attempt to put what God had made for man's use and his delight to its practical application. Everything was planned in advance; he was going to need such-and-such implements and they were laid out ready for use. Because he would have nobody else with him, he seemed peculiar. "We don't know what he's doing in there," they complained. He could not let anybody know. Other people would inevitably get in the way—if not physically, he would be conscious of them mentally, instead of having a mind completely open to any idea. Since they did not understand what he was up to anyhow, he could not dissipate his energies with explanations and conjectures. He was sailing uncharted seas and, though he might have a vision of what his landfall would look like, he could not tell for sure, and he might have to change his direction if the wind blew too strongly from another direction.

One who had his first sight of Professor Carver in the laboratory in his typical pose, leaning over a little in an abstracted kind of way, was bound to recognize him as a great man. Though this fact sometimes escaped those who lived in the shadow of the mountain—whose eyes were, through habit, bent to the ground they had traveled, and could not be raised to see the top, visitors almost inevitably felt that. They were aware of his restless, groping spirit seeking light. His intentness gave the impression that he had a fixed idea; that his span of life was limited. But if only he had time to work out his plans he knew he would have something to pass on.

Mr. Washington, as always, wanted to make the fullest use of human material. It was not a question of whittling the wrong-shaped peg to fit into the existing hole; somewhere in the world was a right-shaped hole for every human being, where his fullest potentialities could expand and be utilized. Such a situation he sought for Professor Carver, as evidenced by a short note he wrote on February 22, 1904: "Professor Carver. When you get this I want to speak to you about the Carnegie Institute for encouraging original research. I think that in some way this organization should be of some service to you in giving you a chance to do original work."

Nothing resulted from this, however, and a time came when Professor Carver felt so harassed and burdened by the weight of executive duties that he considered the need of removing to some other locality where he would be less hampered in his creative experimentation. This experimentation was unique and much too valuable to be lost to the school. The Agricultural Department could be placed in capable hands which would leave his at liberty. Consequently, the Board of Trustees decreed he should be relieved of departmental and classroom duties, except for some evening classes in botany, which he himself wanted to keep. He was to continue to serve as an information bureau, as director of the Experiment Station, and to extend his lecture trips; for the rest, he would be free to lock himself in his laboratory and follow his creative genius for research.

The Institute was a self-contained town of itself now, with what amounted to a city hall in the administration building, a post office, bank, church, library, power plant, shops, water and sewerage systems—all the accouterments of a modern town. And as it grew, the farm land was pushed further out. The old Slater-Armstrong Building which had once been "the finest in the South" had been outgrown, and was turned over to the Home Economics Department. A new agricultural nucleus was needed on the outskirts, and in the building contributed by the Milbank Memorial Fund in 1909, Professor Carver's laboratory was set up with more adequate equipment than he had had heretofore. And it became known as God's Little Workshop.

His chemical laboratory was no more important to him than his proving plant or hothouse; he employed them all as a housewife employs her stove. They were tools, and he never quarreled with his tools, but took what he had to make what he wanted.

The creative mind was hard for some people to understand; its working seemed to be illogical because, of necessity, it broke away from conventional thinking. The creative mind asked so many questions and seemed so eccentric that its owner was frequently branded queer or downright crazy. The professor had his own rule of behavior for this creative mind of his, which was to keep its mouth shut, its ears closed, and its eyes open.

He was himself a manifestation of the spirit of orginality, but he did not consider that these powers were his alone. He did not say, *I* am going to do so and so, but looked for Divine direction. And he believed devoutly that a plan was inherent in everything if one could just be patient and wait for it to show itself. According to his notion, at the back of all manifestations, and that did not exclude the scientific, was one Cause, one Creator. The seeker after truth did little but draw aside the veil and think God's thoughts after Him. "I discover nothing in my laboratory," Professor Carver said. "If I come here of myself I am lost. But I can do all things through Christ. I am God's servant, His agent, for here God and I are alone. I am just the instrument through which He speaks, and I would be able to do more if I were to stay in closer touch with Him. With my prayers I mix my labors, and sometimes God is pleased to bless the results."

When the decision had been made, one of Professor Carver's first acts was to notify Secretary Wilson, who was still his counselor, of his changed status. Early in 1910 he received the reply:

Department of Agriculture
Office of the Secretary
Washington, D.C.

MY DEAR CARVER,

I am very much pleased with your letter and to find that you have been promoted to a higher class of work. Research, of course, is the highest class of work connected with agriculture. Research, of course, is very difficult, . . . to wrest from nature some of the secrets that have never been known before. . . . I will send you a copy of my annual report. I wind it up by saying that science unapplied is a dead thing. The science that you work out in your laboratory must not be allowed to go to sleep or to go to the grave again.

I am very glad indeed that this promotion has come to you. You certainly have worked for it and earned it. I remember when I first met you, you said you wanted to get an agricultural education so you could help your race. I had never known anything more beautiful than that said by a student. I know the taste you have for painting and the success you had made, and I said, "Why not push your studies along that line to some extent?" You replied that that would be of no value to your colored brethren. That, also, was magnificent. Now you have a fine opportunity, being the foremost colored man the world knows along the lines of agricultural science, to do your people good, and that has always been in your mind.

In a month or two I shall have been here for fourteen years. In looking back over what I have been doing, I have come to the conclusion that it was worth doing, and that there is no justification for a man's holding a position in the Federal or State Government service unless he has succeeded in making his service valuable to his fellow men.

So go on, my dear Carver. You are not going to surprise me by anything you may elaborate, because I know the thoroughness of your fundamental training. The old doctors around Ames did good work with you, and you are a very industrious student.

Wishing you the full realization of your highest and holiest aspirations, I remain, your friend,

(Signed) JAMES WILSON

# CHAPTER XVII

## *"I Heard from Heaven Today"*

*Boll weevil, where you been so long?*
*You stole my cotton, now you wants my co'n.*

THIS WAS TO BECOME the universal plaint of the Southland. The dangerous little beetle began creeping up from Mexico into Texas in 1904. It would inevitably continue its insidious spread. Professor Carver, the mycologist, saw the danger long before it got in its deadly work. By 1910 the boll weevil was unmistakably on its way and very close. He issued a warning: "The boll weevil is advancing this way at a rapid rate. Better get ready."

Getting ready, to Professor Carver, meant not merely preparing to combat it; so few control measures could be taken. Spraying with calcium arsenate was only a specific if applied to each individual cotton plant, and the price was almost prohibitive for the poorer farmers. But by planting early and cultivating and gathering early they might stand a better chance of escaping some of the ravages. It was "important that every farmer look ahead and secure cotton of the greatest vitality, the fastest growing, and the earliest ripening." Speed was of the essence, if anything were to be saved.

He had always taken advantage of a short cotton crop to pound home the moral of the inexpressible evil of depending on one crop. An abundant crop was as disastrous to the farmers as a poor crop; any crop was disastrous, if they only knew it.

To be happy the farmer must raise his living at home. Professor Carver described how he had walked in unexpectedly on one family, just in time for supper. And supper had consisted of ham raised on the place, butter, also homemade, two kinds of canned fruit, eggs, and syrup on biscuits made from flour which had been purchased from the surplus.

Should the boll weevil prove as destructive as it had elsewhere, and there was no reason to suppose it would not, the slipshod farmer would be forced, willy-nilly, to learn intelligence and thrift. Thus it might prove to be a blessing instead of a curse.

"Help must come, and that right early," thought the professor. Nothing could stay the weevil, but he urged them to prepare for it by planting less cotton and, to take the place of a cash crop, planning to raise a surplus of cowpeas, sweet potatoes, and peanuts to sell.

Of the leguminous crops the cowpea had proved itself the poor man's bank as a soil and health builder. The fuzzy velvet bean, which grew well, but not extensively, was an excellent stock food. Few people in this country, with the notable exception of Professor Carver, had even heard of the soybean until 1907 when the Department of Agriculture instituted experimentation on imported plants and tried adapting it to American soils and climatic conditions. Professor Carver had already tried his own hand at experimentation, and successfully. This was because he was personally interested and not because he thought he could suggest anything so radical to Southern farmers, who would not know how to cope with this strange and unfamiliar plant.

They had, on the other hand, grown up with the peanut—knew what it looked like, when it flowered, how it tucked itself into the ground. All they had to do was enlarge those little patches they were used to cultivating for the children and increase them into acres.

Peanuts are indigenous to South America. *Mani,* as they were known in Quecha, as well as pottery images of them have been found in Peruvian tombs by archaeologists. Apparently they were well liked by the Incas, to have been buried with the dead, and by the archaeologists, also, who roasted and ate their finds. We know, too, they were relished by the conquistadors, who carried them to Spain, whence they found their way to Africa as early as the seventeenth century and came back again to the New World in the slave traders, as the chief food of the captives. "Goober" is one of the few African words that have survived in this country.

Thus the peanut might be considered native to African descendants. It was easy to plant, easy to grow, easy to harvest; in fact, it grew almost by itself. Being one of the few crops which could stand successfully long, dry periods, in drouth it just curled up and waited for rain, and then raced to maturity. Though primarily a tropical plant, it adapted itself easily to the temperate zone. Unique among the Leguminosae, after the flower withered, the stalk stretched, bent down, and forced the young pod into the soil, where it ripened. This explained its name in England, "ground nut," and in France, "*pistache de terre*," and its botanical name, *Arachis hypogaea*—Greek words meaning "weed" and "under."

The peanut almost equaled sirloin for proteins and potatoes for carbohydrates, and was inferior only to butter in fat. Professor Carver had started publishing recipes for cooking peanuts for the table before 1913, but these were constantly being augmented, and the bulletin was in its sixth edition by 1916, carrying directions for growing and one hundred five ways of preparing it for human consumption.

Every girl at the Institute, no matter what trade she was studying, had to learn cooking and practice homemaking. Taking fourteen of these recipes, Professor Carver instructed a class of senior girls who were studying dietetics in the varied usages of the peanut, and they served a five-course luncheon to Mr. Washington and nine guests—soup, mock chicken, creamed as a vegetable, salad, bread, candy, cookies, ice cream, coffee—all from peanuts; and as varied and tasty as one could ask.

Coffee County, Alabama, accepted Professor Carver's warning literally and shifted from a cotton- to a peanut-growing community. It had been on the verge of bankruptcy in 1915 because of the ravages of the boll weevil, but after its change of heart and manner, within four years it became the most prosperous county in the state. Its chief town, Enterprise, put up a twenty-five-thousand-dollar shelling plant in 1919, and acknowledged its indebtedness to Professor Carver by erecting a three-thousand-dollar monument in a little grassy square in the center of the town. The legend on one side read: "In profound appreciation of the boll weevil and what it has done. As the herald of prosperity, this monument was erected by the citizens of Enterprise, Coffee County, Alabama." By 1934 the county held the world record for production, perhaps inspired by the tinkling fountain and the miniature lady and her lights. At any rate, she stands as a symbol of gratitude for deliverance from cotton bondage.

But this success came later—after Professor Carver had solved another problem which had arisen.

Many individual farmers had been persuaded to grow Leguminosae comparatively early. A very few owners had planted a large acreage of peanuts which were ready for market. But what market? The Southern system, including the banks, was geared to cotton. Enough peanuts to fill the paper bags at carnivals and circuses were already being imported from the Far East and had been for years. Who would buy these additional peanuts?

Among the owners in this predicament was a widow who had been managing a large plantation. She had recognized as logical all the arguments against the one-crop system and the necessity for another cash crop. She had planted peanuts. She was puzzled and put the problem squarely up to Professor Carver. Now that she had reached this stage, what was she to do? She had peanuts in quantity, but no buyer.

Professor Carver went away from that conversation greatly troubled. He felt he had made a blunder; he had not thought far enough. He had offered only a half truth, and a half truth was no better than a lie. He could not believe that he was fundamentally wrong about the two crops—sweet potatoes and peanuts—on which he had crystallized his efforts, but somehow they would have to be fitted into the sorry scheme of things. They still could be made the lifesavers of the South if markets could be found. It was up to him to create those markets.

In native plants, mineral wealth, and man power, which form the bases of national wealth, the southeastern section of the United States was better favored than almost any other part of the globe. Yet it remained among the poorest. Race and class fears in this land of neglected opportunity made the communities sterile. Professor Carver did not think merely in terms of helping to lift his people, but all people who were in need. The Negro and the South were interdependent; if the South could be rehabilitated, the general scale would rise.

One important way was to build up native industries. Even though the South would probably remain largely agricultural, a really prosperous agriculture needed many new industries for processing products, supplying its equipment, and balancing its economy.

Professor Carver retired to God's Little Workshop to wrestle with the immediate question. In his solitary moments he meditated long over the implications of the boll weevil, and decided that God had sent it in order to develop a New South—a South of factories as well as farms.

He devoutly believed that a personal relationship with the Creator of all things was the only foundation for the abundant life. He had a little story in which he related his experience:

I asked the Great Creator what the universe was made for.

"Ask for something more in keeping with that little mind of yours," He replied.

"What was man made for?"

"Little man, you still want to know too much. Cut down the extent of your request and improve the intent."

Then I told the Creator I wanted to know all about the peanut. He replied that my mind was too small to know *all* about the peanut, but He said He would give me a handful of peanuts. And God said, "Behold, I have given you every herb bearing seed, which is upon the face of the earth . . . to you it shall be for meat. . . . I have given every green herb for meat: and it was so."

I carried the peanuts into my laboratory and the Creator told me to take them apart and resolve them into their elements. With such knowledge as I had of chemistry and physics I set to work to take them apart. I separated the water, the fats, the oils, the gums, the resins, sugars, starches, pectoses, pentosans, amino acids. There! I had the parts of the peanuts all spread out before me.

I looked at Him and He looked at me. "Now, you know what the peanut is."

"Why did you make the peanut?"

The Creator said, "I have given you three laws; namely, compatibility, temperature, and pressure. All you have to do is take these constituents and put them together, observing these laws, and I will show you why I made the peanut."

I therefore went on to try different combinations of the parts under different conditions of temperature and pressure, and the result was what you see.

Valuable contributions to the sum of human knowledge had already been made by Professor Carver in many fields—botany, mycology, genetics, agriculture, dietetics. From the time of his arrival at Tuskegee he had also been experimenting with the most vital of all—creative science. Now he was beginning to devote his energies to it in earnest. He saw the development of man as falling into three stages: Finding, Adapting, Creating. First was the utilization of things Nature had provided; the second was characterized by a rearrangement of the materials—stones, ores, fibers, skins, metals—on which industry was based, so they might assume a more useful role; third was the transformation of those materials into more and in some instances entirely new ones for the protection and comfort of man.

A very large proportion of any farm crop was inedible and therefore sheer waste. His answer to the surplus problem was simple and direct. "Find new uses for this waste, and thus enlarge the usefulness of the product to mankind."

Professor Carver abhorred waste, and from his laboratory by-products rushed into the vacuum. He had a vision in which he saw that farms could be transformed into something more than mere food factories; they could become a source of the raw material of industry. This was an idea which was to capture the imagination of millions when it was advanced by white industrialists thirty years later.

When the cowpea was brought into the laboratory it did not prove to have the potentialities of the velvet bean, from which he made flour, starch, stains, dyes, wood fillers of different colors, ink, and, from the stalks, a substitute for excelsior packing. Because of his great interest, he was lecturing on the soybean and the derivatives he had found—flour, meal, coffee, breakfast food, oil, milk—long before it had been picked up by Midwestern growers. However, for industrial purposes he could not emphasize the soybean because of Southern unfamiliarity.

He concentrated his efforts, therefore, on the peanut, and from this storehouse of wonders combinations in many curious and uncommon forms poured in a never-ending stream—gastronomically, from soup to nuts: a dozen beverages, mixed pickles, sauces (Worcestershire and chili), meal, instant and dry coffee, salve, bleach, tan remover, wood filler, washing powder, metal polish, paper, ink, plastics, shaving cream, rubbing oil, linoleum, shampoo, axle grease, synthetic rubber. If the Institute prepared a list, it was out of date before it could be printed. Some offered immediate possibilities for commercialization, some might be only curiosities, but you never could tell.

The peanut was 32 per cent oil and the oil particles lacked the gelatinous membrane common to animal fat; hence, a hydrogenator or catalyzer could be used to reduce the peanut oil to oleo. The fat globules could be broken to a lesser or greater extent to produce milk which would not curdle in cooking or when acids were added, and which contained all the elements of cows' milk, being low only in calcium. Cream would rise upon it which could be turned into butter without souring. The cream could be removed to produce buttermilk, and from either an inexpensive, palatable, and long-lasting cheese could be manufactured; where a hundred pounds of cows' milk made ten pounds of cheese, the same amount of peanut milk made thirty-five pounds.

This milk proved to be truly a lifesaver in the Belgian Congo. Cows could not be kept there because of leopards and flies, so if a mother died her baby was buried with her; there was nothing to nourish it. Missionaries fed the infants peanut milk, and they flourished.

To conserve the enormous waste of other than the edible portion of crops, Professor Carver had investigated the potentialities of the majority of Southern harvests for uses other than human consumption and began studies to "find ways of utilizing the millions of tons of lignin and cellulose that were being discarded yearly as invaluable material."

He thought it would be interesting to transform dull sawdust into shining slabs of synthetic marble. When he had added the adhesive and pigment and given it a high polish, it was strong, substantial, and weatherproof. Its production would offer an inexpensive way to utilize the waste of lumber mills and at the same time bring a colorful richness into the homes of those who could not afford to live in marble halls.

Toward the same end he made serviceable wallboard of caladium, wistaria, peanut shells, pine cones, banana stems, cotton, pecan hulls, and many other Southern plants.

He had for some time been interested in native fibers and their commercial possibilities. Such vast amounts of spruce were going into the ever-increasing amount of newsprint that inevitably the available supply of forests was going to be reduced to a dangerous point. In 1910 he produced a paper from slash pine, extracting the fiber by hand, since he had no mill. Though the amount was small, it did point the way to anyone who cared to follow. From yucca and peanut skin he produced paper as fine as linen, which might even be used for cloth. He tried his hand also with spiny mallow, tomato stems, the prickly *Sida spinosa,* and thirteen other native plants. From the bare skeletons of cotton stalks left standing in the fields from season to season he made paper and rope and fiber rugs.

When he was exhibiting at a fair he was always on hand early to arrange his exhibit, and this happened one morning at Montgomery. Two white farmers who had their own exhibit already prepared were wandering about to look at other showings before the gates should open and the public flock in. They stopped before the large booth filled with rugs, and nothing but rugs, of Professor Carver.

One farmer lifted up a label, read it, and then shot out a stream of tobacco juice. He looked at another label and spat again. "Well, I'll declare! Okra stalk, eh? Made outa okra stalk. S'pose that's so? Here, you"—and he beckoned to Professor Carver, who was hanging around, interested to know what their reaction would be—"d'ya know anything about this exhibit?"

"Yes sir. It's mine."

"You made it?"

"Yes sir, just what you see."

"He says okra stalk," the man exclaimed to his companion, and poured out another stream of tobacco juice and shook and laughed. "Okra stalk! Well, glad you found some use for it; 'tisn't fit to eat!"

Professor Carver's work was not confined to class or race. Since only the whites were landowners and had capital it might be considered of greater significance to them because they could make immediate use of it. They seldom did, however, though he attempted to bring more of the South's mineral wealth to the attention of those who were in a position to exploit it.

Alabama was surpassing rich; her marble was comparable to that of Italy. The remarkable development of cement manufacture was due to the practically inexhaustible deposits of limestone. The exploitation of her coal and iron resources had been begun in the latter part of the nineteenth century, but these, as well as most of the zinc and bauxite, were owned outside and shipped outside. The South would make a bid for Northern capital and then resent it when it came.

Meanwhile, other types of mineral wealth were still lying dormant. In his rambles Professor Carver picked up lumps of pure malleable copper, the basic copper carbonate called azurite, 90 per cent pure cyanite. He followed a deposit of bentonite, which could be used to de-ink newspapers and thus make them usable again, and found it to extend into a large and exceptionally pure deposit near Montgomery and as far south as Mobile. Among the raw materials virtually begging to be brought to the uses of man were heavy oxides of iron, manganese, graphite, sugar quartz, and "glittering everywhere" were heat-resisting, non-conducting micas, so necessary in the electrical industry and very effective for decorative purposes. Professor Carver found calcareous tripoli and siliceous tripoli, from which he made a universal scouring powder, and clay fine enough for talcum powder, which could be borated, thus providing an opening for some enterprising manufacturer.

Much of Alabama's mineral wealth lay in its clay deposits: clays of rare beauty and real commercial value. Here in abundance was white clay produced by the decomposition of feldspar, ready to hand for molding a fine kaolin—which in Chinese means high hill.

Once when Professor Carver was invited to Indiana to give a lecture he happened to see a vase which had been bought for twenty-five dollars. He admired it so much he set about to discover the source of the porcelain, and traced it to Georgia. In that state and in Alabama china clays were being sold at a low cost to manufacturers in the North; the finished wares were then purchased by Southerners at a high price. He wanted to see this industry carried on in the South itself. Now and again a jug factory would spring up, make a few churns, jars, crocks, vases, and flower pots, sell them out, and then mysteriously disappear, leaving nothing permanent behind.

As an experiment in ceramics he built himself a little potter's kick wheel and shaped vases, decorating them with charming tree and flower sketches. He was not a potter, but merely desired to prove to Southerners who might see his wares that china clays could be mined and processed.

Along with other leaders of thought, both white and colored, Professor Carver realized that as long as the policy of the South remained faulty, the basis of her economy would remain weak. As long as her farm population remained below the highest cultural level it was capable of attaining, the culture of the entire region would remain deficient. He was dealing directly with farmers, the barometer of the nation's progress. He was showing them, at first hand, how they could individually improve their standards and, even though desperately poor, make for themselves a native culture.

At a flat-topped desk in a little upstairs room in the agricultural building, piled with pamphlets, mail, bottles, rocks, plants, and glue, he painstakingly worked out wallpaper designs colored with clay and thirteen subtle color combinations for cold-water washes. Bulletin No. 449, issued from Washington in 1912 by the Federal Government, reports on his washes and repeats his directions.

These washes, however, merely covered the surface. The woods commonly in use for furniture and inside woodwork were the softer, cheaper ones—fir, cypress, pine—and required stains which would penetrate to the sub-surface. So he produced a lovely, mellow series of these which would bring out the grain and make it glow: burnt straw, citrus, cocoa, licorice, lime green, mole, moss, ripe wheat, sea blue, slate, tobacco, zebra.

At the Alabama State Exposition in 1911 Professor Carver

showed an impressive array of clay products, including samples of color washes—red, pink, lavender, purple, green, yellow, blue—and furniture stains. His exhibit of these and a sweet potato which weighed eight and four tenths pounds shared honors with the one-legged man, the high slider, and the balloon ascension.

All of this work Professor Carver had to do from the shoulder. It was hard to get the people to progress. Only a few were really interested, and he suffered many discouragements. He had no appropriation for a demonstration of his stains, but had to use what scraps of wood he could find. He wanted to stain one of the buildings on the grounds, but the superintendent said it wasn't good enough.

However, he was soon given an opportunity. When the Episcopalian church was being built in the town in 1912, architecturally charming but handicapped for lack of funds, paints were priced, and the only suitable one cost four dollars a gallon. The congregation brought its problem to Professor Carver, and from his laboratory he sent to his white friends a stain which cost seventy-five cents a gallon. That was thirty years ago and, with the passage of time, the wood has put on richness, depth, and luminosity. This was Professor Carver's first sizable demonstration of his stains, and it gave him heart to sound again a hopeful note of manufacturing possibilities.

The exhibits of Professor Carver were a visual means of focusing public attention; he was lecturing in pictures. The astute Mr. Washington recognized the propaganda value of this type of production when put on view at fairs as an example of what a Negro mind was capable. The two of them were standing on the broad steps of the dining hall, just as Washington was about to start on a trip to the North.

"Have you completed your Macon County exhibit?" he asked.

"No, it will never be completed. But I have at least two freight carloads ready."

"I'm certain your Macon County exhibit will do more to

convince Southern white men of the value of Negro education than anything that has come to us." He pondered for a moment, and then suggested, "Why wouldn't it be a good idea to have a train exhibit? We could show it at Birmingham and Montgomery when the Legislature is in session and after that decide where to go next."

Professor Carver agreed that the proposal was worth considering.

"Well, good-by. Let's think it over."

"We'll think it over. Good-by."

And that was their final parting.

Booker T. Washington made his last speech in New Haven on October 25, 1915—an appeal for race understanding. He was brought back to Tuskegee to die, November 14, having given his life in the service of the Institute. The townspeople of Tuskegee mourned his passing as sincerely as the colored folk to whom he had dedicated himself.

Frederick Douglass had died just before the momentous Atlanta speech. He had led his people out of slavery. Washington had taught these freed men how to live as free men in mastering trades and agriculture. On the third of these great guides—all born to be slaves—Professor Carver, the quiet scientist, devolved the duty of conducting the race on to the next step by putting the laboratory at the disposal not merely of the farmer but also of the industrialist.

Theodore Roosevelt came down to deliver a eulogy on his friend Washington. When the memorial service was over, and before the mountain of flowers had withered, he sought Professor Carver to say good-by. As they walked together arm in arm to the train which was to take Roosevelt away he said half-humorously, "I think you do things much as I do, though that may not be a credit to *you*. You study first, then come to a decision, and then stick to that decision. We can neither be worked, walked, nor talked down." He, too, recognized Professor Carver's significant position and, more seriously, he added, "There *is* no more important work than that you are doing."

Founder's Day at Tuskegee Institute was established in 1917 and has been held in commemoration every year thereafter on the Sunday nearest April 6, which was as close as anyone could guess at Washington's birthday. Ex-President Taft, Judge Landis, Jane Addams, and similar friends of the underprivileged were there to evidence respect for the memory of a great man. The campus had become one of the most beautiful to be found anywhere, dotted with bursting redbuds like small, pink, low-lying clouds. Dripping wistaria, white and purple, loosed its fragrance on the clear, spring air. When such days come to Tuskegee, of almost unearthly charm, one person will greet another with, "Lovely weather we're having." And the response is, "Yes, a regular Booker Washington day."

The presence of their principal still pervades the school. If something occurs which should not have occurred, the old people say that Booker Washington must be sleeping. And if a door bangs when no man is near it, then Washington has just passed through, keeping an eye on things as he used to do. His gravestone is a rough-hewn boulder of granite, but his monument is one of the noblest ever erected by man, Tuskegee Institute itself.

# CHAPTER XVIII

## *"Down Came the Heavenly Manna"*

PROFESSOR CARVER could not think with equanimity in terms of anything that involved controversy or contention. This applied not merely to his immediate surroundings and petty disputes, but to the larger aspect of war. However, when the war came in 1917 he issued a plea to Negroes to join hands, hearts, and interest with the rest of the nation. "A race that will not prove itself indispensable when the world is in a crisis does not deserve and need not look for recognition in times of peace and prosperity."

His Tuskegee boys had something more than muscle and something more than song, and his hopes were fulfilled as he watched them set out to join Negro companies, one of which bore a banner, "We are going to show the world that fast black won't run." They were carrying on the tradition, in the same spirit of earnestness and devotion as the Negro sergeant, William Carney, in the Civil War, who had assured his commanding officer, "With God's help I will bring back the colors with honor, or else report to Him the reason why." Though wounded in head and legs he had fulfilled his promise and, as he returned, he proudly announced, "The old flag never touched the ground." The first man to die in the American Revolution was Crispus Attucks, a Negro; the first man in the A.E.F. in 1918 to receive the Croix de Guerre with star and palm was Henry Johnson, a Negro.

Professor Carver served his country after his own fashion, accepting the war as a challenge to help further the ways of peace. The United States had been dependent on Germany for its chemicals, fertilizers, and dyes. In fact, Germany supplied the commercial world with aniline dyes. When the war stopped importation, industries that required dyes—printing, paint, paper, leather, and clothing—were suddenly thrown back fifty years and had to return again to using natural colors, such as fustic and cochineal.

To be sure, thought Professor Carver, aniline dyes were the best, but could not vegetable dyes be perfected? He started across the fields and over the hills and into the swamps in search of the trees and flowers which would readily yield their latent colors. From leaf, root, stem, and fruit of twenty-eight plants he squeezed 536 dyes which could be used on leather, cotton, wool, silk, and linen and which would not fade in washing or in light. If they could stand up under the fierce Alabama sun, they would stand up under anything.

These were merely basic colors. Only a professional and technical expert who understood cross-dyeing could deal with them properly. The head of a great dyestuffs firm offered Professor Carver a blank check for him to fill in, saying they would equip a laboratory if he would take charge of it, at his own salary. This offer he declined, but he was pleased that he might have given them something with which to proceed. A woman from the Department of Agriculture spent several days going over his records and then wrote an enthusiastic report—without, however, mentioning his name. Then the United States Government confiscated the German patents, and the crisis was over.

The possibility of a food shortage loomed in 1914 as it did in 1940. War had set many extra mouths gaping with hunger, and Tuskegee joined in encouraging that part of the world over which it had influence to raise more food to win the war. In the Pavilion was held a public-school exhibit of onions, beans, cabbages, collards, and radishes, with such slogans as, "A bountiful food supply spells strength and victory," and "No hungry nation can long protect its flag." There was the flag, in which turnips and beets made up the stripes, and scrubbed and shiny potatoes twinkled as stars.

He was walking back from the Milbank Building one afternoon when a tramp, miserable and forlorn and concave where he should have been convex, materialized out of the bushes and edged up. "Could you give me a dime for something to eat?"

Professor Carver fished out the ten cents and watched the man elongate his legs in the direction of the shops, less than a quarter of a mile away. Sadly he shook his head, which was growing gray over the shortsightedness of his brothers and sisters on this earth who would not see what their eyes beheld.

"It's pitiful, pitiful," he said to his companion. "Between here and that store there's enough food to feed a town." He pointed to the weeds growing beside the road and to the wild plums overhead. "And a balanced diet too."

It was uphill work persuading more than a handful of farmers of the value of raising vegetables—of fighting King Cotton with such a puny weapon as logic.

But Professor Carver hearkened to Isaiah, who had hearkened to the Lord: "The voice said, Cry. And he said, What shall I cry?" Then the voice told him what to say. "All flesh is grass, and all the goodliness thereof is as the flower of the field." Isaiah had his ear to the ground, and by listening Professor Carver heard also. The voice said to him, go and get it, so he did.

In most places you had to put your foot down carefully as you stepped out the cabin door or it would crush a cotton plant—and that meant crushing what represented money. But along the fence rows weeds sprouted luxuriantly; and a wild vegetable by any other name would taste as good.

One definition of a weed was any plant growing in ground that had been cultivated, usually to the detriment of the crop; it was economically useless and possessed exuberant growth. Well, said Professor Carver, all weeds were plants, all plants could be weeds, but no plant need be a weed—not if you reduced the definition to its essentials; a weed was a plant out of place. Okra in a cornfield was a weed because it was out of place. So was the cocklebur in a wheat field, but in its proper place it could become an important medicinal crop.

As for the exuberant growth of weeds, Nature scattered billions of seeds. Only a few survived; the weaker perished. It was the law of life. Some plants were cultivated carefully, guarded from fungus diseases and insect enemies. But often the wild plants were more palatable than the cultivated ones, which had been robbed of vitality by coddling. The lowly ones without the fence had strength of character; they would dare to come up earlier than the tenderly nurtured within the enclosure, and would still be flourishing when the short growing span of the latter was finished. You did not have to hoe around them or pick bugs off or spray; they were there because they had already mastered the rules for survival.

In their respective seasons Professor Carver had for a long time included wild vegetables in his own diet—clover tops, dandelion, wild lettuce, chicory, rabbit tobacco, alfalfa, thistles, bed straw, pepper grass, wild geranium, purslane, hawkweed, Flora's paintbrush, water cress, shepherd's-purse. The dainty chickweed, which was pretty as to appearance and delicate as to taste, could be happily combined in salads or stews, cold or hot. Curled dock made as good a pie as its cultivated cousin the cultivated rhubarb. From sour grass, or old-fashioned sheep sorrel, he made not merely pies but confectionery and paint.

A little earlier than asparagus in most localities, the tender shoots of the pokeweed poked up through the soil. These were as delicate and delicious as the asparagus tips, which they resembled, as was also the swamp milkweed. Evening primrose, so pink as to be almost red, grew in masses.

Lamb's-quarters, choicest of vegetables, was scattered over the temperate and subtropical sections of the country, and was available from early until late summer. It made an immense amount of green stuff, was tender, crisp, and cooked easily. Before McCollum tested it on his rats and announced it contained the Fat Soluble A—one of the newly discovered and much-needed properties called "vitamines," Professor Carver had proclaimed its high medicinal value.

Most wild vegetables had a short season in which they were tender but, being robust in flavor, they would keep well. The housewife could pack them in cans or jars and have shelves full of winter succulence. And, since jars were hard to come by for the really poor, they could be dried. That way they were practically imperishable and required little storage space. Dehydrating wild vegetables seemed an excellent way to save the country's granary from the nibbling mice of waste.

The crop of peaches was overabundant that year, so Professor Carver advocated drying them. "We have become a tin-can people and like to have things come to us in convenient packages. Now we must rediscover many of the old ways of saving food; this so-called reversion will actually spell progress."

One of the results of his simple dehydrating technique he called fruit leathers: reduce the overripe fruit to a pulp, roll it out like a piece of piecrust, dry it, and then cut it into strips and tuck it away in jars. This was an old Pompeian confection, and his method was merely a revival.

Professor Carver ventured a prediction: "Fifteen hundred years ago the sweet potato and the peanut were grown. But from then until a few years ago baking, frying, and boiling represented nearly the sum total of the processes through which the sweet potato could be carried. Peanuts were commonly considered fit only for monkey food. But recently we began the real discovery of the sweet potato and the peanut and out of these discoveries is going to come the opportunity for making the Southland the richest and most prosperous section of America."

Over and over he reiterated that if all vegetable foodstuffs were destroyed except these two strictly Southern products, the peanut and the sweet potato, we could live on them alone and be perfectly hearty, and we would still have a perfectly balanced ration for man and his animals—starch and sugar from the sweet potato and protein from the peanut—and both could be prepared in so many different ways that "the palate will not tire nor the digestion suffer from a monotonous sameness."

His most extensive researches at this time involved sweet potatoes. He had previously tried out various means of reducing the storage losses on this perishable but valuable food which were militating against its becoming a money crop, and had made a multitude of products, from shoe polish to rubber which could be vulcanized.

But just now the ingenuity of the people was being tested to find economical, nutritious, and palatable foods. Germany was supposed to have some six hundred and fifty substitutes, and could we not find a few to fill the shortages? Germany made egg white from fish protein, Professor Carver made egg yolk from a Puerto Rican sweet potato. From the same vegetable he concocted tapioca, a breakfast food, and a delicacy which tasted like ginger. He manufactured a syrup which was comparable to Midwest corn syrup in quality and lower in cost, and vinegar and domestic alcohol.

Another way to make the most of the sweet potato was to utilize its starch content as a flour; and he developed three types; the first two, from cooked sweet potatoes, could be produced by the housewife who possessed no more equipment than her rusty, broken, little wood stove and table and meager kitchen tools.

By adding one third of this sweet-potato flour to two thirds of the regulation wheat flour, the dining hall at Tuskegee Institute was able to eliminate two hundred pounds of wheat flour or, to put it differently, save twelve dollars a day.

The United States was short on wheat; much of it was being sunk in the Atlantic by submarines. Flours from barley, rice, corn, chestnuts, cassava, and Irish potatoes had all been tried and pretty generally pronounced unfit for making bread such as Americans were accustomed to.

In January of 1918 Professor Carver was summoned to

Washington "to demonstrate the products of the sweet potato with which he has been successfully dealing during the past year," and exhibit its possibilities, "especially as a breadmaker." He had several meetings with different groups of Army bakers, chemists, dieticians, technicians, and transportation authorities.

These last were invited to the conclave because his work in dehydration was of especial interest to them in wartime. Successful dehydration of foods would not merely insure their keeping indefinitely, but greatly decrease both weight and bulk—all of which factors were of vital importance when cargo space was so limited.

Most of the experts were inclined to be somewhat skeptical at first. But after Professor Carver had actually made the bread in the bakery for the committee to sample, as he modestly mentioned, "they were greatly interested and pleased with it." They decided the sweet potato was the greatest conserver of wheat flour that had yet been found and that it could also help conserve sugar.

A Washington daily reported that he "appears devoted to the task of producing new uses for the products of the soil to bring about a greater consumption." It commented on his pleasing personality and admired his handling of words with a view to their precise meaning.

In this interview he had said, "I do not like the word 'substitute' as applied to my products. I prefer to let each stand on its own merits." According to his interpretation, the word tended to imply that such a creation was not so good as the real thing, but was used only on sufferance when the real thing was not available. Synthetic, on the other hand, was "a fourth kingdom of Nature, entirely within the control of man, beneficent when compatible elements are joined, and of deadly destructiveness when incompatible elements unite. We can see," he predicted, with that prescience which was one of his outstanding characteristics, "that a new world is about to come into existence. It will be the synthetic world.

The big laboratories will eventually be moved to the farms where they can be close to production."

A few enthusiastic observers decided immediately that the sweet-potato acreage must be increased, and began to plan for a large drier, costing in the neighborhood of four thousand dollars, to be erected somewhere in the South to handle ten thousand bushels.

Professor Carver returned to Tuskegee meditating in a pleased way on how he had in some measure been able to prove that the better a man were educated the better could he serve his community and his country by showing that their interests were identical. Firmly he held to the belief which was to be put to the test in 1940 that, a nation being made up of individuals, the problem of one is the problem of all and one group cannot long prosper at the expense of another; each man is the keeper of all his brothers wherever they may be on the globe, and an evil which afflicts one man afflicts all men everywhere.

The sweet-potato bulletin he published that summer was reprinted in agricultural and home-economics journals, in dailies, weeklies, and monthlies, in the *Literary Digest* and the *Ladies' Home Journal*. He was called "the Negro wizard of agricultural research in chemistry." One publication remarked that this quiet, resourceful, hard-working, extraordinary black man of genius was returning convincing, positive answers to those who were seeking to find new industrial outlets for the growing population of the South; his exhibit showed he had caught the vision of a greater industrial South, and that he was interested in doing the basic work of finding new uses for ever-ready materials.

Sweet-potato flour was used in camps to augment wheat flour. At its current stage of production it could fill the gap in the shortage, but when normal production was resumed, it was more expensive than wheat. A bill for an appropriation of $250,000 was pending in Congress, a large part of which was to be allocated to propaganda in instructing the public concerning the potentialities of the sweet potato. But when the war crisis was over both the drier and the propaganda were dropped for twenty years.

When a reporter inquired of Professor Carver concerning the attitude of the public toward his discoveries, he answered, "The discoverer must pass through three stages at least, each of which is important and quite natural. The first is the 'knocking' stage. Any new article offered to the public must meet certain hostile critics who say, 'This thing is no good; the man who puts this claim forward is very foolish; we don't want this newfangled thing; the old things are good enough for us.' Everybody rises up against it, which is really a very good thing. The new product must meet successfully all the hostile tests. It must prove its superiority.

"Then follows a stage of total apathy, when everybody apparently conspires to remain silent. Those who know the facts concerning the discovery and know nothing against it just keep quiet or say, 'Let this new thing die a natural death.' Those who don't know the facts lose their interest in opposing it.

"However, there always comes to a really valuable and significant discovery that interesting third stage—a stage in which many people, including the former critics and apathetic observers, tumble over each other trying to boost the discoverer, his discovery, and everything connected with the project. Once it has survived the second phase, everyone rushes in to exploit it, and you can be sure that the commercial development will take care of itself."

As Professor Carver offered each of his new products for display someone inevitably asked, "Now you have it. What are you going to do with it?"

And he answered, "I've done all I intend to. My interest is scientific and not financial. If an investigator goes into business, he ceases to be an investigator—that is the business of the businessman."

"How are these products to be placed on the market?"

"I don't know. It's for the people to take these products

and create the supply and demand. There must be a demand for every article supplied."

Cost figures were no concern of his, and ideas came crowding so fast he lacked time to work on any one thing too long. Mr. W. Wade Moss, a young chemist who spent some time in his laboratory, wrote in the *Manufacturers' Record,* July 1930, that the professor was a prospector seeking gold, but when he had found it he left it to miners to dig for the metal. He accomplished the thing he was intended to do, which was to inspire others, and he abandoned each new trail at the stage where its value became obvious, that they might pick it up and carry it along.

Very seldom did he take out any patents, and for much the same reason. If he attempted to patent every product he would be surrounded by patent ghouls and would get little else done. But, chiefly, he did not want to benefit specific persons; his products should be available to all.

Though the professor's mail was phenomenally large, he tried to answer it promptly. He was always ready to help anyone who asked. From all over the United States, from Australia, South America, the Philippines, China, India, Africa, Japan, and Russia, came emissaries or letters. An American from Mohandas Gandhi's ashrama came to consult him about improving the Indian diet by the use of peanuts, vegetables, and nuts growing in India.

Sometimes the letters inclosed checks. Perhaps a Florida peanut grower's crop had been damaged by disease; Professor Carver identified the fungus and suggested control measures, and the man forwarded a check as recompense. Or a cotton mill acknowledged its indebtedness with a hundred dollars. Back would go the check, in which he had no interest, and the solution, whether it was how to dye cement or turn peanuts into linoleum. It might take time to assemble the information for a reply, but he could not write a letter fast enough to return money. There was no charge; his aid was without price.

The best things, said he, could not be bought or sold. Their value lay in human effort and devotion; the medium of exchange was brotherhood, and the compensation was service. As for the additional money, what would be the good of it to him? His business was to create things, not buy or sell them. Having no use for more, he would only be troubled about the proper means of its disposal, and this would distract him from his work.

Professor Carver still received the fifteen hundred dollars a year he had received when Booker T. Washington had asked him to join forces in helping to build a race, but even his salary checks meant so little that months would go by without his depositing them.

He was profoundly disturbed by the emphasis most other people placed upon money. When Julius Rosenwald presented the teachers who had been at Tuskegee a certain number of years with an honorarium, all were jubilant except Professor Carver. He bluntly called it a handout and declined his, though politely. He appreciated the spirit which had actuated the gift, but his attitude was the same as when he was a boy and someone had pitched him a quarter for a five-cent job. It smacked of the days when white people threw a coin to a slave very much as they would throw a bone to a dog.

This was the sort of "oddness" that continually surprised other people, and he thought despairingly, "How long must one be with a person and still not know any more about him than on a first meeting?" To him, it was entirely reasonable that he should want to be paid only the salary the school had agreed his services were worth.

He had come to the conclusion that the unthinking and exaggerated value placed upon money was the most destructive single influence in the world. Where money could be put to a constructive use, however, he welcomed it in amounts small enough to be comprehended by the people with whom he had to deal. When a friend sent him a small Thanksgiving present, he replied that he himself had plenty to eat, so he proposed to dispense it as he had similar sums.

For instance, he had given a dollar to a former student who had been unable to make his way at his trade, saying, "I want to see what you can do with this." The man had purchased a hen for fifty cents, a setting of eggs for fifteen cents, and spent the rest for feed. When he reported to Professor Carver, he had saved fifty-one dollars, which he had paid on a lot, and had seventy-five hens still bringing him an income. This, according to the professor, was a proper expenditure of money, because it enabled the man to earn, and only that which was truly earned had any lasting value.

The work of Professor Carver had reached the ears of Thomas A. Edison, deaf to the common sounds which stimulated the auditory nerves of most mortals, but hearing acutely the inaudible sounds of progress in science. He wrote from Florida and sent Miller Rees Hutcheson, his chief engineer and right-hand man, to talk with the professor. He himself planned to stop at Tuskegee on his way North, but an emergency called him back earlier than he had expected. However, on the strength of Mr. Hutcheson's report, he made a formal offer for Professor Carver to join his laboratory staff. The salary named was in six figures, but the professor was asked not to divulge its exact amount, so he never did.

This fabulous sum presented no temptation. His salary was enough for his modest purposes, and in computing "enough" what was the difference between one and one hundred thousand dollars? He simply stated, "There was nothing to talk over, and I thanked him in a letter."

His reason for declining seemed adequate. He was a solitary worker and would be out of place in a large organization so foreign to him, no matter how important it might be. For the same reason and in the same gentle manner he continued to decline all other invitations to move elsewhere. He still had too much to do at Tuskegee. He had been brought there by Washington, and he could not be faithless, now that Washington was dead.

Once he had given out his information on a product, he

usually dropped it; he must go on, and had no time to bother about who was going to receive the credit. Some people lived from what others accomplished. One man came with an offer from one of the great rubber companies. He himself was not a chemist, but he was in a position to command the services of research men. And when they were finished with a problem, the result was his, while they remained anonymous.

Professor Carver could not accept the offer. He had no desire to receive anything personally, but he did want his race to be recognized through him. He had devoted twenty years to the Southern colored farmer, and, as he said, "If I were to go, my work would not be known as mine, and my race would get no credit. I want it to have the credit of whatever I may do."

His eminence in his chosen field of knowledge was first recognized abroad when, in November 1916, he was elected a Fellow of the Royal Society of Arts, an honorable scientific body of Great Britain, founded in 1754. Professor Carver never sought to determine how this had come about, but he believed the suggestion could be traced to Sir Harry H. Johnston, who had spent considerable time studying the work of the "Wizard of Tuskegee" while on a visit to America some years before.

This distinguished novelist, naturalist, and expert on African affairs paid a signal tribute to George W. Carver in his autobiography, *The Story of My Life:* "One of the most interesting personages at Tuskegee was Professor Carver, a full-blooded Negro, who spoke English as though he had been brought up at Oxford. He was the Professor of Botany. I had not time to sound his knowledge of the botany of Africa or Tropical Asia, but no one I ever met in the New World taught me so much about the plant distribution in North and South America."

Again in his book, *The Negro in the New World,* Sir Harry said: "He (Professor Carver) is, as regards complexion and features, an absolute Negro; but in the cut of his clothes, the accent of his speech, the soundness of his science, he might be the professor of botany not at Tuskegee, but at Oxford or at Cambridge. Any European botanist of distinction, after ten minutes' conversation with the man, instinctively would deal with him *de puissance en puissance.*"

# CHAPTER XIX

## *"Go Tell Doubting Thomas"*

FOR SOME YEARS Professor Carver had shown his products at country fairs, and a few Washington officials were acquainted with certain aspects of his work, but the pool of general awareness was still small, and he was unknown to businessmen—even to those who were attempting to make their fortunes from peanuts.

In 1919 the acreage devoted to peanuts, first planted commercially in 1917, had been greatly stepped up; more of these little legumes were being consumed than in all the preceding years of their history in the United States. Despite the increase in peanut growing, Southern industry lagged far behind. One spokesman deplored the fact that though more than 25 per cent of the home-grown variety came from Alabama, the state could not boast a single processing plant, whereas New York, where the peanut was not raised at all, had the largest plant in the world.

Southern peanut men recognized that though the domestic industry was valued at approximately eighty million dollars, it was as yet only in its infancy; they wanted it to continue expanding in a hurry. Toward this end they met in May at Atlanta and organized the United Peanut Associations of America.

One of its first purposes was to build up a greater demand through advertising. But one member intelligently remarked that the public, and themselves also, should first be educated; some people thought the peanut grew on bushes, some were afraid of Oriental peanuts because "they might bring in bubonic plague," and almost no one knew anything about the properties of the peanut. This bold spirit went on to make a suggestion. "There is an old colored man in the Tuskegee Institute by the name of Carver. I went down to see him and had two hours of the most interesting time in his laboratory. This old man has produced from the peanut a peanut milk, though he disclaimed at once that he did not expect to put the cow out of business." He proposed they should have Carver come to a meeting and describe the things he had made.

"The old man" at this time was about fifty-five but, since his hair was gray, to most Southern minds he fitted into the "uncle" category.

Some of the members were horrified at the suggestion. What! Have a nigger tell them about their business? But others were open-minded enough to be willing to take a chance, and they proved to be in a majority. After some argument it was finally agreed that Carver might show them what he had done with the peanut.

The United Peanut Associations were to meet in Montgomery in September 1920, to deliberate upon the immediate safeguard needed by such an infant industry. The Republicans were back in power and about to institute a new tariff bill. It looked as though the cradle of Democracy, as the Democratic South proudly called itself, were going to be left out.

Nearly half of the American-consumed peanuts, or about thirty million bushels, were imported from the Far East, China grown and Japanese processed. The present duty was only three eighths of a cent a pound on unshelled and three fourths on shelled. This afforded no protection whatever, they said. They feared Southern farmers might have to discontinue raising peanuts if they had to compete with Oriental importations on these terms; they required at least four and five cents respectively, a levy which would more nearly equal the difference in the cost of production in the countries which employed coolie labor and the cost of production in the United States.

It would not be an easy matter to secure this increase of duty, because Southern congressmen were likely to hew to the party line and reaffirm the traditional policy of the Democratic party in favor of a tariff for revenue only.

The United Peanut Associations foregathered on Monday, September 13, at the Exchange Hotel, the same building from which the Confederate Congress had sent the telegram instructing the batteries to fire on Fort Sumter. Senator Oscar W. Underwood and Congressman J. Thomas Heflin offered their views, not too encouragingly, to the group of shirt-sleeved men who had removed their coats. It was almost unbearably hot.

Tuesday morning early Professor Carver arrived in Montgomery. He was an expert packer. He could fit an astonishing amount into a small space, but his twenty-five or thirty bottles nevertheless bore considerable weight. Laden with his heavy cases, he presented himself at the hotel.

The doorman interposed his bulk. "What do you want here?"

"I want to see the president of the Peanut Associations."

"They're over at the City Hall."

So Professor Carver picked up his burden and trudged over to the City Hall in the stifling heat. In response to his inquiries he was sent to one person after another and finally was informed that the peanut men had been there but had left. He lugged the cases back again to the hotel. The doorman would not admit him—no niggers allowed.

"But they are expecting me!"

The doorman shook his head.

"Well, then, will you be kind enough to take a note in? I must get in touch with them."

He wrote a few lines explaining his non-appearance, and a bellhop disappeared with it inside while Professor Carver waited outside on the sidewalk. At last he was taken around the back way and up the freight elevator to the room where the meeting was being held. Although he was tired and perspiring after an hour of tramping and blundering around and waiting, no hint of his discomfort appeared in his manner as he stood before the peanut men to present his gift which would bring them prosperity.

Professor Carver opened his cases and extracted bottle after bottle, making known its contents as he did so: leather stains, from intense black to tan and russet; wood stains—peacock green and malachite green among many others; Worcestershire sauce. He informed them that a three-and-a-half-ounce glass held enough peanuts to make a pint of very rich milk, or a quart of "blue john" or skim milk. He held up buttermilk; cream made for ice cream, smooth and fine; evaporated milk; fruit punch.

He explained one of the reasons why he liked to hear the country folk talk—he could learn much from them. "My mother," one man had told him, "used to make the finest coffee out of peanuts."

"I asked her about it," went on Professor Carver, "because I had tried and was about to give up. She said take it out and let it cool and then roast it again. So I began an intermittent process and found that developed the flavor." Then he showed them peanut coffee, instant coffee, instant coffee with cream.

"I thank you for being allowed to contribute in a small way," he finished, "and wish you Godspeed."

*The Peanut Promoter* for October 1920 reported that the biggest thing at the Montgomery Peanut Convention had been the address of Professor Carver. "Coming before the convention with doubts lingering in the minds of the audience as to the advisability of having one of the negro race come before them, he soon had their minds off of that thought and closely following every statement made giving the results of his experiments with peanuts.

"After he had concluded they forgot that he was of the negro race and were loud in their approval. A gentleman in the audience promptly arose and suggested that the Association offer to Mr. Carver any assistance that he may need that can be given by the Association in securing patents for his products. This was unanimously adopted, for which Mr. Carver thanked the members. Dr. Carver verily won his way into the hearts of the peanut men."

Recess was declared and all came forward to examine the products. When they had resumed their seats, Congressman H. B. Steagall spoke. "If I had been here yesterday when Senator Underwood and Tom Heflin were addressing this convention I should have felt at home and free to speak without embarrassment, but following the speaker who has just addressed this meeting I certainly do feel out of place and greatly embarrassed, and especially so if I attempted to talk about peanuts in a way to instruct anybody. No man who has heard this address here today could stand in the face of the argument that here is an industry not profitable to the section of the country directly interested in the growing of peanuts and their protection, but here is an industry that touches the necessities of life throughout every nook and corner of the nation, and certainly if there ever was an infant industry that could plead a case before Congress, certainly we ought to make out a case perfect before the Ways and Means Committee and make out a case of protection for this industry. When the time comes that this question must be thrashed out before the American Congress I propose to see that Professor Carver is there in order that he may instruct them a little about peanuts, as he has done here on this occasion." (Applause)

The peanut men put on their coats, and the meeting ended with a resolution "thanking the Chamber of Commerce for the hospitality extended by the grand and glorious city of Montgomery."

Professor Carver packed up his bottles once more, grasped the cases in either hand, and hastened to the station to catch his train for home.

The following January Professor Carver received a telegram from the Peanut Associations which read, "Want you in Washington morning of twentieth depending on you to show Ways and Means Committee possibilities of the peanut." He replied that he would be there, and he was, to attend the hearings of the General Tariff Revision before the Committee of Ways and Means of the House of Representatives.

Most of Saturday, the twenty-second, he sat listening, becoming more and more shocked and more and more horrified. He had never been in such a place before, but he had expected the proceedings of what he had assumed was an august body to be carried on with dignity and decorum. Instead, he found the men offering argument were harassed and bulldozed and treated as though they were scamps. He was extremely embarrassed to hear people talk to one another like that, virtually calling each other liars. He soon realized that they had all submitted briefs two weeks in advance, which were now being picked to pieces. No one had told him he should have submitted a brief. Almost in consternation he thought, "Do I have to go up against that?"

It was nearly closing time, four o'clock, and the committee was listless and tired and bored. The members had been listening all day to figures and statistics on walnuts and pecans. Word was sent over to clear the docket immediately. They brightened up a little; it would soon be finished.

The Virginia Carolina Co-operative Peanut Exchange attested that a protective tariff on peanuts was the only thing that would save the sandy land farmers from ruin.

Then George W. Carver's name was called. Observing a Negro making his way forward, one Congressman remarked, "I suppose if you have plenty of peanuts and watermelons you're perfectly happy?" Professor Carver was accustomed to this sort of gibe and ignored it.

As he reached the platform, Chairman Joseph W. Fordney warned, "Your time has been cut to ten minutes."

The professor knew he could not begin to show his exhibit in that length of time; it would take almost as long to unpack. Nevertheless, he began to open his bag of tricks, talking as he did so, employing his old technique of making his audience laugh. "I've been asked to tell you something about the extension of the peanut, but we'll have to hurry if we are to extend it, because in ten minutes you will tell me to stop."

Confused questioning was tossed at him, which consumed precious time, and he was cautioned, "Three minutes are gone." He had been worried and had not known quite what to do; ugliness always made him nervous. But now a familiar imp entered into him and he began to feel devilish. He grinned disarmingly. "You took those three minutes, so I suppose you'll give them back to me?" A ripple of laughter broke out.

Smoothly but swiftly he continued to unpack. Out came flours, hulls ground and made into meal for burnishing tin-plate, and a chocolate-dipped confection. He held up one of these, saying, "You don't know how delicious this is so I will taste it for you," and popped it into his mouth. When the laughter had died he launched into his theme: "The sweet potato and the peanut are twin brothers and should not be separated. If all other foods were destroyed, these would provide a balanced ration for man." He showed them a sweet-potato syrup which could be used as a binder for the peanut bar, then he pulled out stock-food hay, bisque for ice cream, meal, a diabetic breakfast food.

The professor was barely started and his time was over, but Congressman John N. Garner spoke up, "I think this is very interesting. I think his time should be extended."

Approval being unanimous, Professor Carver continued. Peanut skins, he said, had some of the properties of quinine and from them also he had extracted thirty different dyes.

One member questioned, "Could we get too much peanuts?" They began to argue among themselves regarding the respective merits of oleo and butter and the possibility of antagonizing dairymen by the production of too much peanut oleo.

Mr. Garner broke in by asking, "What do you know about the tariff?"

"Tariff?" replied Professor Carver. "This is all the tariff means—to put the other fellow out of business."

The committee burst into uproarious merriment, Mr. Garner jumped out of his chair and spun around on his good leg, and Mr. Fordney exploded, "Go ahead, brother, your time is unlimited."

Imperturbably, Professor Carver continued. Some time ago he had started to extract milk from the peanut. He held up the bottle of milk, on which everyone could see cream had risen.

The argument began again about the advisability of a tax which would allow peanuts to compete with dairy products. When it had subsided a little Professor Carver lifted another bottle. "This," he said, "is for ice cream."

"How does it go in a punch?" called someone.

"I will show you some punches."

Then he pulled out buttermilk and evaporated milk. He explained that the peanut made one of the best cereal coffees and showed one already combined with cream and sugar. He held up a bottle of Worcestershire sauce, pointing out that the original had been based on soybeans, but the peanut sauce was just as good. Then came cheese and an oil which was a by-product of milk. This, he said, he had just made and was looking forward to its future use with a great deal of interest.

Someone asked, "Do you make all these products yourself?"

"Yes," was the answer. "That's what a research laboratory is for."

"Haven't you done something with sweet potatoes?" called someone else.

"One hundred and seven to date."

Mr. Garner spoke again. "I did not catch that statement. Will you repeat it, please?"

"Yes indeed," said Professor Carver. "I said one hundred and seven, but I have not finished working on them yet.

The peanut will beat the sweet potato by far. I have barely begun on it."

He went on pulling rabbits from his inexhaustible hat. "Here is the latest thing, a face cream soft and fine as almond cream. It is a vanishing cream and will take any perfume. And here is one for massaging infants to fatten them. It is much more readily absorbed by the skin than olive oil."

In rapid succession out came a bottle of ink, dehydrated milk flakes which could be dissolved in hot water to form milk again, a relish, mock oysters, curds which could hardly be distinguished from meat. Professor Carver had captured his audience so securely that he suggested with a wholly spurious meekness, "I have two dozen or so others, such as wood dyes and stains, but if my time is up I'd better stop."

Nobody paid any attention. Instead, Mr. Garner reverted to his previous statement about sweet potatoes and peanuts. "I understood you to say that if all other foods were destroyed a person could live on sweet potatoes and peanuts?"

"That is correct, because they contain the necessary vitamins. Together they form a natural food for man and beast. There is everything here to strengthen and nourish and keep the body alive and healthy."

Professor Carver had talked for an hour and three quarters instead of ten minutes. His listeners were curious to know more about this man who could so hold their interest.

"Mr. Carver, what school did you attend?"

"Iowa State. Secretary of Agriculture Wilson was my instructor for six years."

Congressman John F. Carew voiced the opinion of all. "You have rendered the committee a great service."

Mr. Garner added, "I think he is entitled to the thanks of the committee." One and all rose to their feet and applauded, standing.

Mr. Fordney polished off this most remarkable tribute with, "We want to compliment you, sir, on the way you have handled your subject."

While the professor was tucking away his bottles and jars Congressman Alben W. Barkley asked whether he could send them a brief. "The proceedings are ready for the printer now," he said, "but we'll hold them up if you can get it here. We'd like to have that."

Accordingly, on the train that night the professor wrote out a statement beginning, "These products may be of little or no value as far as the paramount issue confronting your committee is concerned." And it ended, "My appearance was not to discuss the tariff. I have nothing to sell; I will manufacture nothing. I simply came to add my little bit if possible. I feel sure you gentlemen will guard and put proper restrictions upon every interest that arises in harmful competition with ours without any suggestions of mine."

Though he had not discussed the tariff at all, his exhibit had been a far more powerful argument than any number of words and figures he or anybody else could have produced. As a result, the committee wrote into the Fordney-McCumber Bill the highest tariff rate the peanut industry ever had —three and four cents a pound for unshelled and shelled peanuts respectively. Undoubtedly he had performed a signal service for the South.

The peanut men, through their trade magazine, *The Peanut World,* quite genuinely and sincerely acknowledged that indebtedness in the May 1921 issue: "With profound pleasure and pride we dedicate an entire page to that incomparable genius to whose tireless energies and inquisitive mind the South and the country owe so much in the development of the peanut trades, arts, and industry. His contribution to the common fund of human knowledge in the field to which he has devoted his life is simply immeasurable. In the mental laboratory with which he has been so generously endowed he has been enabled, through the physical laboratory, scientifically applied, to be a benefactor not only to his own but to all races. He has been virtually a miracle worker, and we believe *The Peanut World* would be remiss in its duty did it not pay him this tribute, small in comparison to what he has done for all of us."

Verily Professor Carver had won his way into the hearts of the peanut men; he had struck oil.

They did not want to lose their grasp upon him, and the next fall invited him to show his peanut products at the Greater Four County Fair at Suffolk, Virginia. The Suffolk Negro Business League presented him with a set of china dishes, one large and four small, shaped and painted to look like the half shells of peanuts. They could have been used as ash receivers, but Professor Carver did not smoke. Tobacco, said he, was neither food nor drink; man became a part of what he took in, and narcotics did nothing to build up the system. Furthermore, if God had intended the nose to be used as a chimney He would have turned the nostrils up.

So his dishes were used to receive dust, but he was grateful, nevertheless, for the appreciation the gift signified.

Sporadic recognition of Professor Carver on his home ground began slowly to come. A few of the brighter citizens of the South awoke to the fact that cultivating Professor Carver, for whom they had an intimate, personal affection, would be good business. A former governor, a railroad president, the president of a chain of stores, and a former mayor of Tuskegee, organized the Carver Products Company, to serve as a holding company for various operating companies which would manufacture, among other things, paints and stains. They included in the contract a clause stating that Professor Carver should receive 10 per cent of the net profit. The venture set out with big ideas, and they actually started to incorporate the Carver Paint Company, but no one individual would put up sufficient money to earn money, and none would leave his own business and devote himself exclusively to that. The Carver Products Company died before it had properly commenced.

But Mr. Ernest W. Thompson of Tuskegee remained the professor's individual, assiduous companion—though never so far as the dining room—producing him here and there where his products could be pushed to the fore. To give them wider publicity before a wider group than fair goers, an exhibit was arranged in March 1923 on the roof garden of the Hotel Cecil in Atlanta. The West Point Railroad sent a special car to the Institute to transport the professor, his boxes, and a few pictures painted with clay colors, and Mr. Thompson accompanied him. There for three days at three-thirty each afternoon he lectured and demonstrated peanuts, sweet potatoes, and clay, to all comers, and they were many.

One Atlanta paper wrote up an interview in some amazement at the spirit of youth which animated him, as though he were a young man just starting out in life. He was equally amazed at this point of view. He was only sixty-three and of course he was eager to get certain things done! Why should he not have vivacity?

As a matter of fact, laughter eddied about him most of the time. When the others teased him or played pranks on him, he would go after them swiftly, catch and spank them soundly, enjoying this foolishness as much as they. He was full of anecdotes and stories—many of them on himself—which he told with gusto. He retained his gift for mimicry, though he never could quite twist his tongue to the Southern dialect.

A constant source of joking revolved about his habits of dressing. They had not improved. Just before he had set out for Washington someone had suggested that he buy a new necktie. He had promptly retorted, "A new necktie won't help me to answer their questions."

He seemed to cling with especial fervor to an old, shabby cap. His younger companions at Atlanta hunted all around for a silk cap, and finally paid seven dollars for the best the city could produce. Then they chucked his old one out the window.

Some sort of function was to be held the last evening, and Mr. Thompson went to the professor's room to see whether he were dressed. The professor was looking for his cap. He was persuaded as far as the front of the hotel, and there he balked. He sat on the running board of the limousine drawn up to take him to the party, and refused to budge. He was positively not going to wear the new hat! "I've stood for your smoking and drinking, but I will not stand for stealing. I want my cap!" They had to give in and went hunting in the alley until they had found the old, disreputable object. And not until it was safely on his head again would Professor Carver enter the car.

Seven years after Professor Carver had been elected to Fellowship in the Royal Society he was the recipient of another honor. This, too, was more classical, though no more welcome, than the thank-yous of businessmen. On September 4, 1923, he went to Kansas City to receive from the hands of the Attorney General of Kansas the Spingarn Medal for distinguished research in agricultural chemistry. This medal, established by the author and publisher, Joel Elias Spingarn, in 1914, was intended to be a stimulus to the ambition of colored youth, but it had the further purpose of focusing the attention of white Americans on the achievements of Negroes, and the professor esteemed the award as tending to remove bitter racial disparagements.

Shortly afterward, at the invitation and under the auspices of the Y.M.C.A., he made a lecture tour of white colleges in North and South Carolina. Though he spoke not a word concerning race but adhered strictly to that most impersonal of subjects, science, its primary aim was interracial good will.

No colored person had ever stood on those platforms before. Since this was an experiment that had never been attempted in the South, the Y.M.C.A. secretary who accompanied Professor Carver part of the distance asked the heads of the various colleges to write him personally what they believed the response had been.

The replies, which were not intended for the professor's eyes, varied according to the traditions of the different schools. One president wrote: "His humor, his profoundly religious spirit, his humanitarian impulses, and his wonderful discoveries and knowledge fascinated our students. He will create in our white people a deeper respect for the possibilities of the colored race wherever he goes." And another: "To see a man as black as Dr. Carver and yet as able as he is, comes as a distinct shock to Southern boys and jars them out of their conviction of the Negroes' absolute inferiority."

But by no means all were thus jarred. At one school the faculty were afraid to attend and, in another, many of the students cut chapel rather than listen to him. The head of the latter offered the criticism that Carver took too long to get to his subject. The reason should have been obvious. Professor Carver could practically feel the icicles dripping from the hall, and it took him some little time to warm his audience up to the point of losing their antagonism. Presently the ice began to melt under his spell, and he had a very pleasant reception afterward.

For two weeks he maintained his barnstorming trip, riding by day in dirty Jim Crow cars and speaking every evening. Once he was so tired he fell asleep by an open window and when he reached Spartanburg he had a sore throat. As his lecture ended his voice did also. From then on he had a very trying time, having his throat treated at each new town by a different doctor in the daytime so he could be heard at night. He kept going, wading through the lecture periods as best he could.

The constriction of his vocal cords was due in part to nervousness; it was not easy thus to wear himself down before audiences which were practically always hostile at the outset, and a tremendous exertion was required to maintain the light touch which would win each one over. He had broadened the sympathies of some, but he had to leave again with many still unwon.

His only comment on the tour was typical in its disregard of personal trials and immediate disappointments and its emphasis on the long view, which would surely bring about a change for the better: "The most gratifying thing I have found in my years of work is the ever-increasing demand of the youth of the country for knowledge. The crying out for education is the greatest assurance of the strong foundation now being laid for our America of the future."

Professor Carver returned to Tuskegee with his throat closed and a recurrence of the laryngitis to which he had always been subject. Johns Hopkins Hospital could offer little encouragement in the way of a cure. Nobody knew what to do for it, and it persisted way into the summer.

One Sunday morning he heard a visiting missionary, who himself had come home to die of tuberculosis, describe the conversion of a little girl just before her untimely death from pulmonary disease and malnutrition. The sad little story touched Professor Carver deeply, as another evidence of a wasted life. Perhaps the peanut could have prevented this waste. He did not hear the rest of the sermon; instead, the question, "Can't you do something?" kept repeating itself in his mind. He did not usually perform any work on Sunday, but this time he went straight to his laboratory and started an experiment. In a very short time he had a possible remedy.

Creosote, a powerful antiseptic, had long been accepted as an integral part of the treatment of pulmonary cases, but when emulsified with cod-liver oil it was so abominable to the taste that many patients could not swallow it. Professor Carver blended beechwood creosote with peanut juices in a stable emulsion. This was actually pleasant to take and combined the properties of an excellent medicine with a nourishing food which would assist the process of cure. He treated himself with the preparation, and it succeeded in curing the hacking cough from which he had suffered for six months.

The Women's Board of Domestic Missions of the Reformed Church in America was to hold its forty-second anniversary meeting in New York November 19, 1924, at the Marble Collegiate Church on Fifth Avenue. The professor, who might be considered an unofficial missionary in the South, was asked to be one of the speakers.

Before this audience of some five hundred, three or four

individuals talked on mission work among Indians and Southern poor whites, and then Professor Carver rose. At his appearance, a titter rippled through the church, but shame immediately silenced it.

He was to address a religious body and had prepared his thoughts accordingly. This mission, like his own, was to give aid to human beings in need, according to Christ's precepts. To these people he could speak freely what was in his heart, and for the first time publicly reveal his spiritual conception of his own work.

He came to his lectures straight from his laboratory and, consequently, the latest discovery in which he had there been absorbed usually still held his conscious attention. So he told of the conversion and death of the child who, he felt, had died needlessly when on every hand was growing the peanut, the magic plant that might have saved her life, and described its efficacy in clearing up his own cough.

The audience that first had laughed was absorbed by his earnestness as he spoke of God's bounty and man's indifference to the great gifts; man had not touched the fringe of earth's possibilities. "Thou madest him to have dominion over the works of thy hands; thou hast put all things under his feet." What had been done with the peanut and sweet potato could be done with everything else, because God had said that every herb and plant could be made of use to man. "God is going to reveal things to us that He never revealed before if we put our hand in His," he said. "No books ever go into my laboratory. The thing that I am to do and the way of doing it come to me. I never have to grope for methods; the method is revealed at the moment I am inspired to create something new. Without God to draw aside the curtain I would be helpless."

After a brief silence, forgetting the nature of the building in which they were seated, the audience burst spontaneously into applause.

The Baltimore *Sun* next morning considered the event sufficiently noteworthy to merit an editorial and said it was refreshing to find a chemist who did not feel it necessary to bar God out of the workshop. And it was pleasant to find him devoting himself not to the devil's work of producing destructive combinations, but to new means of meeting human needs.

However, inimical and contemptuous forces were, as usual, in action. The New York *Times* also elevated the news item to the rank of an editorial. But this editorial writer, who had not been present, had placed a different interpretation on secondhand information: "It is for chemists to determine to what extent he [Dr. Carver] is worthy of recognition. He seems to have done useful work. And therefore it can be claimed that he has shown abilities of a sort not present in many of his race. It is therefore to be regretted that he should use language that reveals a complete lack of the scientific spirit. Real chemists do not scorn books and they do not ascribe their successes, when they have any, to 'inspiration.' Talk of that sort will simply bring ridicule on an admirable institution and on the race. All who hear it will be inclined to doubt, perhaps unjustly, that Dr. Carver's chemistry is appreciably different from the astronomy of the once-famous Reverend John Jasper who so firmly maintained that the sun went around a flat earth."

Professor Carver was bewildered and hurt by the misinterpretation. He had not said that inspiration took the place of books. What he planned to do was not in books, so why take them along? Creative chemistry was so named because no one had created the same thing before. But the creative chemist had to be thoroughly well grounded, having all the science he had learned from books and experience in the forefront of his mind and in his fingers before he could see the possibilities. Then he could take what he had pulled to pieces and put it together again in the new way desired. The result depended on the individual chemist's ingenuity and patience—and the help of God. This was not conceit, quite the contrary.

The professor had no intention of answering the *Times;*

he had no wish to engage in argument. But Mr. Thompson insisted that the matter was too important to let pass; he must take the opportunity to set the paper right. Under this urging he wrote a letter:

I regret that such a gross misunderstanding should arise as to what was meant by Divine inspiration. Inspiration is not at variance with information; in fact, the more information one has the greater will be the inspiration. In evolving new creations I am wondering of what value a book would be to the creator if he is not a master of analytical work, both qualitative and quantitative.

He had seen taros and yautias in the market, and had seen also many possibilities in developing them.

I know of no one who has ever worked with these roots in this way. I know of no book from which I can get this information, yet I will have no trouble in doing it. Proverbs 3–6: "In all thy ways acknowledge Him, and He shall direct thy paths." Intelligent people now believe in a God. I am not alone in this. May God deepen and strengthen our religion as a race rather than destroy it.

The *Times,* which was unable to prove the non-existence of God, did not print the letter, but the press services picked up the story of Professor Carver's talk and carried it the length and breadth of the land, into the foreign-language papers, and as far as the *Manchester Guardian* in England and the Colombo *Daily News* in Ceylon. It appeared under such headlines as Chemist Attributes Success to Divinity, Gives Credit to God, Negro Professor Aided by Heaven, Inspired by Providence, Colored Savant Credits Heaven, Credit to Divine Revelations, God His Book of Knowledge, God Reveals Secrets, Divine Guidance, Credits Divine End, Divine Inspiration, Divine Aid, Divine Impulsion, and so on, and so on, and so on.

With the too common impetuosity of the press, some reporters included in their stories the statement that Professor Carver was on the trail of a "cure" for tuberculosis. This he promptly, categorically, and publicly denied, but it received the customary fate of denials—it was ignored.

Professor Carver left the controversy as to whether scientists were commonly atheistic or agnostic to the newspapers; they could continue arguing the so-called conflict between the scientist and religionist which existed, some believed, not so much in the minds of either, but in the minds of the stand-bys who wanted to see a fight. As a matter of fact, the individual astronomer, chemist, or botanist might doubt dogmas and avoid churches, but a fair share could be found who agreed with Einstein that no legitimate conflict could exist; Einstein stated his view precisely, that "Science without religion is lame, and religion without science is blind."

The professor went serenely back to his labor at Tuskegee the day after the lecture. He had a little allegory which applied to skeptics and finished them off neatly: "Here is a thirty-candle-power light bulb, and I place beneath it a burning candle. In order for the light of the candle to be noticed it will be necessary for the light bulb to be put out or for the candle to be increased thirty times. It will be much easier to put out the bulb than it will be to build up the candle. The same is true of some people. When one outshines the others, they do all they can to discredit his work. The candle is the little bit of folk—too narrow and with no concept."

Whether newspaper readers agreed or disagreed with Professor Carver's religious beliefs, his name had spread far beyond the circle of those who knew him merely as a friend of the farmer. But this sort of fame did not abate in the slightest his continued services to the South.

Early in 1925 a sort of super-fair, the Southern States Exposition, was held in Grand Central Palace in New York, its purpose being to present the potentialities of the South to Northern capital. No such fair would be complete without Professor Carver, and he was invited to show his wares. His exhibit in a modest nook of the building attracted wide attention.

When reporters thronged about him, he stood in a corner with his hands folded, his bright eyes searching the faces before him. "Are any of you from the *Times?*" he asked suspiciously. He had grown wary of press misinterpretation, and he did not wish to be classed among those who, for the sake of fame or money, rushed into print with the first ideas that came into their heads.

Though he was wont to say that Science was Truth, he recognized also that man's part in it was merely a groping toward that Truth. Anyone was at liberty to make a supposition. If he were sure of his facts he would say "yes" or "no," but if he were not sure he would say, "probably so," "I hope so," or "investigations to date have proved so and so." He might have been working on something for months, maybe years, but not until he was thoroughly satisfied would he give out the information. Then they could fire into it as much as they pleased. He was exceedingly careful not to make a direct statement—even though it might seem correct at the moment —from which there could be no appeal and which could be upset by the light of further knowledge the next day or the next year. This should be true of all scientific advance, but was particularly necessary in his case.

His discoveries, with the exception of his mycological work, did not properly belong in scientific journals. They were not revolutionary in themselves. Anyone with the proper education could milk the peanut or abstract paper from suitable fibers, or rubber from the sweet potato or any other vine which secreted latex. His special contribution was to expose these hidden properties in plants to the public view and, by dramatizing them, serve as a signpost pointing the way for those who had the facilities to incorporate them into the contemporary pattern of living. All this he would do, but he did not by any means wish himself to be dramatized at the expense of his integrity.

At the Southern States Exposition *The Manufacturers' Record* offered a prize of five thousand dollars to the state showing the greatest manufacturing possibilities and, with Professor Carver on hand, of course it went to Alabama.

What happened to that five thousand dollars? The professor wrote to the Alabama chairman, but no answer was forthcoming. Nobody seemed to know where it went or what had happened to it. Presumably it was turned over to somebody who did not know any more about what to do with it than was already being done and used it as any other little donation would be. He drew a moral from this incident. So many people in the South claimed, "All we need is money." But if each one had ten thousand dollars he would not be a bit different. Money was not what was needed. Suppose large sums were just turned over to the South? What would they be spent for? You can spend wealth, said Professor Carver; you can get rid of it, but not usefully unless you have planned how it can make you grow. What the South actually lacked was manufacturing wisdom.

# CHAPTER XX

## *"Let Us Break Bread Together"*

THE SPIRITUAL WOUNDS of a Negro are as infinite in number as the sparrows that fall, and are no more to be counted. Over and over, on trains or in restaurants, Professor Carver would see a white person advancing upon him with a determined air and think, with dread, "Oh dear! Here it comes!" To his retiring nature the conspicuousness which arose from his being a Negro was painful in the extreme. His personal welfare was the least of his concerns, but he did shrink from the embarrassment of being publicly singled out for insult. It shocked him each time he encountered it, no matter how thoroughly he had braced himself to meet it.

None of this, however, stopped him from going where he felt he must go; if he had something to do, he went ahead and did it. Prodigious feats of lecturing and traveling were performed by Professor Carver during the '20s.

Such simple questions as where one is to eat or sleep, which present themselves to most travelers, were knotty subjects to him in the Southern states where a Negro's right to comforts and conveniences was not recognized. If he were thirsty he could not drink from a public fountain, but must climb down the stairs to the basement to a fountain plainly marked "For Colored"; and if a meeting were being held on an upper story he must climb up the stairs or go round to the freight elevator.

There was always the problem of where he was to spend the night. Local laws often prohibited him from sleeping under the same roof with a white man. The larger cities had colored Y.M.C.A.s, but in the smaller towns he had sometimes to tramp for hours to find a place in which to stop. He was truly tired by that time, and, the accommodations being decidedly inferior, he could not always rest well even then.

Professor Carver's trips were usually a curious mixture. While he was in transit to or from the place of meeting he experienced extreme discomfort, both physical and mental; with a strange irony he could never escape, he might have to sit, desperately sick and longing for a place to rest, even in the big public lobby of a hotel while the management was deciding he could not be admitted. But the very next day, while he was on the platform, he would receive the greatest acclaim. No matter how carefully the numbers of his hearers had been estimated in advance, the hall chosen was seldom large enough; often there were more outside than in. Charmed with his dry humor and whimsicalities, audiences listened and marveled, though he observed no one rushing to meet the challenge of producing a better South.

Though Professor Carver had to catch innumerable trains, it was his proud boast that he had never missed one. Of course, if someone else were making the arrangements or engineering the departure, he might have to hustle getting there, but with such assistants or in spite of them, he had never been left at the train.

He was unsurpassed in the art of packing. He carried no brief case, but wrapped his papers and documents compactly and neatly into a bundle, tied with a string, and he could fit more into that bundle than anybody before or since his time. He had never had anyone to look out for him—mother, wife, or sister—so he had learned to look out for himself. Once when he was making ready to go to Washington he omitted his eyeglasses. Since he used them only for reading, they were not a constant necessity. But he was chagrined at the oversight and remarked to one of his friends that he guessed he ought to have married. Of one idiosyncrasy he was never able to rid himself: nine times out of ten when he went anywhere he left his nightshirt behind him. He would write to the hotel and say he was sorry, but always he had a guilty feeling that he had no business to be so forgetful.

Over the years this advocate of God in Science continued to appear before Southern schools with varying degrees of success, depending on the amount of prejudice already existing, never certain beforehand what sort of reception he might encounter. After he had spoken at the Blue Ridge Assembly the students were lined up beside the bus which was to take him to the station. He passed between them saying good-by, but many of these young men who were studying for the ministry drew back; they would not perform the Western rite of brotherhood by shaking hands.

Again under the auspices of the Y.M.C.A., he toured some dozen colleges in Mississippi, a state distinguished for the highest degree of prejudice and the lowest degree of literacy in the country. Signs were frequent: "Nigger don't let the sun set on you in this town," and he was warned that he ran the risk of being mobbed.

In most places the students listened attentively and respectfully to his discourses on the peanut and the sweet potato, "The lifesavers of the South," including the University at Oxford, where Senator Theodore G. Bilbo published a little paper. And in it the senator said he did not know what the proud University of Mississippi was coming to. It had had that peanut nigger from Tuskegee making an address. He could not understand what a nigger would have to say that would interest white Southern boys, much less white girls.

But white girls elsewhere spoke their own minds on the subject. Professor Carver's appearance before the Woman's College was canceled at the last moment, and the president forbade students to attend the hastily organized meeting in the colored high school. In a school paper they apologized for the discourtesy to which they had been forced and registered an objection, very heartening in its determination:

As the events of the past week have shown, we were a bit hasty in last week's editorial "Another Step Forward" in predicting that the South's outlook was broadening, that race prejudice was a thing of the past. We wish that such a condition did exist—it should exist, but the protest raised against Dr. Carver shows that it is still a state to be attained in the future. So far the South has only a superficial, a very superficial, coating of tolerance. A casual observer would think that enlightenment had come. We thought so too. . . . Some of us are inclined to tuck our heads with shame and deplore the fact that we dwell in a state so backward in certain respects as Mississippi. . . . But instead of sitting down and blushing we should be up and doing something about it.

Professor Carver's Mississippi tour was proclaimed "the greatest accomplishment for interracial good will so far achieved in the South," and when he went on to Panama City, Florida, the Southeastern Peanut Association meeting there adopted a resolution: "Our South has proven to be your South."

This sentiment, however, was shared by very few other businessmen, and on the whole Professor Carver felt the South was missing much by its inferiority complex. Years before, when he had been exhibiting at a fair, a state governor kept coming up to his stand and asking oblique questions. The governor was going to make a speech that afternoon proclaiming the potentialities of the great Southland, but he would not ask directly for what he wanted, because he would then be crediting a Negro with knowing more than he did; that he was unable to do. He was typical of so many of his compatriots; they would go without rather than acknowledge they were beholden to a Negro.

Professor Carver's mail was piled with requests for information, but by letter was not the most satisfactory way to obtain it, when the source was immediately at hand. As elsewhere over the country, businessmen's clubs were usually luncheon clubs meeting in hotels, and those were the times and places they heard new speakers and exposed themselves to new ideas. Professor Carver could not enter their hotels nor sit down to table with them. They could have learned much from him, but custom erected a barrier between themselves and this knowledge.

Often they asked to borrow his exhibit, but this he never would allow. He had two good reasons, either of which would have served. He would not have his exhibit handled by anyone other than himself—he packed it himself, unpacked and set it up, and then repacked; no other hands could touch it. Always present was the danger that someone would take it to pieces, help himself to what he wanted, and perhaps misuse what he had stolen. And he had a second reason: he did not ask that they recognize himself, but did insist that Tuskegee be recognized.

Professor Carver's information was for the legitimate use of anyone who asked for it legitimately. But he would not go round by the back door to offer it to anyone not honest enough to get it fairly and squarely. He was reminded of the most important lesson he had learned in geometry at Ames: you can't arrive at a right result from a wrong hypothesis. If the information were not honorably come by it would, in the long run, do the recipient no good.

If people desired his exhibit desperately enough they were obliged to give in and invite him. This accounted for his appearance in many places where no other Negro had ever been before.

It was not necessary to journey abroad to be subject to the pain and terror of having been born not white. Tuskegee had become the center from which stemmed many Negro activities designed to fill the gaps in the social structure. Partly due to the unhealthful conditions under which they were forced to live, the life expectancy of colored people was lower by several years than that of white. Though their population increase had not kept pace with that of the rest of the country, they still numbered nearly a tenth of the total. Because this "tenth man," too, became ill, and few white nurses were willing to attend him, Booker Washington had very early started a three-year course of nursing for girls. Since then it had seldom been able to meet the demand. The Institute had not considered itself qualified to have a medical school, but had from the outset maintained a hospital.

In 1913 Mrs. Charles E. Mason, whose husband was one of the faithful trustees, had presented the John A. Andrew Memorial Hospital in honor of her grandfather, a governor of Massachusetts. This hospital had served a large section of the South which lacked facilities for treating Negroes.

Then when a hospital for Negro veterans, who could not be admitted into white institutions, was projected shortly after the war, Tuskegee was its logical location. In exchange for one dollar the school presented the Federal Government with 400 acres of land, and Vice-President Coolidge came down to dedicate the buildings.

Charles W. Wickersham, a trustee of many years, was in charge of the proceedings. Mr. Coolidge would say, "Good night" and "Good morning" and "Pass the salt," but for the rest he let Mr. Wickersham do all the talking. Mr. Wickersham was fairly stumped by the lack of enthusiasm and general flatness of the atmosphere. He went out into the kitchen of the guest hall to see whether he could stir up any animation through that channel.

"You know," he remarked to the cook, "I can't get the Vice-President to talk."

"Well, Mr. Wickersham, there's two things: I got quail, fixed up the Southern way. And if that don't work, wait till he sees Professor Carver."

Sure enough, when Mr. Coolidge saw Professor Carver, he asked question after question and fairly talked up a breeze.

But when he had gone away, a truly ominous storm of major proportions gathered at Tuskegee. The great Federal hospital and its ample pay roll were plums too ripe to be left unharvested by Southern politicians. They were determined it should be staffed by white doctors, and advanced the argument that Negro doctors, who were not very numerous anyhow, had no experience in treating psychopaths. This was largely true, because Negro physicians could not intern save at very few hospitals of the country. However, they were intelligent and they could read medical literature, and this was one place where they felt they were entitled to receive coveted and necessary experience.

They were determined, and the Imperial Wizard of the Ku Klux Klan was full of anger; he issued orders from Atlanta.

The night the Klan rode two hundred Negro soldiers were stationed on the campus, home from the war they had helped win for democracy, which now seemed a somewhat hollow victory; they were waiting, not too hopefully, for rehabilitation. More men stole in from the hills. The shadowy parade ground was filled with shadowy forms. A menacing silence held the campus as the parade of automobiles, shrouded white figures on the running boards, came down the road. Through the slits in their government-owned sheets the Klansmen were aware of the dim, immobile figures, shoulder to shoulder in the dark, ready to defend Tuskegee. The cars swept through the campus, out to the highway, and ignominiously returned whence they had come.

So the Klan rode and vanished. And the Veterans' Hospital, designed for Negro patients, was staffed throughout by Negro physicians and nurses.

Though the discussion of such events was discouraged among the students, the riding of the Klan is among the folk tales of Tuskegee. One of the pioneers was telling the story to a newly inducted member of the faculty. "You young people," he said, "are eating white bread now."

"But it is still bitter bread," replied the young man.

Bitter bread it would remain until the racial attitudes changed. These were roughly two. The first was fear on the part of white people whose economic status was low enough to be threatened by any rising economic scale among Negroes. This fear expressed itself actively in bullying. On plantations within twenty-five miles of Tuskegee the riding boss, "the man on the big horse," regularly whipped so-called tenants precisely as the overseer of seventy years before had whipped slaves—because it was good for them. And, as they also had done seventy years before, landowners and professional men who were not economically threatened regarded Negroes with condescending amusement and affection. Those they had grown up with and who had tended them were "dear old uncle" or "dear old auntie."

A contentedly secure middle class which would automatically maintain a balance between the social extremes was lacking, and hence the system remained feudalistic—that of master and serf. In the main this stayed virtually unaltered through the long lapse of years, with the vital exception that the landlord no longer had any obligation to care for Negroes coming under his jurisdiction.

To keep alive such a system it was necessary that its adherents recognize no variations within the Negro race. A shopkeeper of the town who had a bare elementary education would say of Tuskegee's dignified Ph.D.s, "The Institute 'Nigras' know their place and we never have any trouble with them"—the word being a polite compromise between nigger and Negro conceded to Northerners who had been known to object to the former.

Some were uncomfortable about the situation. One man would not come to the Institute at all, but transacted his business at a distance. "When we visit you," he said, "you do everything possible to make us comfortable and extend every courtesy to make us welcome. We cannot return these courtesies; therefore I will not accept them."

It was easy to say, "Why doesn't someone break the vicious circle by inviting Negroes whom he knows to be his equal in education and culture to his home?" But custom had the sanction of many years' usage. It could not lightly be upset. No one, not even a minister, dared to make the first breach. If a "foreigner" who came from the North to settle among them attempted to treat the Negro on anything like an equal footing, he himself became outcast. A teacher at a neighboring school took that stand and very soon his "services were no longer required," and he had to move elsewhere.

Many white visitors to Professor Carver's laboratory, when they saw brain and hands, joint tools working in harmony together, said that he was a genius, a law unto himself. Since he had been acclaimed elsewhere as a great man, they were safe in acknowledging what they had instinctively felt. To explain their bemusement, they averred he had not a single characteristic of the Negro, not one—as though all Negroes could be lumped together. This was nonsense, and Professor Carver dismissed it as such. Of course he was a Negro, according to the best obtainable evidence a full-blooded Negro, and his emotions were those of a Negro.

Students of such matters attempted to trace his physical characteristics, which differed considerably from the more usual West Coast Africans, to a particular tribe or tribes and arrived at various hypotheses, but nothing authentic could be definitely established. They did agree, however, that no white blood appeared to have altered the strain.

Not all Southerners by any means subscribed to the same point of view regarding Negroes. Each being an individual, each had his individual reactions, depending on the influences to which he had been exposed, but far too many shared the more or less common attitudes.

Gardeners had no ax to grind, and botanists and mycologists with scientific impersonality acknowledged an expert when they encountered him. They would agree with Professor Carver himself when he said, "If you have nothing but complexion to recommend you, you have no recommendation. If you know anything, you recommend yourself."

Just after he returned from his appearance before the Ways and Means Committee in Washington he attended a farmers' convention. A white man said to one of the officials, "I understand that man Carver that's created such a stir—understand he's coming."

"Yes, he'll be here. If he says he's coming, he doesn't fail."

"Well, I want to know is he a black man? All your big men are two thirds white, and I can understand where their intelligence comes from."

"You come and you'll be satisfied with his complexion."

The man sat right behind Professor Carver on the platform. At first he was not going to listen. But then he straightened up and finally rose and peered at the exhibit with the rest. His mouth fell open, and nobody knows when he closed it. His final comment was, "Is Carver educated or is he a freak?"

Perhaps he was both.

So many people came to Tuskegee and exclaimed with avid curiosity, "I want to see Carver, I never saw him, I want to see Carver!" They wanted to know, "Is he bright or dark?" He was used to loud asides from those who seemed to assume he was an inanimate object lacking a sense of hearing. "My God, is that him? You can see there's something unnatural about him." It made no difference to them whether he were suffering agony of mind or in a mood to be amused.

As he grew older it was chiefly the interference with his train of thought that exasperated him, but the irritation made him more conscious of the implications of their intrusion. He had to protect himself and safeguard his patience and time by declining the honor of being put on view.

Professor Carver's becoming a recluse was occasioned in part by the unhappiness he had suffered. If you encounter a sleeping lion, you do not kick it awake, particularly if you have nothing with which to defend yourself. Because of the nature of the task he had set himself, he was unable to stay off the trail used by the lion, but when he was not actually obliged to venture forth and travel that precarious path, he could shut himself away from the howling jackals. He did not dislike people, as such, but when they had nothing in common, why bother? He had much better put in his time doing things to help them if they would but take advantage of it, making his contribution to those big enough and broad enough to accept it without qualification.

He could not learn to like a person; he liked him immediately or not at all. Certain words could not be described—love, hate, joy, sorrow—they were just words, and their meaning was understood only by each individual who experienced them. His aversion to certain people was equally indefinable. But if he encountered one whose nature seemed evil, he thought to himself, "Beware of him. He's doomed." And instinctively he turned his head away in order not to see what was there.

He knew their secret thought, "Here's a peanut-headed nigger speaking," and occasionally he wished they knew that he knew; they could not throw water in his face and make him believe it was raining. But no mere words would alter their opinions, so better just let them go their way. He remained unimpressed by the fulsome chorus of admiration and the often-repeated exclamation, "How happy you must be to do all this for other people!" His reply, if he had made any, would have been, "Have you yourself taken the time to kick even one stumbling block out of my way to make my path a little easier?"

But he did not speak.

As a Negro, Professor Carver was cut off from so many experiences which would have enriched his life; he missed so many things that he considered beautiful and important. Once when he was in Montgomery, having a little time to spare, he ventured into a park, first looking to make sure there was no sign saying he could not enter. He was contentedly examining the grottoes and the flowers when the park keeper strode forward. "What are you doing here? Don't you know niggers ain't allowed? Get out!"

When Paderewski came to Montgomery, he could not hear the master play, because Negroes were not permitted in the theater. And when the Kress collection of Italian paintings and sculpture was on view there, he was barred from seeing them, though he longed to do so. He might, perhaps, have been permitted to enter the gallery, but he would have been stared at and commented upon beyond endurance. He could not enjoy beauty in the midst of ugliness.

He felt the same thing when the pipe organ was dedicated in the Methodist Church in the town of Tuskegee. The organist came out to the Institute to invite him to come and hear her play.

"Thank you," he replied, "but I think I'd better not."

Two times she returned with the same request; she had asked the minister and he said it was all right, and then the leaders of the congregation had also agreed. Nobody was going to make a fuss about it.

He repeated his answer. "I appreciate your asking and thank you again. But if your playing is to be in tune, nothing untoward must enter in and mar its grace. If I were to step inside your church, there would certainly be some individuals who would make me feel not welcome. By the time the hustling and bustling and looking around at me and wondering, 'What's he doing here?' were over, and a suitably removed place had been found for me to sit, *I* would not be in tune. The best thing within me could not respond. So I think I had best stay at home."

Seldom did he indicate what was in his heart and mind on this subject; when white people came to the Institute chapel they were made particularly welcome, but no colored person could worship God in a white church. Once, however, when a group of ministers asked him what they could do to better race relations, he did deliver a short sermon, stating solemnly and frankly, "Your actions speak so loud I cannot hear what you are saying. You have too much religion and not enough Christianity—too many creeds and not enough performance. This world is perishing for kindness."

Professor Carver had in abundant measure and as a natural gift the kindliness toward other human beings of which he spoke. Once he was waiting for his train at Chehaw and saw a man firing an engine, trying to shovel coal and clumsy about it because he was crippled. His ever-ready sympathy was touched. "May I help you?" he asked.

The man looked up and saw it was a Negro making the offer. "No!" he snarled.

Professor Carver merely said, "Excuse me," and did not trouble the man any more. This was his habitual reaction to such incidents. When people bothered him, he only said, "Never mind, they don't understand. It doesn't make any difference." And when a storekeeper said roughly, "What d'ya want, Uncle?" he silently turned and left the place, maintaining his tight-lipped, formal manners.

On this same trip Professor Carver encountered forcible demonstrations of the two prevailing attitudes of the two prevailing classes. He was on his way to the World's Peanut Exposition being held at Windsor, North Carolina, and Mr. Thompson accompanied him. Some forty miles from their destination they had to transfer. The bus they were preparing to mount had no room for colored. Professor Carver would have been stranded had not Mr. Thompson's authority made a place for him.

During the exposition itself two young fellows, both very drunk, approached the glass cases in which Professor Carver's exhibit was sheltered. "Come on, Bill!" exclaimed one. "Want to see the smartest nigger in the world? Don't be ashamed to shake hands with him. I did."

Bill spoke to Professor Carver directly. "I suppose you know you're a nigger?"

"Yes. I know."

In that sort of mind there existed nothing to which one could appeal. Some people were so big you couldn't whip them and others were too small to reason with. Of course you could say, "He didn't agree with me so I knocked him down," but then you fell to his level. Petty persecutions were the manifestations of small and mean persons who, by exercising them, proved themselves inferior.

Professor Carver proceeded about his business in the serene knowledge that not he but they were being degraded. "There are three kinds of ignorance," he sometimes said. "The first is the old-fashioned, 'don't-know' ignorance. The second, which is worse, is the 'don't-know-and-don't-care' ignorance. And the third is 'cussed' ignorance, which is the worst of all." Those who were afflicted with the last-named ignorance laid a curse upon themselves; by making themselves ridiculous in the eyes of dispassionate observers they stultified themselves.

He expressed this sentiment again in his own idiom: "I feel most strongly that we have no right to ask God to change fixed laws of the universe. If we plant oats, we must expect to harvest oats and not corn or beans. If we sow hate and wrongdoing in our lives, we must expect to reap the awful results."

For himself, he was not particularly concerned with behavior patterns; his interest was not related so much to why people did things as it was to how. If they disappointed him, he simply crossed them off the list. He maintained at least a surface disregard either of open insult or condescension of the "dear-old-uncle" school. Most of the pan was skim milk and must ever remain so.

More often than not something occurred to reassert his natural merriment. An old colored lady from a far section in the hills used to come in each morning very early at the same time to see the exhibit. "Handsome as I was," the professor mourned, "she paid no attention to me." Peering through her glasses, she would read the labels out loud. "Shoeblack!" How wonderful that was, and so was coffee and so was milk. By the fourth morning she had worked her way through to the paints. "Paints made from peanuts!" She pushed her sunbonnet back and her spectacles up. "Mebbe so, but Ah don' b'lieve it. Ef he'd jes lef dat off Ah mighta b'lieved it!"

On his journeys Professor Carver picked up his own particular kind of fun where he could find it. Time and again he entertained himself by standing on the platform solemnly waiting for those who were to meet him to distinguish the scientist in the trappings of the apparent farmer. Often his own people set an undue store by dressing smartly or even too flamboyantly, and he leaned over backward not to do the same. The reception committee would turn away from the nondescript figure alongside some boxes, little cap squashed down on his head, and say, "I guess Dr. Carver didn't come."

He was proceeding once toward a chautauqua in Richmond when his familiar imp took possession of him. Day was just beginning to break as the train approached the city, and the porter waded through women and children and banana peelings, shaking the men whose tickets in their hatbands proclaimed they were supposed to get off at Richmond. Professor Carver had no hatband because he had no hat, only the little cap. When the train had pulled into the station three gentlemen attired in frock coats and white gloves came through. He scrounched down in his seat as though he were asleep, and looked so unpromising that the porter let him slumber on.

The train was about twelve miles out when the conductor stopped in the aisle and asked for his ticket. "What are you doing here?" he demanded.

"I'm riding," said Professor Carver innocently.

The conductor dressed down the porter for not having called him, and then said, "We're nearer Hanover than we are Richmond, but we'll back up." He added doubtfully, "There's a return train at twelve, but we'll back up."

However, Professor Carver took pity on him, said there was a man in the town ahead he wanted to see anyhow, and he would take the twelve o'clock back. So the conductor did some telegraphing and Professor Carver was placed on the return train. This time he really did descend at Richmond and was duly greeted by the three frock-coated gentlemen. Their appearance amused him so he had to tell funny stories all the way to his destination so he himself would have an excuse for laughing.

He thoroughly enjoyed his private joke and deflating pompous individuals by taking them down a buttonhole or two. At one of the hotels, where what seemed a necessary compromise was being made between having him an honored guest and segregating him, the proprietor himself came up to his room where he was to have his dinner to see that the linen and silver were correctly arrayed. There must be no laxness in serving such an honored guest. With pencil poised he went through the menu. Would the doctor care for a portion of this or would a select bit of that tempt his fancy? And when he had gone down the list the doctor quite sweetly said he would like a little bit of turnip greens and some fat pork.

A new group of white businessmen—a doctor, a druggist, a lawyer, and a college president—were again attempting commercialization of Professor Carver's products, this time with his peanut and creosote remedy, which was copyrighted under the name Penol. Though he would not allow exploitation either by the use of his name or his picture, he again looked on benignly and spent two weeks in the Sharp and Dohme laboratories supervising its preparation. This venture actually proceeded as far as manufacture, but again no one had the business acumen to abandon his own business and devote himself exclusively to that. Finally the bank failures and the depression left the town of Tuskegee without capital.

Mr. R. H. Powell, one of the members of the Penol Company, like Mr. Thompson, was secure enough in his position to be able to sponsor Professor Carver, in the interests of building up the business. Shortly before the stock-market crash, Mr. Powell arranged for him to talk on peanuts before the Lions' Club of Columbus, Georgia.

The professor, naturally, could not attend the banquet. A waiter came to his room to tell him dinner was being served, but he sent his regrets; he had already had his supper and was still busy preparing his talk. When he was summoned a second time, he went down.

Unfortunately the dinner guests, practical men, eighty or a hundred of them, who seldom thought of anything except making money, had not yet finished. However, they ignored the solecism, and Mr. Powell made a glowing introduction. "I am a Southerner, with all a Southerner's traditions, but I want to say to you young people, now is the time to begin thinking along other lines—lines of opportunity for all people." This was accounted a brave thing for a Southerner to announce publicly.

Journalists, who wrote for the weeklies and monthlies as distinguished from reporters who wrote for the dailies, began to "discover" Professor Carver. They sought his name in Who's Who and found that he had been born a slave and ended with the Fellowship, a gulf which had never been bridged by any man. Drama leaped to the eye. *Efficiency Magazine,* of London, published an editorial: "If I were asked what living man had the worst start and the best finish, I would say Dr. Carver. It is a great loss to us that we have no one like him in England."

American journalists sought him at Tuskegee, but he could not reminisce as one with a happier past might have done. He had buried his memories and wished them to remain buried; only a painful psychological struggle could exhume them. He saw no good reason for undergoing this ordeal, particularly in view of the results. Usually he had little to say about himself, save perhaps a placating anecdote in the interests of politeness. The journalists emerged with stories which were half fantasy—as they imagined they should have been. He himself, with only the mildest curiosity, read the reports and watched the legend grow, making no effort to correct even the obvious inaccuracies. He was entertained by the effusions, as he often was when he rose to speak on the lecture platform. He frequently started his talk with, "I like to hear myself introduced because I learn so many things about myself I never knew before."

The journalists variously referred to Professor Carver as the "Wizard of Tuskegee," the "Negro Burbank," "Columbus of the Soil," and a black worker of white magic, but many also were tripped by the snare of associative pattern words. Since he was an object of affection he fell into the "plantation darky" or "well-loved" category; he was commonly described as "old" and his walk as "shuffling."

The "humble" peanut and the "lowly" sweet potato were firmly tagged with these adjectives, though no one ever explained why the amino acids of a peanut should be any more humble than those cut from the belly of a steer, or the glucose of a sweet potato more lowly than that of a grape. "Humble," too, was Professor Carver himself, though no one who knew him well had ever seen him bow in humility before anything except the manifestations of Nature and his God.

He was not, however, arrogant. That trait he left to those who called upon him.

As late as 1940 a reporter from the *Piedmont* of Greenville, South Carolina, went seeking an interview and had this to say:

> The Doctor did not ordinarily receive visitors; he was too busy. But at my insistence he did so, with courtesy. Today he is Dr. George W. Carver and Southerners, with their customary understanding of the race problem, have no hesitancy in saying "Dr. Carver." . . . Dr. Carver arose as I entered. His hands were filled with books or papers or something. I nodded, making myself known. Dr. Carver returned the greeting. His hands still worked with the papers, showing that he was a student of the South and knew what to do under the circumstances. I tell this because many, like myself, may have wondered about the details of such an interview. . . . In appearance he resembles hundreds of the antebellum negroes who were a common sight in the South a few years ago. . . . Just an old negro humbly, respectfully talking to a visitor.

The picture had a brighter and more hopeful side, however. Julia Collier Harris, daughter-in-law of Joel Chandler Harris, wrote a eulogistic editorial in the *Enquirer-Sun* of Columbus, Georgia. A biologist of repute had said Dr. Carver was "an avatar, an embodiment of the genius of his race, a vessel, as it were, into which the peculiar gifts, tendencies, and possibilities of generations of the Negro race, far back to ancient times, had been distilled."

To those who had spent so many years with Professor Carver at Tuskegee he would always remain "The Professor." But most people had fallen into the habit of referring to him as "Doctor," originally to avoid the forbidden "Mister," and then, when Northern papers had been pleased to copy, out of respect for his scientific status.

It was eminently fitting that his first college, Simpson, was first to recognize him academically, by conferring an honorary Doctor of Science degree in 1928. Its president, John

L. Hillman, said that Dr. Carver was Simpson's most distinguished son, and these were probably no idle words. When a later president, John Owen Gross, visited Tuskegee in 1941, he amplified this statement even more significantly, "Among the cherished memories that Simpson College will always possess is the consciousness that it did not fail him when he came knocking for admission. It will always rejoice in the fact that it did not make race or color the basis for entrance."

# CHAPTER XXI

## *"The Hind Wheel Runs by Faith"*

SOUTHERN GALLANTRY had stood up nobly under physical combat but had faltered most ignobly under economic competition. So long as the South merited the amused contempt of more enterprising sections of the country, it would continue to suffer under what it called "the strangle hold of the North." Absentee ownership and prohibitive freight rates undoubtedly existed, but these could be overcome by a sufficiently determined effort.

With unabated faith Dr. Carver continued to reiterate that the "Let-George-do-it" type would perish from the South. Eventually Southerners would stop blaming their inertia on this "strangle hold." They would be forced by circumstances to co-operate and would get the habit. They would finally realize they must join hands with the rest of the country and all go along together to keep their belated rendezvous.

Wherever Dr. Carver might be, though it were on a stuffy train, he did not deviate from his accustomed practice of rising at four; the dawn does not come twice to wake a man. Through smoky windows he could see the sun awake and light the face of Nature, and even in the fleeting glimpses thus caught she spoke to him of how she manifested herself. Or, if he were already established in a town as of the night before, he was up and out into the country whenever it was at all possible, to see what this particular bit of the earth's surface might have to offer. Then he could tell those who would attend upon his words what wealth they possessed right there at home.

Immediately after the Armistice the country had been threatened with a serious shortage of drug crops, and in the summer of 1919 the United States Department of Agriculture asked Dr. Carver to make an investigation of medicinal plants native to Macon County that might profitably be raised there. He had compiled a list, with botanical and common names and the usable parts of the plant, of a hundred and fifteen, many of which were already recognized by the United States *Pharmacopoeia.* This he had published in the hope that some farmers would be inspired to turn a portion of their acreage over to the cultivation of medicinal and potherbs, with advantage to themselves and to the drug industry.

Since that time he had always in his journeying kept a weather eye out for vegetable drugs. "An overland trip recently to Marianna and Panama City, Florida, impressed me favorably with the possibilities of a factory for the manufacturing of drugs from the multiplicity of roots, barks, herbs, etc., which I saw in considerable quantities. Some of these could be cultivated and made at least a fine supplement to other farm crops, or even paying crops of themselves." He offered reporters a list of fifty Florida plants with their history and the current price. "This does not include all I saw, and more extensive search may disclose many more. But I trust enough has been said to awaken into activity a much-neglected industry."

At the conclusion of a ten-day tour of Virginia he repeated a similar exhortation. "I am filled with enthusiasm and hope," he said to Virginians. "I thought of the challenging manufacturing opportunities for pharmaceutical drug laboratories and made a list of fifty-six medicinal plants of value."

The fall of 1927 he attended a Negro state fair at Tulsa, Oklahoma, to demonstrate what lay wrapped in the rough and brittle shell of the peanut. One morning early he trekked up Stand Pipe Hill and came back carrying in his hands twenty-seven indigenous plants containing medicinal properties. At that day's lecture he showed them. " 'Where there is no vision the people perish.' I found down in Ferguson's drugstore seven patent medicines containing in their formulas certain elements also contained in these plants on Stand Pipe Hill. The preparations were shipped in from New York. They should be shipped out from Stand Pipe Hill."

Dr. Carver made little differentiation between colored and white audiences; what applied to one should apply to the other, and the varied kinds of opportunities should be available to all. At another talk during fair week he said the whole theory of geological science was going to be revolutionized, and the change would mark the end of dry holes. "Someone will state oil is here and oil is there, and oil will be where he lays his finger. It might as well be one of you."

His natural inquisitiveness had led him to the West Tulsa Refinery of the Mid-Continent Petroleum Corporation. Waste always attracted his attention, and the large amount to be found here, even after the benzene, gasoline, and naphtha had been taken from the crude oil, was no exception. He asked that samples of sludge be sent him at Tuskegee for experiment. It was done, and from this sludge he produced many shades of dyes and an asphaltic rubber.

Constantly Dr. Carver sought to excite the South into interest in learning to develop its own resources. After another visit to Florida he came back emphasizing veneers. "I was especially interested in the lovely palms, varying in size, appearance, and usefulness from the charming little zamias to the majestic royal types. The wood from some of these, when cut into thin plates and used as a veneer, makes a wood so distinctly odd and beautiful in grain that it has to be seen to be appreciated. I have several small panels made from the procumbent stems of one of the Sabal types, which never fails to elicit exclamations of surprise and delight at a type of beauty all its own. From this angle alone there is wealth in these roots and stems, if developed commercially."

Dr. Carver could not speak of the mineral and vegetable possibilities of the South in very loud tones, because the voice of a Negro lacked authority. But he did state the facts whenever he had the chance. The Atlanta *Constitution,* the Birmingham *Reporter,* and the Montgomery *Advertiser* all faithfully published his reminders that opportunity lay at Southern doorsteps. The *Advertiser* went further; it issued an excellent brochure called *Negro Scientist Shows "Way Out" for Southern Farmers,* written by Osburn Zuber, an associate editor.

Occasionally the small cry was heard in the wilderness of indifference; not all Southerners, of course, preferred the easy way of laying upon the past an excuse for the failures of the present. It was costing a small industrialist a large sum to clear his land of palmetto. Could Dr. Carver suggest any use to which this waste might be put? Dr. Carver could and did; he made veneers that were soon being manufactured and bringing prosperity to a furniture factory.

Those who had hearkened most attentively, the peanut men, had profited the most, and their loyalty and gratitude to Dr. Carver were proportionate. Mr. Tom Huston of Columbus, Georgia, employed very concrete methods of acknowledging his debt. He had sent a chemist, W. Wade Moss, over to Tuskegee to consult Dr. Carver about the oil settling out of his peanut butter. Mr. Moss stayed off and on for several years, returning between times to Mr. Huston with his information.

Mr. Huston was lavish with appreciative gifts. Once he brought a sealskin blanket. Dr. Carver thanked him and put it in moth balls at the bottom of a trunk, where it apparently remained.

Another time he asked, "What do you want most?"

Surprisingly, Dr. Carver replied, "I want a diamond."

"If you want a diamond you shall have it."

Mr. Huston procured a fine stone, had it mounted in a platinum ring, and dispatched it to his friend. He asked Mr. Moss to find out whether Dr. Carver had liked the present.

"Where's your diamond?" asked Mr. Moss.

Dr. Carver opened his geological specimen case and there it was among the minerals.

As a final tribute Mr. Huston wished to make a gift to Tuskegee Institute. He sent a sculptor, Isabel Schultz of Baltimore, to design a bronze wall plaque of Dr. Carver's head.

The light sprinkling of cropped hair seemed a scant covering for Dr. Carver's orderly brain, and the flowing mustache of his youth had long since had its wings clipped. But the beak of a nose still dominated the square chin and triangular eyes, which had retreated further under the high forehead, wrinkled like a hound's. Those hazel, almost green, eyes had lost little of their keenness. Only when he was reading did he perch spectacles on his nose, ample to hold more sturdy affairs than these small, old-fashioned, gold-rimmed glasses, the broken bows held together with black tape and a piece of copper wire.

Dr. Carver's hands and mind were busy at something else while he was supposed to be sitting for his portrait. Miss Schultz kept asking, "How does that look?" but he was disturbed by the interruptions and, without even glancing up, responded, "How do I know how I look?"

The plaque was finished and ready to be presented by Commencement of 1931. Dr. Robert Russa Moton, who had been called from Hampton Institute at the death of Washington to guide Tuskegee on its way, considered it right and proper that an occasion should be made of the presentation. But when Dr. Carver was told he must don cap and gown, he rebelled.

"I won't wear it!" he said emphatically.

"Yes, you will!" retorted Dr. Moton equally emphatically. "I'll put it on you."

Thereupon Dr. Moton chased Dr. Carver up the driveway, past Washington's tomb, and almost to the hospital. But Dr. Moton was big and powerful and Dr. Carver was not. Dr. Carver came back wearing his gown and mortarboard, the tassel on the wrong side as usual.

Seventy-five per cent of Dr. Carver's vast correspondence, averaging one hundred and fifty letters a day, asked for advice and help. A man might inquire about peanut-butter-making machinery when the letterhead showed he lived only a few miles from the center of the peanut-butter-processing country. Just reading such letters took up a good deal of Dr. Carver's time, and he had to expend more time in answering them. They would start, "I know you're busy," and then ramble on for pages. A good rule, he said, was just to look at the last paragraph; what was really wanted would be contained in that. He did not follow this rule himself, but answered them all in scrupulous detail, and neatly marked them as such.

With considerable amusement he once caught a visitor eying this accumulation in some astonishment. "You are looking at my truly awful desk, but I don't feel so bad about it as I once did. I once had a Chinese assistant who classified this conglomeration as 'orderly disorder.' " This statement was amply proved as he dived like a terrier into the pile of papers and pamphlets and books which towered well above his head when he was seated and, after only a few moments' rummaging, emerged triumphantly grasping the particular thing he wanted.

Of the remaining 25 per cent of his letters, most were petitions to speak or broadcast, though there was also a miscellaneous smattering of this and that. In one mail would come an application to borrow a painting, a definition of the word "American," a biographical sketch of himself from Nyassaland, or a prayer someone wanted in a book.

His answer to this last was simple:

My prayers seem to be more of an attitude than anything else. I indulge in very little lip service, but ask the Great Creator silently, daily, and often many times a day, to permit me to speak to Him through the three great Kingdoms of the world which He has created —the animal, mineral, and vegetable Kingdoms—to understand their relations to each other, and our relations to them and to the Great God Who made all of us. I ask Him daily and often momently to give me wisdom, understanding, and bodily strength to do His will; hence I am asking and receiving all the time.

The letter, as it did in 1930, might contain a request from the USSR to come to Russia and help with the agricultural program. He declined this invitation for the same reasons that had directed him when he declined other invitations to leave Tuskegee, but John Sutton, who had been one of his assistants, went in his stead.

The voluminous mail Dr. Carver received from his boys, both colored and white, compensated for some of the more troublesome epistles and was, as he said, a sweet thing to live for. Several of the white lads in town were devoted to him, and one or another was usually trailing him in and out of doors. When they went away to school, he remembered their birthdays and they kept in touch.

His interest in young people was as fervent as ever; he was not concerned with the pigmentation of their skins but with their youth, and in doing what he could to see that each started out in life with his best foot foremost. Circumstances sometimes hampered him; he could help the races independently, though never together. A German youth attending Antioch College had read about Dr. Carver and hitchhiked down to Tuskegee for the purpose of studying with him. Alabama law promptly sent him away again; he was not permitted to learn alongside colored boys.

Segregation must always, in fact, be taken into account. A man in Mexico who raised a million coconuts a year asked Dr. Carver to come down and conduct an experimental laboratory for him. Dr. Carver saw in this a chance to give a boost to a young white friend from the University of North Carolina. He replied that he could not stay away from Tuskegee permanently, but he would come down for a short time, bringing an assistant with him. After two weeks the young man should be able to continue on his own and Dr. Carver would leave him there. The planter wrote back that he regretted the fact but, the young man being white, he could not work in the same laboratory with Dr. Carver. And that, so far as Dr. Carver was concerned, closed the correspondence.

When the parents of local boys were perplexed, they, too, sought the wise understanding which had resolved some of their sons' difficulties. Lloyd G. had been one of his devotees, and he had got the boy a job in work he liked. Then Lloyd's father asked Dr. Carver whether he would have a talk with his younger son, Fred, who had been studying electrical engineering at the Georgia School of Technology but did not seem happy about it.

"If he has any inferiority complex about white and colored people," responded Dr. Carver, "don't bring him. He may not like me."

But the boy was brought, and they talked a bit. Afterward Dr. Carver reported to Mr. G.: "You'll never make an electrical engineer out of Fred. He's a fine young chap, but he's not doing what he ought to do. He could string wires and climb a pole, but when I think of an electrician I think of Edison. He'll never make an Edison; he isn't fitted for it."

"What is he fitted for?"

"He can come out here and I'll coach him along a little. Then we'll see."

"If you're sure you don't mind, I'll let him walk around after you, but I'll charge him not to bother you."

Fred did this for three months, and Dr. Carver, just to give him a perspective view of Nature and try to find out where his natural aptitudes lay, started him sketching. When he saw the pencil drawings, he let him begin on color and take the results home.

"That," Dr. Carver announced to the worried parents, "is what Fred is fitted for."

Fred was placed in a position where his artistic gifts could have expression in the commercial world, and he speedily proved that Dr. Carver had been right.

From very early days the simple country people, seeing Dr. Carver with his hands full of plants, had assumed he was an herb doctor; they had carried their sick children to him, and he had given them counsel as to where they could find proper medical aid.

Sometimes the white boys who seemed to be forever hanging around had muscular afflictions, and these he himself could help. He called up his old technique of massage at which his fingers had been so magical when he was rubber for the athletic teams at Ames.

One boy had been kicked on the kneecap by a horse. The ligaments had been torn and in healing had tightened and made one leg six inches shorter than the other. Dr. Carver rubbed the leg daily with peanut oil, and in six weeks the boy was walking with only a limp. In a year he was striding along perfectly, and shortly after that he began pitching for his college baseball team. Then came an infantile-paralysis victim, and Dr. Carver began to work on his withered leg with the same spectacular success. The lad gradually shifted from crutches to cane and was eventually playing football.

Dr. Carver had had additional confirmation of the efficacy of the peanut massaging oil he had long ago developed for fattening infants. To some of the white women of the town he had presented a face-cream preparation with a peanut-oil base. They had been delighted over its texture until some who were inclined to gain weight brought it back saying they could not use it; it made their faces fat. If peanut oil would nourish healthy facial muscles, why might it not do the same for atrophied muscles? Perhaps it would be more effective as a rubbing oil than the mineral or cottonseed oils which were then a part of the routine care for infantile-paralysis victims.

Poliomyelitis had hit the country a few years before, suddenly and with astounding force. Doctors had watched its hideous trail helplessly, and terror had mounted among parents. Dr. Carver happened to tell one day of the two boys he had treated and remarked that one of them was now playing football. He added that peanut oil might become an aid in treating the aftereffects of poliomyelitis.

December 31, New Year's Eve of 1932, the Associated

Press picked up the story. Instantly the word of possible salvation spread and he was deluged with tragic letters imploring him to send them the "cure." His correspondence reached truly alarming proportions, and answering it became an almost insuperable task. During the month of January alone he received 1,495 letters. Messages came by telegraph, special delivery, and long-distance telephone. Chemists, doctors, scientists, and quacks wanted to get in contact with him; masseurs and health-resort directors begged for instruction; shysters offered counsel and legal advice; manufacturers sent contracts—"just sign and return." He was swamped with appeals for a pint, a quart, a gallon of the oil. It would have taken a factory to fill the demand.

Of course he had to say he had no "cure." He was profoundly embarrassed, because again his denial went unheeded.

But hope would not be denied. There began a rush to Tuskegee of frantic parents bringing their crippled children. They came from Georgia, Florida, Mississippi, Tennessee in a continuous stream. Automobiles were lined up outside his office from dawn until long after sundown. His week ends were completely given over to these pathetic victims. Sunday after Sunday, all day long from seven in the morning to five in the evening, until he was exhausted, he labored—rubbing, rubbing, rubbing.

Since Dr. Carver was not a medical man, he kept in close touch with physicians, that nothing might go wrong. Physical therapists, however, could learn much from him. He would run his long, sensitive fingers over the afflicted area and say, "Life ends about here," isolating the muscle so accurately he might have been dissecting it out.

Perhaps the healing touch lay chiefly in his own hands, but of some two hundred and fifty cases he treated, from boys of thirteen to middle-aged men, all showed improvement of the nervous systems and collapsed muscles, sometimes of a seemingly miraculous nature. One man had been pronounced incurable; he was completely helpless and could speak only disconnected words. But Dr. Carver soon had him walking and talking almost normally. And the muscles of those Dr. Carver treated began to increase rapidly, by actual measurements.

In 1939 the National Foundation for Infantile Paralysis had raised sufficient money from the President's Birthday Balls to make its first large grant. Crippled children whose skins were dark could not be admitted to the Georgia Warm Springs Foundation, so a poliomyelitis center was established at Tuskegee, and the brilliant young orthopedist, Dr. John W. Chenault, directed it. He continued the experimentation. On one leg of one patient cottonseed oil was used, peanut oil on the other; the former increased around the calf only a quarter inch, the latter, one inch.

For his own use Dr. Carver had made up a series of ten oils of varying weights and viscosity, because skins also varied in their absorptive powers. But these were not for sale. Anyone could purchase a gallon of peanut oil at any drug or grocery store. If he would make no profit on potentially commercial products, certainly he would make none on therapeutic oils.

The General Education Board of the Rockefeller Foundation, which made extensive grants to Tuskegee Institute, found it difficult to understand why Dr. Carver's assistants should receive larger salaries than he, but he had never asked for an increase over his original one, and it had never been suggested. "I guess if they thought I was worth more than that, they would have offered it," he said. This was in fun, but he had little need of money and continued to be negligent about cashing his checks. They were tucked away in a trunk or loose in the clutter on his desk. Sometimes when he was going through the accumulation of papers a check would fall out dated six months before.

The fiscal year was up in May, and the treasurer of the Institute would appeal to Dr. Moton to see that Dr. Carver's checks were cashed before the arrival of the auditors, so that the books could be balanced. But Dr. Moton merely threw up his hands. "I can't do anything with him. Nobody can."

At the beginning of 1933, when banks were crashing all over the country, including the two in Tuskegee and the one at Ames in which Dr. Carver still kept an account, someone was kind enough to be concerned over his savings and inquired as to whether he knew the banks had failed. "Yes," he replied. "I heard about it. All I have is in those three. I guess somebody found a use for the money. I wasn't using it." He had lost something like forty thousand dollars, but beyond making this statement he never discussed the matter.

One of the Tuskegee banks was paying fifty cents on the dollar and offered him a certified check for the amount. "No, thank you," he replied. "I put in one hundred cents on the dollar." They offered him cotton; he could store it awhile and sell it when prices were better. "No, thank you. I didn't put cotton in the bank." Finally he was prevailed upon to accept a farm near Tuskegee in part payment. He had little interest in it and did not even go to see it. He had never had any financial luck with cotton. If he sold a bale, he usually did so at a loss, and then the next day the price would go up. Eventually he did, however, realize a certain amount on the farm itself.

Three resistless changes had been for some time tending to place the farmers of the Southern states in an even more deplorable position than ever before.

Time was when the country had a virtual monopoly on cotton, but other nations went into production to make themselves more self-sufficient, until the United States became only one of fifty. Also, the manufacture of artificial fibers which were superior to and cheaper than cotton was on the increase; rayon had become the third largest textile. And, finally, mechanization, though slower there than in other forms of agriculture, was beginning to spread over the cotton fields.

In the long run machinery relieves much of man's drudgery, but the first effects can be disastrous unless plans are made beforehand to take up the slack. From the beginning of the twentieth century manufacturers had been experimenting with mechanical cotton pickers. The steel fingers of one of the latest models, tried on flat Mississippi land, could do in a day the work of a man's hand requiring three and a half months.

But tractors and pickers could not negotiate the small hillsides of Alabama and Georgia. King Cotton had grown restless from the irritating beetle bites. He had spread westward to Texas and Oklahoma where the boll weevil was not so severe and where the wide spaces did not hamper mechanization. The cotton growers of the Old South were condemned to the most primitive of all forms of agriculture, employing small implements and hand labor in competition with the mass production of the Southwest. These were not merely onerous but ruinously expensive. Where plowing and planting four rows with a tractor cost only five dollars an acre, the same amount with one mule cost over a hundred dollars.

With the production of rayon going up in the '20s the price of cotton went steadily down. Southern warehouses were choked with bales that nobody would buy, and they overflowed into the streets of almost every little town. There they stood, season after season, their numbers slowly but relentlessly increasing. Somebody must find new uses for this unwanted commodity.

Early in the decade Dr. Carver began to indicate the possibility of absorbing some of the surplus in road building. Later, this general idea was put into effect in South Carolina, where an experimental stretch of road was laid, using tar and rock and a layer of cotton fabric and then more tar and gravel on top. The cotton served to bind the asphalt together in much the same manner as steel bars in concrete.

But Dr. Carver had a different plan, which was to mix asphalt with cotton linters immediately after ginning, thus eliminating the cost of labor and machinery for weaving the fabric. So he made paving blocks of this intimate mixture which would greatly cut down the wear on the asphalt of secondary roads and greatly increase the resiliency, and invited highway engineers to lay a mile of test road. The blocks had the added advantage of utilizing about forty bales to the mile, whereas the woven cloth would use no more than six to eight.

Another use for the cotton excess Dr. Carver advanced at this time was in wallboard. He had already made insulating and building board from yucca stems and leaves, sunflower stalks, cornstalks, sawdust, spent canna stems, and cotton stalks. But now he laid special emphasis on the superior board, light and strong, he had constructed from short-staple cotton.

These were suggestions for the future. Nothing could prevent the debacle of 1930. Calamity struck the already impoverished South with greater force than anywhere else in the country. The price of cotton dropped to a new low, practically starvation level. Cotton farmers were sinking fast, and blaming them for their helplessness would not remedy the situation.

A new day dawned in the South in 1933 with the advent of the Roosevelt Administration. The North, as represented by the Government at Washington, had tardily excised the hideous cancer of slavery, won the Civil War, and "freed the slaves." But it had seemed to take the attitude that aftercare was not the business of the surgeon. It had metaphorically washed its hands of the South without first disinfecting the wound, and the germs of trouble had festered deeply ever since, insidiously debilitating the entire country. No less than a human being could a country maintain its efficiency if one member were diseased.

At last, however, the full might and authority of the Federal Government was going to take a hand in this rehabilitation business with which Tuskegee Institute had been so long struggling. Because of that long struggle, certain things had been learned which could be handed on to the powerful newcomer in the field of salvation.

The summer of '33 Secretary of Agriculture Henry A.

Wallace went South. "Earnest Henry," he was called in Washington—a name well earned, because he was in sober earnest about the rights of human beings to happiness. He was traveling from state to state, probing into the evils that some cure might be found, and Dr. Carver invited him to stop at Tuskegee.

In his address at the Institute, Secretary Wallace reminisced affectionately of the days when as a little boy he had trotted by the side of the ardent young botanist, George W. Carver, across the wide expanse of the Iowa State campus, discovering the pleasures of delving into the mysteries of growing things and developing a kinship with them.

Then he went on to explain what the new Administration had in mind to do—to improve the machinery of social adjustment and to balance production. Success would be dependent upon a right feeling in the human heart. An unrelenting fight must be carried on against prejudice, greed, hatred, fear, and ignorance. No matter what laws might be enacted they would fail of their purpose if the heart were not right. More was needed than science and economics; spiritual insight must be added before matters could be set straight.

Dr. Carver had little to say to this intention save a fervent Amen. He spoke only a few words: "I haven't any good excuse for being here except that I was ordered to come. However, I want to quote a passage to you. 'Seest thou a man diligent in his business? he shall stand before kings.' I want to impress that on the young people. Such a man is Secretary Wallace."

Secretary Wallace's promises were speedily put into effect. One of the first acts of the Federal Government in that first troubled year of hog-killing time was to throw out a life line by instituting a "program" for cotton.

As fast as such agencies as the Agricultural Adjustment Agency, the Tennessee Valley Authority, and the Farm Security Administration could be put in operation, the Federal Government began to help the South to help itself on an enormously increased scale. Agents advocated diversified farming, soil conservation, balanced diets through home vegetable gardens, home ownership—all the things Dr. Carver had advocated forty years earlier. But at last the familiar words were being spoken in tones of authority.

Thousands of colored and white families were rehabilitated simply by removing them from submarginal lands which had been worn out by cotton to a few more productive acres, a weathertight house, and a sanitary privy, and by advancing a mule and a plow, some seed, and some fertilizer. Almost 100 per cent they paid back this investment in human salvage and became self-respecting units as families, earning their own way in the social economy.

Secretary Wallace came that way again in 1936 to look over the drought area, and again he stopped to see Tuskegee and Dr. Carver and to talk to five thousand assembled farmers and educators, and explain how the Administration was trying to bring about "a more uniform if less spectacular prosperity." He reiterated his faith in a better human product, and the new president of the Institute, Dr. Frederick Douglass Patterson, responded with justified pride. "Seventy years after abolition we find that Negroes have worn well the responsibilities of freedmen. They have participated with courage and enthusiasm in all the measures looking to human betterment, in proportion as they have been accorded the privilege."

## CHAPTER XXII

### *"To See How the End Will Be"*

FROM TIME TO TIME it was thought seemly that Dr. Carver should have an assistant. Sometimes they found his idiosyncrasies too hard to cope with; sometimes, on the other hand, they could not even grasp his purposes. They were satisfactory in greater or less degree, but they were assistants chiefly in name. They participated very little in his work, which remained as private and individual as before. He had been alone for so long it had become an ingrained habit; he was psychologically unable to delegate authority to others. Unless he performed an act himself with his own hands, he did not feel he was sufficiently familiar with it.

Another assistant came in the fall of 1935, a young man recently graduated from Cornell University, Austin W. Curtis, Jr. Dr. Carver opened the door of his laboratory a little way, greeted him pleasantly enough, told him he could look around and get adjusted, meet people, and find out how things were done at Tuskegee; over there was a room he could use. Then he closed the door again and dismissed Mr. Curtis from his mind.

Mr. Curtis looked around as he had been told. Among other things he observed the seed of the magnolia grandiflora. It contained oil, which might take the place of palm oil in soaps, so he began pulling it apart and putting it together again. Occasionally he reported progress to his superior, who received the report in silence. If the young man were perplexed about a problem and asked about it, Dr. Carver asked him a question in return, and by the time

*Courtesy of P. H. Polk, Tuskegee Inst., Ala.*

Dr. Carver in his study

Dr. Carver with his assistant, Austin W. Curtis, Jr.

PRESIDENT FRANKLIN D. ROOSEVELT GREETING DR. CARVER

the brief colloquy was over, Mr. Curtis had answered his own inquiry himself.

Mr. Curtis continued doggedly but cheerfully investigating the possibility of making synthetic leather from pumpkins and increasing the stock of vegetable colors. In about two months the situation had altered appreciably. He had proved he was a man of Dr. Carver's own sort. He was invited to tell what he had accomplished, and what further he had in mind. Then Dr. Carver would make suggestions as to method, discuss the findings already reached, and make more suggestions as to how they could be improved.

Advice and helpful criticism followed the neophyte through all the necessary phases of the work, including lecturing. After Mr. Curtis had made his first speech, Dr. Carver commented upon it. "Your delivery was fine and what you had to say was excellent, but people didn't understand you. Bring it down to earth." And he repeated his old maxim, "Don't put the fodder up so high the people cannot reach it."

At last someone had been welcomed not merely into Dr. Carver's laboratory, but also into his heart. He believed there was something providential in the coming of this young man, so intensely serious about his work and extremely competent at it, who was at the same time a genial companion; he was proud of him and loved and depended on him as his own son. Dr. Carver was over seventy now, and here was young strength in which he placed utter confidence, one who fully realized the significance of his work and could be counted upon to carry it on. And the affection was returned in full measure. Mr. Curtis accompanied him everywhere, seeing to his comfort, shielding him from intrusion, and acting as his official mouthpiece.

The very charming relationship existing between them often expressed itself through keeping up a merry fiction of the need for stern disciplinary measures. If Mr. Curtis reproved Dr. Carver for standing out in the cold without a coat on, the older man would say, "It surprises me how I managed to live all these years without you. If you keep on aggravating me I shall lose my sweet disposition. Last night I lay awake worrying about you, tossing and turning and rolling for fully half a minute!"

He would remove his glasses and look at his "Cub" and say severely, "You don't suit me at all."

And the Cub would retort, "Sir, they say I grow more like Dr. Carver every day."

"That's a fairy tale. You're enough to worry the horns off a mule." Then he would tuck his hand into the arm of "my dear boy" and go off to see how the paint project was coming along.

Ocher which Dr. Carver ground from clay by hand in crude bowls and with wooden pestles ranked with the most expensive French ocher. Nevertheless, he did not desire nor expect his products to compete with established manufactures. He advised Mr. Curtis, "Don't put yourself in a false position. At best a farmer can get the sand out with a sack and a bucket of water, and take a paddle and stir up the oil. Commercial companies grind paints from twenty-four to forty-eight hours. You can't place stirring with a case knife beside this."

On the other hand, the paint companies could not solve the paint problems of the rural population in the South, and these problems were as immediate as they had ever been. The homes were fashioned of unfinished lumber—of green pine with a high resin content—and its rough boards and open pores would drink up commercial paints, whether expensive or cheap, by the gallon. The color washes were for decoration, but a preservative which could be made by the farmer himself from waste products was needed. Dr. Carver had long ago unearthed the pigments; now a vehicle must be discovered.

Linseed oil and tung oil were out of the question because of their costliness. Although mineral oils were not considered as satisfactory as vegetable oils, nevertheless, a possible carrier might be found in discarded motor oil, for which Dr. Carver had already found a number of uses, including a rubberoid. Students brought in clay of all the colors to be found in near-by fields, gullies, and cut banks—red, yellow, gray, purple, white. These were mixed with the oil, and after nine months of exposure to all kinds of weather no changes had occurred which the eye could detect.

This was laboratory proof, but the paint must be put to the test on the actual object for which it was destined. One day a new student in the home-economics class rose and told her little story.

Her father's farm, three miles from the center of the campus, had come under its inspiring sphere of influence; by following the agricultural tenets advocated there he had saved a little money. He wanted to make his home more attractive and more enduring. Some bushes had been planted in the yard and flowers in tin cans adorned the porch, but the building itself was drab and dingy. It needed decorating and defenses against the inroads of time. His daughter, however, longed to go to school. This also seemed important.

Pride in ownership and the desire for more education were still, as they had been seventy-five years before, marching companions. A choice had to be made, and higher education won. The money had gone for her tuition at Tuskegee. Every day she walked the six miles to the seat of learning and back to her shabby home. If a demonstration were wanted for the durability of the paint she would offer her father's house. The offer was accepted, and buckets and brushes soon transformed it.

In the course of time Mr. Curtis also developed interior paints which could be fitted into the low-cost housing projects of the TVA and FSA or distributed through co-operatives at an almost unbelievably low figure. Not merely did the houses so treated relieve the hideousness of the Southern scene, but they had a remarkable effect on the morale of those who now lived in homes fit for white men.

Mr. Curtis bade fair to become a worthy successor to Dr. Carver in experimentation in the new synthetic world which was rapidly opening out. Until the advent of the machine age, most of what man used for food, shelter, clothing, transportation, and trading came directly from the farm, but then mines took the place of farms as the source of raw material for the iron monsters, and the farmer suffered from lack of sufficient markets. The farmer collectively being the largest buyer, when he was unable to exercise his buying powers, industry suffered in proportion.

Eventually the whole world suffered. Most of the mineral resources of the earth had been explored and tapped and would be exhausted in the course of time if they were not husbanded. Nations which lacked such essentials as iron and oil and coal went to war to secure the coveted treasures. They called it *Lebensraum,* but if substitutes could be made in the laboratory from materials which would otherwise be wasted, room for living would be available to all; the primary cause of war would be eliminated.

Synthetic plastics were practically as old as agriculture itself. They were made in the shadow of the pyramids from cooked starch, and celluloid collars antedated the twentieth century, but it took a world war to disclose their infinite potentialities to American industrialists. From 1918 on, the chemical industry made greater technological advances than even the automobile or aviation, and the great chemical companies which fed it, by getting in early, rapidly built up fabulous fortunes.

The petroleum industry and the packing industry had learned to utilize much of their waste, the former in dyes and drugs and the latter in soaps and fertilizers, but insufficient investigation had been made of the by-products of agriculture. Not so long ago cottonseed was considered a nuisance around a gin. It was burned or dumped into the river to get it out of the way. Then it was discovered it could be used in cooking to take the place of lard. By 1919 there were fifteen or so products from cottonseed which were more valuable than the lint itself, and before 1940 a "bald-headed" cotton had been specially developed in Texas which produced a multitude of seeds but practically no fiber.

When Dr. Carver was a student in Iowa, he had seen the genesis of the application of science to procedure in agriculture. From the time he first began to practice this at Tuskegee he had also seen and practiced the next step, of applying science to its by-products. In the nineties he was pioneering in finding new industrial uses for products of the soil, though his work suffered the delays incidental to any pioneering.

Eventually, however, others began to believe that the kingpin of peace and progress was the farmer. Merely appropriating money to relieve his distress or trying to create an artificial scarcity of food by plowing under were emergency measures; a program was needed which would be constructive instead of destructive.

Dr. William Jay Hale, consulting chemist of the Dow Chemical Company, had radical ideas on the subject. A hundred years after the cataclysmic Industrial Revolution, the world was experiencing another, equally momentous and far-reaching—the Chemical Revolution.

For the new science that would usher in the new age of reason he coined a word, which first appeared in print in 1934 in his book, *The Farm Chemurgic.* "Chemi," the root from which "chemistry" was derived, originally meant the black earth of Egypt; "ergon" was the Greek word for work. Hence, "chemurgy" could be defined as "chemistry at work," and implied in its make-up was the application of this work to the soil.

The substitution of cellulose for steel could re-establish the farmer's place as a producer of the renewable raw materials of industry without cutting down the numbers of people employed in industry. And the risks to both farmer and industrialist would be reduced because the rate of production and demand could be more accurately gauged. As Dr. Carver had so often said, agriculture could aid industry and industry could help agriculture solve its economic and social problems. Both being basically chemical, they had a natural affinity for each other.

Dr. Hale and the other scientists who had glimpsed the vision of the new world of greater comfort for mankind were dazzled as Dr. Carver had been when he said in 1925, "With all the advancements of science there is still an unlimited field for the creative mind; we have only skimmed the surface. What has been done is nothing to what will be done in the years to come."

Unanimously they agreed that end products of this union between chemistry and industry and agriculture should not be called ersatz or counterfeit because they were not so good as the real thing; usually, as in the case of synthetic rosins in paints, nylon for silk, or molded plastics for steel, they were an improvement upon what had been considered the real thing.

Henry Ford, "once the farm boy tinkering with mechanics, had become the mechanic who tinkered with farms." He had said that "Man's substance issues from the soil and not from the merchant's shelves," and his research men were already converting soybeans into new and strange products, looking to the time when five pounds of soy would replace twenty-five pounds of steel in an automobile. Eventually, each million cars would consume one hundred and seventy thousand tons of agricultural products.

In 1935 a group of farm leaders, scientists, and industrialists chose Dearborn, Michigan, for their meeting place, to discuss agricultural industry—a new and tremendously important step in the application of science to agriculture. The resulting National Farm Chemurgic Council marked the official recognition of the beginning of a new era.

"The first and greatest chemurgist," is the title Christy Borth bestowed on Dr. Carver in his book, *Pioneers of Plenty:* "Long before there was a chemurgic council there was a man who was famous for his chemurgic counsel. . . . At least a quarter of a century before Dr. Charles H. Herty tackled the problem, the scientist in his laboratory made paper from Southern pine. . . . Years before a rocklike plastic made from wood wastes became a chemurgic promise, he made synthetic marble from wood shavings."

The director of the council said they had long known of and held in high regard Dr. Carver's creative research into the unknown realm of Nature, hence they had invited Dr. Carver to address the first Chemurgic Conference. He had been unable to accept at that time, but when the invitation was repeated in 1937 he did attend.

Here and there in the gathering of several hundred manufacturers and agriculturists, including the head of the National Grange, could be found representatives of special fields—an economist and a sociologist, a meteorologist and a physicist. And in the hall outside the luncheon room was Dr. Carver, waiting until they had finished eating and he could deliver his talk "On new methods and principles of farm welfare."

Henry Ford had already been to call on Dr. Carver in his room at the Dearborn Inn. As he poked his head in the door, one look was enough to tell these two all that was necessary of their mental kinship. Dr. Carver was immediately reminded of his earlier friend Lewis Adams, "who could do anything." Here at last was the industrialist with the unlimited funds and the vision—who could see the same ends and believed in them so profoundly that he was putting them into operation; he could make dreams come true—of industry based on the utilization of the non-comestible products of the farm, which would put a greater degree of comfort at the disposal of mankind by bringing what had been considered luxuries within the price range of millions who had previously been excluded. And he sincerely wished Negroes to participate in this betterment.

Mr. Ford had had few close associates in the realm which interested him most, and these were now gone. The names of Thomas A. Edison and Luther Burbank and John Burroughs, whom he had considered the three greatest scientists, were engraved above his executive office and laboratory building, but Carver had taken Edison's place, in his estimation, as the greatest living scientist.

Automatically the devotee of the soybean and the protagonist of the peanut dragged their chairs close together and settled down earnestly to a conversational communion which has continued ever since, either through actual meetings, correspondence, or unspoken ideas. They talked and talked, each finding in the other confirmation of his own beliefs and attitudes.

Perhaps because their habits of thought were so alike, they had certain physical habits that were similar, too, such as in the matter of eating; they even drank the same amount of coffee in their cream. Once, when some newspapermen were conducting a joint interview, one of them said, "Mr. Ford, we want you next." He replied, "No. Just ask Dr. Carver. He knows about me. I agree with everything he thinks and he thinks the same way I do."

They planned to see each other at least once a year. On his plantation at Ways, Georgia, Ford had rooms prepared and always kept ready for the occupancy of Dr. Carver and Mr. Curtis whenever they could visit there. But after Dr. Carver became too ill to travel much, Ford himself always stopped off at Tuskegee on his way between Dearborn and Ways to spend some time carrying on that interrupted but continuing conversation—often in the discussion of fibers.

He named his school for colored children the George W. Carver School and built a guest cabin memorial at Greenfield Village hard by the new dietetics laboratory of Dearborn, which Dr. Carver dedicated in 1942. But, more intimate and hence more significant to these two men who valued the historical associations of the past, he presented Dr. Carver with a cup and saucer from the set his mother had brought to the United States as a bride.

Dr. Carver was distinctly limited in the chemurgic products he could perfect; he had none of the elaborate equipment required for the research into and manufacture of even a plastic button, which seems a simple thing. The Institute had no money to spend in such a fashion. He was still restricted to making things with his hands, as he had always done.

When Mr. Curtis first came and confidently said he needed three hundred dollars for a microscope, Dr. Carver looked at his assistant aghast. He did not in the least begrudge this expenditure from his departmental budget, but he had a startled memory of the days when that amount was the total the school had to run on, and he himself had to go rummaging among trash heaps for equipment.

Though the aim was the same in both cases, it was a far cry from these conditions to the chemurgic program as instituted by the Federal Government in 1938. In accordance with the settled conviction of President Roosevelt and Secretary of Agriculture Wallace, that economics needs ethics and humanitarianism as fellow travelers, a new Federal Bureau of Agricultural Research and Technology was set up which was to be a clearing house for the industrial uses of farm crops. Four experimental regional laboratories were built: in Pennsylvania, Louisiana, Illinois, and California, one in each major farm area, each financed with a million dollars annually to develop new uses for their local farm products.

Dr. Carver's primary aim since coming to Tuskegee had been to lighten the appalling misery he saw about him by relieving the poverty of the South—to substitute for the destroying one-crop system of cotton the two lifesavers which could most easily be fitted into the Southern agrarian economy—peanuts and sweet potatoes.

The cultivation of sweet potatoes had increased steadily until by 1935 sixty-two million bushels were being grown. For the manufacture of sweet-potato starch from culls, some years earlier the Federal Government had opened a pilot plant in Alexandria, Virginia, progressing to a large one in Laurel, Mississippi, the chemurgic city. Various bureaus—Standards, Engraving and Printing, and Chemistry and Soils—got together to add another refinement to the comfort of Americans. Since licking was still the accepted way of applying stamps to letters, they wanted to have the mucilage taste better. They extracted the dextrin from sweet potatoes and tentative trials were made to see whether it could be produced in sufficient quantities to be economical.

The laurel plant produced a starch which Southern textile mills could use for sizing cotton fabrics, superior in quality and having a production cost sufficiently low to give expectations that an important starch industry would develop in the South.

Then the war in 1940 extended the live-at-home program beyond the farmers to the country as a whole. The West Indies and Brazil provided only a small amount of the bitter cassava root from which tapioca was made, and its growth in the United States was limited to Florida. With the hundreds of millions of pounds of tapioca-flour importation from the Dutch East Indies cut off, the Government started to make it from sweet potatoes.

During the long, difficult period of gestation nothing seems to be happening and then, all of a sudden, it does. Other things Dr. Carver had advocated during our 1918 participation in the war began coming to fruition in 1942. One newspaper story announced that every decade brought a new food discovery, and dehydration, which performed a miracle in the field of food preservation, was the current one. In words almost identical with those Dr. Carver had used twenty-four years earlier the reporter stated that dehydrated foods could be flown and shipped overseas and their space-saving and weight-saving properties were impressive. Furthermore, as though the idea had never been broached before, one company sent out word through the press that it was dehydrating cooked sweet potatoes. "Something entirely new on the food horizon is the latest successful process for supplying families with year-round tasty yams.

. . . Imperfect slices of yams are processed into a powder which may be used to make cakes and pies."

The lag between laboratory work and ultimate use is likely to be at least twenty years. Most people thought "old Carver was daffy" when he was writing his bulletins, and few paid much attention to them. Very early he had suggested working peanut shells over the ground to loosen and condition the clay soils of the South and give them organic matter and a better texture, but for years peanut mills continued to burn this valuable material as waste. Not until 1940 were the shells pulverized, sacked, sold, and advertised in seed catalogues, to take the place of peat moss. Actually, they were better, because they held more moisture and contained nitrogen, potash, and phosphate, which were lacking in the peat moss formerly imported from Germany.

The majority of Dr. Carver's bulletins suffered a like neglect in the early days. Plenty of oils and fibers were available then, and it was easier to import them from countries employing coolie labor than it was to compete. But Dr. Carver could look ahead and foresee and prepare, and the information contained in his bulletins was later at hand when it was needed. Not so long ago three Southern banks reissued one of his bulletins without, however, attaching his name to the publication or in any way acknowledging his authorship.

However, he was encouraged by the small things that showed production was beginning to catch up, and with the general recognition of the things themselves. "I'm glad to see progress is being made—that the effort has not been entirely lost." Though it would have been more encouraging if any except the chemurgic people had been aware of his pioneer labors.

From the sweet potato Dr. Carver had produced one hundred and eighteen products. But it was less spectacular than the peanut because it was less versatile—the peanut contained oil. From the peanut, therefore, he was able to produce three hundred products.

He was not alone in seeing the value of these two crops,

and an exact measure of responsibility for their enormous increase cannot be apportioned, but he was the individual who focused attention upon them. Of late years, when he talked in Southern towns, the streets leading to the lecture halls were blocked, and when he made a nine-day tour of Texas the State Legislature adjourned to hear him.

He would be quite content to share honors with the boll weevil, which still cost sixty million dollars annually. For many years soapbox politicians had beat the air over the question of better roads and pointed to the holes into which you could drop a cow. When the Ford car was produced, which made travel by automobile almost universal, the oratory was no longer needed; the good roads appeared by magic. In a similar fashion the boll weevil, a little thing the size of a fly, by increasing the hazards of cotton growing, accomplished what a century of talk could not have achieved in diverting numbers of farmers to the planting of peanuts. They could make money from peanuts as they never could from cotton.

The peanut had not even been recognized as a crop in 1896; now it was among the leading six in the entire United States. Peanuts and soybeans were the only two crops which had increased in value while the total farm income was decreasing.

By 1938 the peanut could no longer be described as "lowly"; it accounted for more than $200,000,000 worth of business. In November of that year, "Whereas the peanut is one of Alabama's chief products," the governor of Alabama proclaimed a peanut week. For three days a festival was held, complete with floats and bands, and Dr. Carver was escorted to the parade by a cordon of motorcycle policemen. By 1940 it was the second Southern cash crop after cotton; and five million acres were allotted for 1942.

Peanut-processing companies had prospered greatly, though few of Dr. Carver's products had actually been commercialized. Yet a third local company was organized by some of the same citizens of the town of Tuskegee as had started the first two. One per cent of the gross proceeds were to go to the Carver Foundation, since he would not accept anything personally. Most important of the products of the Carvoline Company, which also manufactured cosmetics, salad oil, and rubbing oil based on Dr. Carver's formulas, was peanut flour.

Peanut flour contained more than four times as much protein and eight times as much fat as wheat flour. Its high alkalinity made it valuable in maintaining body balance, and its low carbohydrate content, even less than soybean flour, gave it a place in diabetic diets. An excellent source of vitamin $B_1$, peanut flour was recommended by the Georgia State Health Department as a pellagra preventive.

As Dr. Carver watched the ideas he had tended and nourished for so long beginning to flower one by one he continued unremittingly to walk in the early morning and at sunset and gather his mycological specimens and dispatch them to Washington to the Division of Mycology and Disease Survey, the duty of which was to collect, study, identify, and work out the best methods for combating disease.

His same unique contributions continued to appear in the *Plant Disease Reporter,* issued by the Bureau of Plant Industry as a service to pathologists throughout the United States. "Dr. George W. Carver of the Tuskegee Institute in Alabama sent a specimen of *Pandanus javanicus variegatus* attacked by *Diplodia natalansis.* He writes that one large plant, with stalks two and a half inches in diameter, was killed by the fungus. The Survey has no other record of the fungus on *Pandanus.*"

Dr. Paul R. Miller of the Survey has recently said: "I have known Dr. Carver well for over ten years and consider him a rarely gifted scientist and mycologist. His contributions have been countless. His methods of experimentation have not always been orthodox, but his innate ability and tireless efforts have far overshadowed any failure to conform to conventional procedure. His ability as a collector of rare fungi is almost uncanny. I have been with him on collecting trips when half of the specimens found would be the first record of occurrence in the state. This is probably explained by the fact that Dr. Carver is a keen student of nature. Knowing the proper habitat of such fungi, it is easy for him to locate them. He not only knows botany but geology, soils, etc."

In the realm of uncorrupted science, national and racial and color bars are down; all are accepted on the basis of accomplishment. Dr. Carver was so accepted when, on August 1, 1935, in recognition of his many years of brilliant mycological discoveries, he was appointed, as Collaborator in the Survey, to the United States Department of Agriculture.

# CHAPTER XXIII

## *"There Is a Balm in Gilead"*

THE YEAR 1936–37 was remembered as a special one at Tuskegee, dedicated to honoring Dr. Carver and celebrating the fortieth anniversary of his arrival from the West. Those forty years had seen changes at the Institute which the most daring prophet would not at the time have ventured to predict. Physically it had grown from a few handmade, faulty buildings surrounded by dreariness to more than a hundred, distinctive in their stateliness and dignity, set in a great expanse of thirty-five hundred acres of park and verdant farm land. But it was much more than an institution devoted to the education of its thirty-five hundred students; it had become a power in the agricultural South and an enlightening influence in the social structure of America.

Booker T. Washington had set the course, and under the guidance of Dr. Moton, a brilliant educator, the academic standards had risen until it had become duly accredited with a college rating. As he could say with justifiable pride, more and more were coming—"a host of youths, no longer trammeled as their forefathers, these of a younger generation are revealing, in their unabased accomplishments, those latent capacities, hitherto repressed, that must inevitably win for them and their people ungrudging access to the larger opportunities of unbounded America and ungrudging place in the family of races and nations."

After twenty years of devoted service Dr. Moton's health had failed. He had retired in 1935, leaving the captaincy to one of the ablest of the younger generation of whom he had spoken—Dr. Frederick D. Patterson, who had come from Cornell University only a short time before to teach bacteriology and veterinary science.

Dr. Moton once said of Dr. Carver, "He has been an inspiration as a teacher and an exemplification in his own person of the possibilities of the race. Thousands will be his debtor in race understanding who will never know his name."

Dr. Carver had helped change the pattern of Southern agriculture. But by the force of his character, no less than by his achievements, he had performed that far more difficult and subtle act, of enrolling thousands under the banner of good will.

Dr. Carver has been called the greatest single force since the turn of the century in creating racial understanding. Undoubtedly he shared this honor with Booker T. Washington, but his greater life span enabled him to advance the understanding by many degrees. Negro artists, too, have helped enormously to better relations, but a more comprehensive fraternity exists among the arts than in most other walks of life, and a great singer will be listened to by all who love music.

Music was, as it had always been, a vital part of life at Tuskegee. William L. Dawson, a Tuskegee graduate, had perfected his gifts and returned to the Institute as musical director. Like an orchestra leader, with a meticulous and sympathetic touch he played upon the untrained voices of the choir, developing rich harmonies from the melodic strains of the religious folk music of the bottom churches where the students had their origin, and they responded, as he wished, with every shade of emotional intensity. Although the members shifted year by year with graduates leaving and newcomers replacing them, they always maintained the same high level.

As the songs of travail and faith which are known throughout the world by the name of spirituals have been the gift of Negroes who have suffered but never ceased to hope, so the chancel windows in the Institute chapel were the gift of hundreds of striving Negroes, contributing their little sums towards this glorious symphony of color, a symbolic record in stained glass of the progress of the race—toiling out of slavery down in Egypt's land, crossing the rolling Jordan, fighting the battle of Jericho till the walls came tumbling down, climbing Jacob's ladder, ever higher, rising in a superb crescendo toward the star in the east, till they shouted all over God's Heaven. The windows were executed in 1932 in the Lamb Studios of New Jersey, but had been conceived in the hearts of the Negroes of the deep South who were singing all the way out of slavery until they should become an undeniable part of the brotherhood of man.

Commencement in June of 1937 marked the climax of Dr. Carver's commemorative year. The singing choir stood under these singing windows, giving voice most appropriately to the poem Mr. Dawson had set to music—Louise Imogen Guiney's "Out in the Fields with God," "Where ill thoughts die and good are born," and where Dr. Carver had spent a large share of his life.

Throughout the year small contributions had been pouring in, chiefly in dollar bills with a smattering of fives and tens, until two thousand dollars of such subscriptions had been raised to pay for a bronze bust, fashioned by Steffen Wolfgang George Thomas of Atlanta. There would never have been any bust had Dr. Carver been consulted. He did not by any means feel he was ready for one, and he did not want a monument anyhow. But there it was, and at the unveiling, June 2, 1937, he appeared reluctantly. He seemed less tall than when he had arrived in Tuskegee, his head thrust turtle fashion from his bent shoulders, but he was wearing the same suit in which he had graduated from Ames, and the buttonhole, as it had then, flaunted a flower.

The astute young Mr. Curtis detected a means of turning the festive occasion to a practical purpose. Dr. Carver's exhibit of fibers, paints, stains, and peanut and sweet-potato products had traveled widely and been seen by hundreds of thousands of people, but when they were at home they stayed shut up in the agricultural building, where only an occasional guest and a few students were admitted. Mr. Curtis believed they should be on permanent view to all.

He therefore gathered some together, added the stuffed fowl and geological specimens, spread them out in a spacious upstairs room in the new library, and took up his stand there to explain them to the many visitors who had come for the ceremonies. The visitors were impressed, including the trustees, few of whom had ever seen this visual record of a lifetime's achievement; they agreed that the exhibit should be permanent.

The Institute laundry dated from 1914 before the school had attained its present proportions. It was a graceful, compact, one-story building of red brick with a white portico, on the main road between the Carnegie Music Hall and the guest hall. It now seemed out of place to have a laundry thus prominently situated, and the tubs and mangles had been relegated to the eastern edge of the campus, back by the powerhouse. Dr. Patterson suggested to the other trustees that the location and size of the building made it eminently suitable to house Dr. Carver's collection, and the following spring at the annual Founder's Day meeting they approved the George Washington Carver Museum.

The Museum, as it turned out, was probably the means of saving Dr. Carver's life. In the midst of his plans, pernicious anemia sent him to the hospital, abandoning the rooms in Rockefeller Hall which had been his private sanctuary for thirty-five years. The red blood corpuscles had diminished to an almost impossibly low number, and for several months an overtaxed heart threatened momentarily to stop.

In the matter of eating, so important in anemia, he was a difficult patient. The sight and smell of food overcame him. He was physically unable to alter his own deeply ingrained habits to those which, he was assured over and over, medical practice had proved would aid his recovery. He loathed orange juice and lemon juice and vanilla, all of which were employed to mask the taste of noxious medicines; a whiff of any of them destroyed his appetite utterly. Apropos of the dietician he said with a wry smile, "I'm supposed to adjust to her whims, but I have not tried very strenuously, and I don't think I shall."

But the Museum was the only thing of its kind that had ever been projected; it must be carried through, and only he could do it. Threads must be tied, loose ends caught up. He had toiled so exclusively alone that nobody else could know the relative significance of objects scattered among his effects which had an important meaning for him. Much of his work was in the pattern stage, but it must be a completed pattern from which could be fashioned the perfected structure. Had he not felt acutely that there was a master scheme, and that he could not stop until the design was finished, he would not have made the necessary effort to live.

Even when he was in the hospital and practically helpless, he could not ring a bell or push a button for attention. He had always waited on himself and simply could not adjust to service. Though he was supposedly inactive, he would lie propped up in bed with his heart thumping heavily but with his jackknife open, whittling out some idea or other. He had never been as concerned with how long he was going to live as with how much he could do while he was living.

When the red corpuscles began to put in a feeble appearance, he was at last permitted to leave the safeguards of the hospital, and was moved into a separate suite of rooms in the Institute guest hall. There he would have the matron within reach, though he never was known to call on her. Henry Ford had a private elevator installed which would spare him the tax of climbing the nineteen steep stairs, and he was only a few steps from the Museum in which were his new office and laboratory and proving plant, where he tested recipes on wood, coal, gas, and electric stoves and a fireless cooker, using iron pots whenever possible. A small greenhouse had been built on at the back, accessible only through his private rooms, to hold his amaryllis and a few experimental plants.

Heterogeneous was a favorite word of Dr. Carver's because he so disliked heterogeneity in thinking. But in a remarkably short time after he was installed in the Museum, the adjective might have applied to his rooms. When the chaos of paper, rocks, grain, soil, and dried plants became too great and his office so stuffed he could not move around in it, he cleaned house. This consisted of gathering up a huge bundle and lugging it into his laboratory. When that was overflowing, he carried it into the proving room and, when that became impossible, he threw it out in the trash barrel. Then he was in despair, because that very day he was sure to want something he had just disposed of.

The deprivation Dr. Carver felt most keenly was the loss of his dawn and sunset walks, and he wondered wistfully whether he would ever be able to get as far as the new school greenhouse which had recently been built; he had never seen its construction or its equipment or flowers.

With inward protestations he continued dutifully to swallow iron and liver pills by the hundred. He was not a heavy eater, but he was as finicky as ever, and he did like something he could get his teeth into. They said there was a whole ox in four tablets of beef extract; well, it could stay there as far as he was concerned. You could not build a good feeling on hunger. You could not nourish on wind and water, and bees' knees and gnats' heels did not constitute a meal. He liked staple foods, but well prepared. Once when what he called a foul fowl was brought in to him he remarked that you could not season a chicken by pouring a sauce on it any more than you could pour oil over clay and expect it to mix. Or if the tray came in with the toast too well done he would send it back with a note: "No charcoal this morning. If I needed it the doctor would prescribe."

Finally he rebelled openly against pills. You must either take heed of the Bible, said he, or, if you thought it all bosh, throw it all away. He chose to take heed, and the Voice had said distinctly to Isaiah, "All flesh is grass and all the goodliness thereof is as the flower of the field."

In the few feet Dr. Carver covered between his own doorway and the Museum were wild vegetables enough to feed a family. He started to gather and prepare these himself and threw the years away as fast as he threw the pills away. He began to extend his walks further and further afield and considered he had completely vindicated his own method of treatment when he was able to climb a fence going across lots to the new greenhouse.

All his life Dr. Carver had been doing essentially one thing. "Flower in the crannied wall, I pluck you out of the crannies." He had plucked and plucked and here in the Museum was the culmination of his effort—the inseparable thought-and-act life of one individual on parade to constitute an enduring record which would remain when the smoke and the din and the destruction had cleared away: the skeleton of Betsy, one of the first yoke of oxen with which the first fields of the Experiment Station had been plowed and planted; two-foot glass jars of the first fruits of those fields: mammoth vegetables looking as fresh as when he had sealed them forty years before; samples of soils in their bamboo containers; cold-water paints on rough pine boards; stains; wallpaper designs; vegetable dyes; wallboard; Cercospora on leaves and plants; edible wild vegetables; feather and bead and mica ornaments; fibers; mats and rugs; hundreds of lace patterns; vases of native clay; the incomparable blue powder in a pharmacist's jar; samples of cotton and cotton bricks; a fair showing of the seventy-five pecan products; one hundred and eighteen sweet-potato products and a representative group of the three hundred peanut products.

The Museum was designed to be not merely a record of the past, but a means of educating for the future, an encyclopedia of Southern potentialities. Dr. Carver had often said that you had only to go out in the back yard to find the solution to the Southern problems. For thirty years specialists in differing lines had come asking what to do in this case, what to do in that one. Now if they wanted information on ores, here it was gathered together under glass in one volume, as it were; if they wanted to know something about fibers or foods, these also were readily available. Dr. Carver had always preferred to be called an "educator," rather than be tagged with any of the sciences he practiced; botany, chemistry, geology, and all the others were merely several means toward an end. In the Museum he was able to crystallize his group theory of education; by decreasing the extent he was increasing the intent.

As a representation of this most versatile man, the Museum still lacked one of his essential aspects. This was rounded out when a space was partitioned off in which were hung thirty-six of his paintings, in frames of bare wood with no stain, no varnish, no gilt.

The Museum had its annoyances, minor but incessant, which interfered with his peace of mind. He had already been sufficiently troubled by the curious who stood with their faces against the glass, just to see what he looked like, and by the intolerable nuisance of souvenir hunters who ripped the labels off the exhibits or stole anything which had his name on it. Comments upon his clothes, coming from people with a not-too-friendly attitude, increasingly exasperated him as an example of lack of perspective and confusion of important things with the totally unimportant. Time was growing short and the laggards in comprehension were so far behind.

A reporter from one of the national weeklies who came to the opening of the gallery in 1941 called the "Black Leonardo" a toothless old man. "Which," said Dr. Carver, "is nonsense. It was a great pity he didn't ask, then he would not have made that egregious error. If he had taken the trouble to inquire I could have proved I am not toothless. I had my teeth right in my pocket all the time."

With the condescension which of later days had injected a certain amount of acerbity into Dr. Carver's tone, the reporter had also referred to his patched apron. "Here," said Dr. Carver, "it is. A little patch no bigger than a dollar. But he couldn't see the paintings for the patch." Why concentrate on that? What difference did it make? What did it have to do with art? And he added, with a note of despair over the obtuseness of humanity in general, "You would think from the way they pressed against the railings that pictures were made to smell, instead of to look at."

The Museum was regarded by Mr. Curtis as a monument evidencing the respect and reverence due a great man. It would be easy to let it solidify, but in that case it would be no more vital than a statue. It would negate the guiding principle of Dr. Carver's life, which was to go on without cessation and find out more and more attributes of more and more objects and put them to use.

If, on the other hand, it were a live and growing thing, the more fitting a monument it would be to a man whose own endeavors had never become static. It must be elastic and independent as Dr. Carver had been, ready to meet what needs would inevitably continue to arise, dedicated to the solution of practical problems—not in pure, but applied, research.

Many of the things Dr. Carver had started had great possibilities but remained still in the test-tube stage because of insufficient equipment and limited personnel. These alone would be sufficient to keep a staff busy for some time to come. In the chemurgic adaptation of farm products to industry the sciences could not be isolated. Chemistry, botany, bacteriology, entomology, physics, and soil chemistry were all tied up together; the protein or carbohydrate composition of a plant could be altered by changing the composition of the soil through fertilizers. Specialists in all these fields were needed to carry on the work along lines laid down by him, before the pilot plant stage and final industrialization could be reached.

Mr. Curtis possessed the virtue of altruism of the same sort as Dr. Carver's or they would not have been so compatible, and what he had of this quality within himself was enhanced by association. To his mind, progress could not properly be called progress unless others besides himself were furnished the opportunity for research and the opportunity to contribute to the scientific knowledge of the world.

Almost no Negroes had any backlog of money for vacation purposes or even to see them through the period of education without resorting to such menial and small-paying jobs as Pullman porters or waiters or delivery "boys." And once they had graduated only two fields were open—teaching and government employ—both of which were restricted in the numbers they could accommodate.

At the present time the Negro could furnish, as always, the labor for science, but could make small use of it for his own advancement. Negro chemists produced little except a few cosmetics and patent medicines. Over the big commercial research laboratories was an unwritten sign in letters which only Negroes could read, "Do Not Enter." Sometimes entrance was barred by law, but more often by the white worker's prejudice or fear of a threat to his own job.

A Negro youth might therefore become highly proficient in his scientific field while he was at school but, even with diploma in hand, there was no place he could go to put his theoretical knowledge into practical effect. Thus the incentive to study in the sciences was removed because it would lead to nothing; he could not even make a living at it, and an incalculable amount of talent, perhaps genius, was being wasted.

From all these considerations there naturally arose the idea of making the Carver laboratory a research center for promising young Negroes. Using as its nucleus the remaining thirty-three thousand dollars of Dr. Carver, rescued from the depression debacle, the machinery for bringing about this devoutly wished consummation was set up in 1940 and called the George Washington Carver Foundation.

As for Dr. Carver himself, he was still seeking, still learning, though he had long since passed such landmarks as his several honorary doctorates. He carried his honors modestly. Each tribute came to him unasked, and often he was

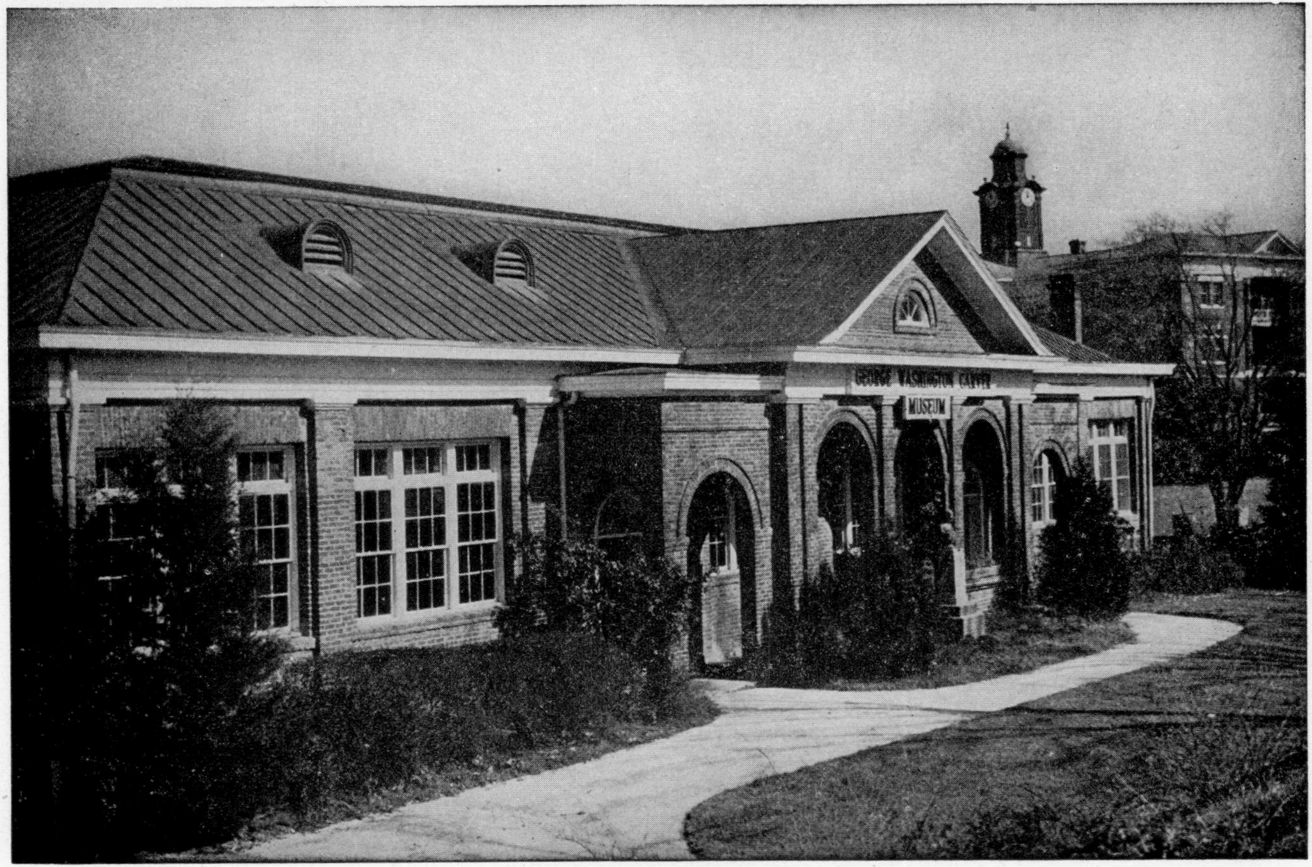


The George Washington Carver Museum

Dr. Carver delivering baccalaureate address at Simpson College, 1941

naïvely unaware of its full implication. Because of a personal shrinking from publicity, he had never sought fame in any form, perhaps not enough for the good of his work. He made the least possible effort to attract attention, and strangers who saw him merely as an individual divorced from his name looked upon him as an utterly insignificant person. Whether the marks of renown came from a comic strip based on his life, or an invitation to address the New York *Herald Tribune* Forum in the Waldorf-Astoria on the subject of "Chemistry and Peace," he took them all in his stride.

This last he was fortunately able to combine in one trip with his acceptance of the Roosevelt Medal for distinguished service in the field of science, in 1939. He was introduced to the two hundred dinner guests in Theodore Roosevelt's New York home with these words: "I have the honor to present not a man only, but a life, transfused with passion for the enlarging and enriching of the living of his fellowman . . . a liberator to men of the white race as well as the black; a bridge from one race to the other, on which men of good will may learn of each other and rejoice together in the opportunities and the potentialities of their common country." With one accord the guests rose to their feet as he received the medal and delivered his simple speech.

Distinctions were piling up like a rolling snowball. They differed widely in prestige, but he accepted them graciously —and then went back to work again.

Eighteen schools had been named for Dr. Carver and, wonderful to relate, a Southern white child. Equally remarkable was the resolution of the United Daughters of the Confederacy extolling him. The Catholic Conference of the South, meeting in Birmingham, disregarded creed in favor of religion and made him the first recipient of its annual award for outstanding service to the welfare of the South. The Variety Clubs of America offered its Humanitarian Award, and the *Progressive Farmer,* a leading Southern agricultural magazine, named him the Man of the Year.

In 1941 Dr. Carver received an invitation from President Alan Valentine of the University of Rochester to be present at the Commencement exercises to receive an honorary degree of Doctor of Science. He had also been asked to deliver, on almost the same date, the baccalaureate address at his old college—Simpson. Thus the years were joined between that place which had first admitted him to education and that which had been the home of Frederick Douglass and a haven of refuge to slaves on their way to freedom across the Canadian border.

His health would not permit both trips. He could travel as far as Iowa, but not so far as New York. Accordingly, the University of Rochester, feeling that it would be honoring itself in honoring Dr. Carver, took an unprecedented step. Dr. Valentine flew down to Tuskegee and a special convocation was held. His citation poignantly summarized Dr. Carver's life: "Scientist, educator, benefactor of your people and America. . . . True to the American tradition, you made every sacrifice to obtain the best education. . . . Recognition came slowly in the world of white men but, when it came, you neither scorned it nor were captivated by it. . . . Because you have opened new doors of opportunity to those Americans who happen to be Negroes; because you have once again demonstrated that in human ability there is no color line; because you have helped thousands of men acquire new confidence . . . I confer upon you the degree of Doctor of Science, *honoris causa,* in recognition whereof I hand you this diploma and ask that the hood of that degree, bearing the color of the university, be placed on your shoulders."

In January 1942 Dr. Carver received an award from the Honorary Birthday Committee of the Thomas A. Edison Foundation for the Advancement of Science and Education which acknowledged only "a few outstanding Americans in the fields of Science, Art, Medicine, and Education, who have made some real contribution to human welfare." The next month the Executive Council of the honorary fraternity, Kappa Delta Pi, announced his election to membership in the Laureate Chapter.

Illness in 1938 had prevented Dr. Carver from going back to Diamond, Missouri, the place where he was born, to join the reunion of the Carver family, his one-time masters, at which he would have been most cordially welcome. Four years later, by order of the governor of the state, markers were put up by the Missouri Highway Commission directing travelers to the "Birthplace of George Washington Carver, Famous Negro Scientist." The white boys and girls with whom he had played as a child were by then very old men and women, but all who could remember the little things he said and did were proud of "our George."

These highway markers have a far-reaching symbolism. In the life span of one man millions of his race who could not read the printed wayside signs, stating how many miles it was to this place or that, can read now, and they know well how far they still must travel and how beset with obstacles the path will be. Seven-league boots were given Dr. Carver, and he covered the distance in one allegorical step, but the others are following swiftly after him.

# EPILOGUE

## *"Coming for to Carry Me Home"*

It was such a little step Dr. Carver had still to take out of the lonesome valley into the Heaven for which he had prepared himself, "Where Sabbaths Have No End."

He wanted to see this book published, and to read the record—a record of which he himself did not realize the full magnitude. When we began work on it more than three years ago, it had not seemed important to him. Being chiefly concerned with the day-to-day job which resulted in service to others, he had given no thought to the marks of fame which might result. He had not even troubled previously to correct the "fairy tales," as he called them, written by people who could not know the facts of his life, because he had never explained himself. And it was not easy for him to remember painful things long buried. But at last it became clear to him that if these matters were put down accurately and truthfully, with first things first and all in its proper proportion, he would be rendering yet another service which it was in his power to make—offering a signpost guiding the way toward a better life for the young of all races.

Dr. Carver wanted to hold this book in his hand, but he could not wait for it. He was very tired, and it was high time he went to rest. As twilight fell on the evening of January 5, 1943, he died, and was buried beside his dear friend, Booker T. Washington. The text of the chaplain of Tuskegee Institute was, "For God so loved the world." Among the sons and leaders in the cause of humanity, George Washington Carver had taken his rightful place.

I am deeply grateful for the privilege of having known

Dr. Carver through the daily communication we had over many months. As we talked together and as I read through his scrapbooks, each day brought stronger confirmation of his true greatness. His sweetness and humor, his wisdom and understanding will be sadly missed by all of us, at Tuskegee and in the larger world, who were ever associated with him. We could work better with him at our side.

And I am deeply sensible of the honor of being the instrument through which his life has been recorded. If this book does anything to hold up a mirror and thereby help make others of his race better understood by white men who seldom look beyond the color of their skins to the living human being, our joint purpose will have been achieved, and George Washington Carver can rest in peace.

# *Bibliography*


Pioneers of Plenty — *Christy Borth*
Black Reconstruction — *W. E. B. DuBois*
American Negroes, a Handbook — *Edwin R. Embree*
Chemistry Triumphant — *William J. Hale*
The Farm Chemurgic — *William J. Hale*
The Collapse of Cotton Tenancy — *C. S. Johnson*
The Wasted Land — *Gerald W. Johnson*
The Books of American Negro Spirituals — *Ed. J. Weldon Johnson*
The Negro in the New World — *Sir Harry Johnston*
The Story of My Life — *Sir Harry Johnston*
Sharecroppers All — *Arthur F. Raper*, *Ira De A. Reid*
Aggrey of Africa — *Edwin W. Smith*
Frederick Douglass — *Booker T. Washington*
My Larger Education — *Booker T. Washington*
Up from Slavery — *Booker T. Washington*
The Negro Year Book (1937–38) — *Ed. Monroe N. Work*
Twelve Million Black Voices — *Richard Wright*
Negro Scientist Shows "Way Out" — *Osburn Zuber*

# Index